MORRISON

MAJOR-GENERAL
SIR EDWARD MORRISON,
KCMG, CB, DSO

MORRISON

THE LONG-LOST MEMOIR OF CANADA'S ARTILLERY COMMANDER IN THE GREAT WAR

EDITED AND ASSEMBLED BY
SUSAN RABY-DUNNE

FOREWORD BY
MAJOR (RETIRED) MARC GEORGE

VICTORIA · VANCOUVER · CALGARY

Heritage House Publishing Company Ltd.
heritagehouse.ca

CATALOGUING INFORMATION AVAILABLE FROM LIBRARY AND ARCHIVES CANADA

978-1-77203-214-7 (pbk)
978-1-77203-215-4 (epub)
978-1-77203-216-1 (epdf)

Copyedited by Kate Juniper
Proofread by Cailey Cavallin
Cover and interior design by Jacqui Thomas
Typesetting by Setareh Ashrafologholai
Cover photograph: Morrison bunker, Passchendaele, November 1917. William Okell Holden
Dodds Collection, University of Victoria.

The interior of this book was produced on 100% post-consumer recycled paper, processed
chlorine free and printed with vegetable-based inks.

We acknowledge the financial support of the Government of Canada through the Canada Book
Fund (CBF) and the Canada Council for the Arts, and the Province of British Columbia through
the British Columbia Arts Council and the Book Publishing Tax Credit.

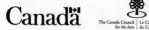

21 20 19 18 17   1 2 3 4 5

Printed in Canada

CONTENTS

In honour and remembrance of all the
Gunners of the Great War—and their horses.

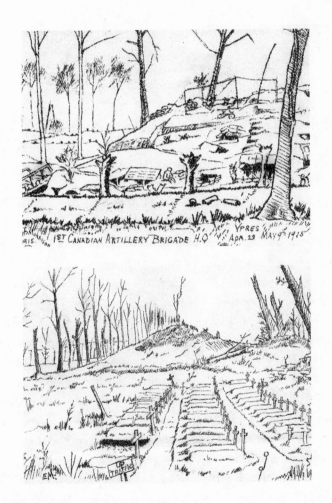

TOP Morrison's sketch of dyke and dugout. FRIPP FAMILY

BOTTOM Morrison's sketch, "Between the Crosses." FRIPP FAMILY

FOREWORD

This is the memoir of one of the most successful artillery commanders of the Great War. His unpublished manuscript lay largely forgotten for almost a century, until Susan Raby-Dunne brought it to light. I have known Susan for many years. We first met while I was still the director of the Royal Canadian Artillery Museum and she was researching John McCrae. I have a great deal of respect for Susan, who is a very careful and thorough historian. I am extremely grateful to her for having involved me in this project, to say nothing of all that she's done to finally enter this memoir into the public record.

Major-General Sir Edward Whipple Bancroft Morrison, KCMG, CB, DSO, was born on July 6, 1867, in London, Ontario. He was known as "Dinky" Morrison to his friends. In his early twenties he took employment with the *Hamilton Spectator* as a journalist, where he eventually became city editor. Morrison joined the 4th Field Battery, a militia artillery battery, in Hamilton in 1897. The following year, he completed his gunnery training at the Royal School of Artillery in Kingston, Ontario. His final average of 87.25 percent was the second highest achieved by any student at the school in the preceding decade.

Morrison moved to Ottawa in 1898, where he took positions with the *Ottawa Citizen* and the 2nd Field Battery. In 1899, he volunteered for service in South Africa. He served with distinction as a lieutenant in "D" Battery, Royal Canadian Field

Artillery, and was awarded the Distinguished Service Order for his actions at the Battle of Leliefontein on November 7, 1900. He returned home from the war in January 1901. Later that year, he published a book about his experiences, entitled *With the Guns in South Africa*. It is an excellent read. Morrison ultimately rose to be the editor-in-chief of the *Ottawa Citizen*. In the militia, he eventually became the commanding officer of the 8th Brigade of Field Artillery in Ottawa.

Morrison married Emma Thacker Kaye Fripp on January 16, 1911. Emma had three children from a previous marriage. Her eldest son, Herbert Fripp, served as Morrison's Aide-de-Camp and worked on his staff for most of the Great War.

In 1913, Morrison left the *Citizen* to take up full-time military duty and become Director of Artillery, in the rank of lieutenant-colonel. It is at this point that the narrative in his memoirs begins.

After the Great War, in May of 1919, Morrison returned home. He was knighted the following month. From 1919 until his retirement in 1924, he served successively as Deputy Inspector-General of Artillery, Master-General of the Ordnance, and finally as Adjutant General. Morrison died suddenly of heart failure on May 28, 1925, at the age of fifty-seven.

Sometime between 1918 and his death, Sir Edward wrote his memoirs of the Great War. He initially produced a handwritten draft. This was then typed into the manuscript that Susan Raby-Dunne later located. It appears that he did review the typed manuscript; however, he clearly did not feel that it was ready for publication, as evidenced by the fact that he left areas of text blank, apparently pending further research. His sources are unknown, but given the time frame in which the manuscript was produced, Morrison would have relied mainly upon his own memory and any personal notes that he had kept (the Canadian Army Historical Section did not even finish sorting the available official material until 1929). While the manuscript was never published, portions were printed as a serial in the *Ottawa Citizen* in 1928.

Aside from proofreading, my part in the project was to go through the manuscript to identify all of the individuals mentioned, and to suggest notes to clarify any military- or artillery-specific text as necessary. In so doing, I relied most heavily upon the outstanding collection of war diaries and personnel records available online at Library and Archives Canada. In terms of secondary sources, I principally used *The Gunners of Canada: The History of The Royal Regiment of Canadian Artillery Volume I 1534–1919* and *Official History of The Canadian Army in the First World War: Canadian Expeditionary Force 1914–1919*, both by Colonel G.W.L. Nicholson;

The History of the Royal Regiment of Artillery: Western Front 1914–1918 by General Sir Martin Farndale; and the four volumes of *The Order of Battle of Divisions*, compiled by Major A.F. Becke as part of the *British Official History of the Great War*. I consulted numerous other sources, the most important of which were selected volumes of the *British Official History of the Great War*, edited by Brigadier-General Sir James E. Edmonds; selected volumes of the *Official History of Australia in the Great War* by C.E.W. Bean; the *Dictionary of Canadian Biography*, edited by Francess Halpenny (particularly useful was the biography of Morrison by William Rawling contained therein); and the Canadian Virtual War Memorial website, maintained by Veterans Affairs Canada.

I owe many thanks to Clive Prothero-Brooks, collections manager at The Royal Canadian Artillery Museum, for his enthusiastic help with my research in the museum's archives. I also wish to thank Andrew Currey at the Australian War Memorial for identifying an officer in the II ANZAC Corps at Passchendaele. With these references in mind, any errors in the notes that I sent to Susan are my responsibility alone.

As I went through the manuscript, I was astounded by the breadth and accuracy of Morrison's recollections. The only exception to this accuracy was during the period of March to June 1915. In this section there were some puzzling statements. There are two possible reasons why Morrison's memory may have been a little less precise in this period. First, he was a lieutenant-colonel commanding a field artillery brigade, and as such did not have the same scope of information and overall knowledge of battlefield events that he would later benefit from as a divisional and corps artillery commander. Thus, his impressions of the period in question may not have been based upon direct experience and therefore may have resulted in some confusion on his part.

The second reason is that Morrison suffered an accidental injury on July 19, 1915, when his horse tripped while he was riding and rolled over him. He was hospitalized from July 19 to July 22 with injuries to his head, chest, and knee. It is a virtual certainty that he suffered a concussion as a result of this accident. It is quite possible that this injury interfered with some of those short-term memories belonging to the preceding months. He was diagnosed as having defective vision in his left eye in 1919 during his demobilization medical, but it is unknown whether this eye damage was related to the 1915 head injury. In any case, inconsistencies in the narrative, rare as they are, have been duly noted; regardless, this memoir remains a breathtaking account of the Great War, in which Morrison's character and abilities shine through.

Sir Edward was a morally and physically courageous man. He did what he felt was right despite the risk of censure by higher authorities, and often moved well forward in the front lines in order to personally view the battlefield. As a commander, he fostered an environment that encouraged innovation—in terms of both the technical and the tactical aspects of gunnery. He was also very demanding, and insisted on the highest standards from the units under his command. The result was that the Canadian Corps led the Allied Forces in the employment of artillery in battle.

In the century since the War, Morrison has been overshadowed by the reputations of three of the War's most brilliant staff officers, all of whom worked for him: Field Marshal Sir Alan Francis Brooke, General Andrew George Latta McNaughton, and General Henry Duncan Graham "Harry" Crerar. These men became the most illustrious of many gifted staff officers who worked for Morrison during the War—though to credit any staff officer too much is a mistake in my view.

The grim reality of the Great War is that there was no shortage of brilliant staff officers in the British Army. What was in short supply were general officers willing to accept the advice, innovations, and plans of their staff. At the end of the day, it is the role of all staff officers to present well-developed plans for approval by their commander, but it is the commander alone who is responsible for the success or failure resulting from the orders issued. Under Morrison's command, Canada's Gunners won all of their battles and truly paved the way to victory for the Canadian Corps.

General Andrew McNaughton was interviewed by John Swettenham on June 3, 1965, for his book *McNaughton Volume 1 1887–1939*. Looking back, with the perspective of a former army commander himself, McNaughton said of his commanding general in the Great War:

> Morrison's forte was to employ the rest of us to do the details of the staff work and technical and scientific aspects of gunnery. He was a good commander and if you could prove your case you got his full and firm support—for ammunition, guns, methods of attack, liaison, and all the things you had to have in general.

In a corps where promotion was based upon merit and underperforming officers were relieved of command, McNaughton's appraisal should come as no surprise. Lieutenant-General Sir Arthur William Currie, himself an artillery officer and very intolerant of leaders whom he felt did not measure up, wrote an entry in Morrison's pay book shortly after the War. Susan uncovered it in her research, and it is fitting here to leave the penultimate word to the General Officer commanding the Canadian Corps between 1917 and 1919, for whom Morrison worked:

> I desire here to record my appreciation of the outstanding qualifications of Maj Gen Morrison, CB, CMG, DSO, as a gunner. He knows his work thoroughly and loves a fight. He is keen, energetic, gallant, capable, and loyal. He is a good organizer, far-seeing, fair, and just.—A.W. Currie, Lt. Gen.

Of course, the truly final word now goes to Sir Edward himself, his voice restored to the history of the Great War through this wonderful book.

UBIQUE

Major (Retired) Marc George

MAY 2017

Lieutenant-General Sir Arthur William Currie's praise of Morrison, handwritten in Morrison's "Officers Record of Services—Army Book 489."

A WORD FROM THE COLONEL COMMANDANT
OF THE CANADIAN ARTILLERY

"But it is still possible for eye-witnesses to bring home to their countrymen some inspiration for their children's children to cherish, and a partial description of those heroic deeds which roused the emulation of the finest troops who took part in the Armageddon of the Great War." — Major-General Sir Edward Morrison

With the centenary commemorations of the battles of the Great War, a new generation of Canadians has been awakened to the tragic sacrifices and extraordinary achievements of their country and its army during that terrible conflict. The part played by the Canadian Artillery was denoted by unsurpassed dutifulness, courage, and stoicism; brilliant tactical innovation; and the world-leading application of science and technology to the utility and effectiveness of gunnery.

In assembling and editing the memoir of Major-General Sir Edward Morrison, KCMG, CB, DSO, Susan Raby-Dunne has brought to light an invaluable primary source—an account of the Gunners' essential contribution to victory, offering as it does the personal experience of a man who fought in the War from beginning to end, in appointments of high responsibility ranging from his pre-war role as Director of

Artillery to his wartime post as Commander of the Canadian Corps at Vimy, Hill 70, and Passchendaele, and throughout the Hundred Days.

Morrison's battlefield virtuosity and personal bravery place him in the forefront of the great Gunners of that era, of which there are many, and constitute an enduring source of pride and inspiration for all members of The Royal Regiment of Canadian Artillery. May I also state here our indebtedness to Ms. Raby-Dunne, not only for her commitment to the memory of Edward Morrison, but also to that of his fellow Gunner and close friend John McCrae, who features significantly in this memoir. She is a true friend of the Regiment.

Brigadier-General (Retired) J.J. Selbie, OMM, CD
COLONEL COMMANDANT
THE ROYAL REGIMENT OF CANADIAN ARTILLERY
MAY 2017

A WORD FROM THE SENIOR SERVING
GUNNER OF THE CANADIAN ARTILLERY

Why do we read memoirs? I think it's because we've discovered someone who interests us and we want to hear their side of the story. Memoirs put us in the mind of the author. We hope to learn things that only they knew, experience feelings that only they can describe, and add their perspective to events we have read about elsewhere. When I read a memoir, I invariably compare myself with the author—could I do what he or she has done? In the case of Major-General Sir Edward "Dinky" Morrison, as much as I'd like to think that I could have done what he did, I must be honest in saying that I know that I could not.

As the Senior Serving Gunner in The Royal Regiment of Canadian Artillery, I am not far removed in function and position from the role General Morrison played at various times in the Great War. Like him, I have served in varying capacities throughout my career, planning for the use of artillery in combat—but never have I done so in the circumstances in which he found himself in the summer of 1914 and over the four years that followed.

This book is not only about an artillery officer; it is about an army officer of the highest calibre. Major (Retired) Marc George has already commented on the praise General Morrison received from Sir Arthur Currie: "He knows his work thoroughly and loves a fight. He is keen, energetic, gallant, capable, and loyal. He is a good organizer, far-seeing, fair, and just." There is not an officer in the army today who does not aspire to embody every word in those three short sentences.

General Morrison takes us on a journey that every artillery officer—indeed, every army officer—needs to experience. With his memoirs we join him at the outset of the War, travel across the quagmire of the training areas on Salisbury Plain, fight through every major battle of the Canadian Expeditionary Force, and end at demobilization. General Morrison speaks to us of the horrors of the trenches without hyperbole, but with sufficient descriptors so that we are at once shocked by the scenes he witnessed and amazed by the courage and spirit of the Canadian soldier. His voice is that of an immensely proud commander, consistently praising the soldiers and NCOs who continued to go "over the top" while grieving the heavy losses they so often sustained. He recognizes the unsung heroes: the stretcher-bearers, the drivers, the ammunition handlers, and the medical orderlies, and he poignantly speaks of his friend John McCrae and what led him to write his iconic poem.

What General Morrison does not do is place emphasis on his personal achievements, nor on the countless times he led from the front, sharing the risk and hardship with the soldiers. His matter-of-factness when recounting a particularly hazardous situation ("Six men who were immediately beside me were killed or wounded") says as much about the degree of danger in which these soldiers served as it does the kind of leader General Morrison was. He is respectfully critical of senior commanders when appropriate, basing his assessment on fact rather than emotion or conjecture. Throughout, it is clear that he believes that the lion's share of the Canadian efforts fell to those who were led: "Never once did the troops fail their leaders unless their leaders first failed them."

From a gunner's standpoint (and I can't resist), General Morrison is remarkably instructive as to the tactics, techniques, and procedures of the employment of artillery during the First World War. He speaks to the innovations of the era that improved effectiveness, gained efficiency, and greatly contributed to the Allies' ultimate victory. Much of what was pioneered under Morrison's command is still fundamental to the modern artillery battle. Indeed, today we find ourselves in another era where emerging technologies demand the same innovative thinking to counter them: armed and remotely piloted vehicles; long-range, precision-guided munitions; combat in complex terrain; cyber-warfare; and information dominance are but a few examples of the challenges faced by the gunners of today.

I began this note by wondering if I could do what General Morrison had done. I still believe I could not. But what this remarkable story also left me with is a strong sense of the things in our military profession that endure, and the lessons that transcend time: good leadership, innovation, courage, humility, professionalism, patriotism, and last but not least, a good sense of humour.

On that note, I'll conclude with this excerpt, written in his usual matter-of-fact tone, in which General Morrison recalls a visit to his headquarters by a breathless, perturbed, and generally unimpressed British staff officer with a message from the Army Commander:

"'General Morrison, do you know that the Army Commander is appalled at the amount of ammunition you have used today?'

'So are the Germans,' I retorted."

Thank you, Dinky.

UBIQUE

Major-General Simon C. Hetherington, OMM, MSC, CD

SENIOR SERVING GUNNER

THE ROYAL REGIMENT OF CANADIAN ARTILLERY

KINGSTON, ONTARIO

MAY 2017

INTRODUCTION

This memoir is long overdue for entering into the record of history—and of Canadian heroes. Its genesis actually began in 2005 with my research into John McCrae: soldier, physician, and writer of the iconic Great War poem "In Flanders Fields." Very shortly after I began that research, the name of Edward Morrison came up. It didn't take long to realize that these two men were close friends, having probably met initially in the militia, and then cementing a lifelong friendship as artillery lieutenants bound for the Boer War in 1899. At the beginning of the Great War, then Lieutenant-Colonel Edward Morrison was Major McCrae's commanding officer and commanded the 1st Brigade Canadian Field Artillery.

Upon performing an Internet search during this time in 2005, I could find very little about Morrison. The first thing that appeared on my screen was a handwritten copy of "In Flanders Fields," apparently given to Morrison by McCrae. By the time I had travelled to Ottawa and spent nine days in the national archives reading everything they had by or about John McCrae, I had found many mentions of Colonel Morrison throughout McCrae's diaries and letters. McCrae expressed the highest admiration for Morrison: his character, his leadership, and his bravery during the Second Battle of Ypres between April 22 and May 9, 1915. McCrae believed that Colonel Morrison should have been awarded medals for his bravery during that time, or at least been mentioned in dispatches, but there was no one of a sufficiently high rank anywhere near the firing line during the battle who might make the necessary recommendations.

While prodding staff at the archives, I accidentally caused the discovery of a single scrapbook that had been misplaced for years. It was a scrapbook containing newspaper extracts of Morrison's unpublished First World War memoir, parts of which had been released as a serial in the *Ottawa Citizen* in 1928, three years after his death. I'd never known of its existence before then. The newspaper columns were glued into the red, leather-bound scrapbook, and I had the staff make copies of the entire thing for me.

The more I learned about Morrison and the Great War, the more astonished I became that he was relatively unknown by anyone other than some artillery personnel, a few war historians, and the most avid military history buffs.

A visit to Beechwood Cemetery made me feel that he had been completely lost to obscurity when I found his gravestone. It was a small, modest marker made of three concentric stone squares, the largest being on the bottom. The cross that had once sat on top of the smallest square was long gone. Black stains discoloured it with something that looked like mildew—*Hardly befitting someone of his stature*, was my thinking. It was inscribed simply:

To the Memory of my Husband
Maj. Gen. Sir Edward Morrison,
K.C.M.G., C.B., D.S.O.
Born July 8th 1865, Died May 28th 1925

There is a discrepancy here as to Morrison's date of birth. On his attestation papers he lists it as July 6, 1867, and that is the date that will be on the restored marker. It seems that the gravestone was designed by his wife. Was the marker of this key military man not considered a worthy undertaking by the Canadian government?

Along with my years of research on McCrae, I began to learn a lot about Morrison, too. I read his excellent memoir of the Boer War, *With the Guns in South Africa*. It was an interesting and vivid account of his time there, and his black wit caused me to laugh out loud more than once. I could only imagine the hilarity around the Karoo campfires with his friend John McCrae, who was also a great raconteur and loved a good laugh.

After publishing two books about McCrae, I turned my attention fully to Edward Whipple Bancroft Morrison. He served in the Great War from the absolute beginning in 1914 to its very end, with demobilization, in 1919. He was in virtually every major battle that the Canadian Forces fought in, and commanded the

Canadian Artillery from late 1916 until demobilization. Upon looking for photographs of Canadian Corps Commander General Arthur Currie, I found that almost every photograph of him during the last hundred days featured Morrison also—often unnamed. Here he was, in photographs variously with Currie, HRH The Prince of Wales, Field Marshal Sir Douglas Haig, and other prominent leaders of the Great War. I even found him on film, talking to another officer in the background as Currie was giving a speech sometime in 1918. How do we Canadians not know more about this man?

My first mission, back in 2008—before I ever thought of writing about Morrison or getting his memoir published—was to put the wheels in motion to have his gravestone restored. That is how I met the Fripps. John and Shaun Fripp were Morrison's stepgrandsons, Morrison having married their grandmother, Emma Fripp, in 1911. John Fripp owned the plot, so I got his permission in writing to restore the marker, and the cemetery generously volunteered to cover the cost. Herbert Downing Fripp, John and Shaun's father, was buried right next to Morrison, denoted by a simple, flat rectangular marker that showed no indication of military service at all. I soon learned that he was also a Great War veteran and Gunner. I had no idea until I jumped into this project that Captain Herbert Downing Fripp had served with Morrison, and in fact had been his Aide-de-Camp.

I came to learn that the Fripps had almost all of Morrison's war memorabilia, including his medals; writings; sketches; a three-hundred-page, typewritten memoir-in-progress; photographs; letters; his blue officer's book, the "Officer's Record of Services—Army Book 489" (containing Currie's handwritten accolade); and other treasures. They graciously allowed me to take temporary possession of several things pertinent to his service in the First World War.

So this is the complete and formerly unpublished memoir of a smart, feisty, dedicated, self-effacing, funny, tough gunner commander in the Great War who "saw the whole show," to use an expression of his friend John McCrae's: "from the soup to the coffee." It's my hope that this project helps set the Canadian historical record of the Great War straight in this small yet significant way.

Susan Raby-Dunne
LONGVIEW, ALBERTA
MAY 2017

PREFACE
By Major-General
Sir Edward Morrison

S o long as Canadians exist as a race, history will credit them with a proud heritage of glory in the greatest of all conflicts of this—or any other—age.

Their prowess in the field could not be over-praised—and not only by the Allies, as the enemy joined in lauding their valour and steadfastness in the field. It was a common saying that the Canadians could not get enough fighting, and by the capture of Mons at the end of the War they could be said to have been in at the death.[1]

As one who served in every field in which our countrymen fought for the Empire in the Great War, the author may claim to have a first-hand knowledge of how our men garnered their glory upon over a score of hard-fought fields.

Of the men of the Canadian Corps, it was proudly said by their Officers, at the end of five years of relentless fighting, that they had never lost a gun nor relinquished a trench that they had failed to recapture.

Of the many fine tributes paid to the "Men of the Northern Zone," perhaps none was quite so finely generous as that of the Third Australians,[2] who met and wildly cheered the victorious Canadians as they came down from the capture of Passchendaele Ridge.

"Good old Canadians—

You are the only ones who could do it!"

---

1   In other words, the Canadians played a key role in the final defeat of the German army.

2   The 3rd Australian Division.

Chapter 1

A FOOL THERE WAS

I t is often said of the announcement of the War in Canada that it came as a great surprise, but it surprised only those who had not been on the *qui vive*.[1] Some had taken warning months in advance, and, foreseeing the strain on Canada's resources, had made preparations on a large scale.

Among these alert and far-sighted ones were Colonel Sam Hughes[2] and the public men who gave him the appointment of Minister of Militia. Among the short-sighted were those who abused him and derided his appointment in the early summer of 1913. From the very first, Colonel Hughes showed his excellent grasp of the trend of events, and gauged aright the dimensions of the rapidly approaching war cloud. Three years before the war he placed orders with British armament firms for about three hundred field guns, and, when the orders were not filled, he filed a demand with the same firms for five hundred field guns and field howitzers in total and two hundred machine guns.

For some reason which I never heard explained satisfactorily, the British armament companies did not fill these orders, with the exception of twenty 18-pounder guns, until long after the commencement of the War.

---

1   On the alert.

2   Ultimately Lieutenant-General, The Honourable Sir Samuel Hughes, KCB, PC, Minister of Militia and Defence, October 10, 1911, until dismissed by Prime Minister Sir Robert Borden on November 14, 1916.

As Director of Artillery I was sent to England to insist on the immediate delivery of this armament, with authority from the Minister to cancel the order unless at least a percentage of the field guns were immediately shipped to Canada. Even under this threat, I received—only grudgingly—from the Vickers Company those twenty 18-pounder field pieces, and these were the gun tubes only. These tubes were later mounted on carriages in Ottawa, for Colonel Hughes had encouraged the Ottawa Car Company to equip their excellent factory for the manufacture of gun carriages, limbers, and nearly all descriptions of military vehicles. This involved the establishment of patterns and the importation of skilled workmen: an enterprise that reflected the great patriotism of the proprietors of the company.

Of machine guns, although the orders had been placed for a year, and though every pressure had been brought to bear, these British armament companies were able to deliver only a few samples. It will be recalled that quite early in the War there were pertinent inquiries as to why the enemy appeared to have a monopoly on machine guns. It is no wonder that, when the First World War broke out in 1914, the British Empire was almost without machine guns. The simple fact is that Vickers, Coventry Ordnance Works, and similar huge armament companies allowed the Empire to be caught without any supply—or visible means of supplying—this invaluable weapon.

It may also be mentioned here that at the outbreak of the War, the British Army was so short of field howitzers and field guns that Canada had to send over in the armada what few surplus guns she had. The twenty field guns that the Vickers people had supplied under pressure, and which had been later mounted on carriages by the Ottawa Car Company, were sent along with an Indian Mountain Battery and two batteries of obsolete 5-inch howitzers, which Major John McCrae had commanded years before the War.[3] He later recognized them, when they were under my command at Bizet near Armentières. All of which indicates how hard-pressed the British Army was for artillery as early as May 1915.

In Canada, for years past, the troops had been kept in a half-starved condition of preparedness as regards numbers and equipment. With the exception of Colonel Sam Hughes, every writer on military preparedness scorned the idea that Canada could ever have an army; that if she could, it would never be able to fight anything above

---

3   John McCrae served in the Canadian Artillery from 1887 to 1905, retiring as a Major. He fought in the Boer War as an artillery officer between 1900 and 1901. The two militia batteries in Guelph were equipped with these 5-inch howitzers. McCrae commanded one of these batteries before he retired.

the prowess of a jackrabbit; and that the idea that it could ever be successfully pitted against the highly trained and magnificently armed troops of any European power would be the idea of a maniac.

But the Minister of Militia had just that idea. In fact, one of the first efforts at preparedness (an event which was almost consonant with the act alleged to have precipitated the War) was a mobilization of Canadian troops by Colonel Sam Hughes: the largest and most effective of its kind ever held in Canada up to that time. It was carried out in a most methodical manner and was in fact a practice mobilization for the whole of eastern Canada, from Lake Superior to New Brunswick. It was subsequently subjected to criticism as an illustration of Colonel Sam Hughes's latest effort at preparing a Canadian army to meet a German war, which, as yet, no one believed would ever occur.

I had been associated with Colonel Sam Hughes for nearly twenty-five years in the volunteer militia service when the War approached, and was then employed as Director of Artillery at the Department of Militia and Defence in Ottawa. Knowing him as long as I had I must admit that I was prepared to number him among the maniacs and numerous other critics of the Minister of Militia, when he one day announced that he was going to raise and immediately train and equip 33,000 troops of all arms and transport them at once to the seat of War. I thought I knew all about the resources of our militia, especially of the arm to which I belonged, and while I carefully assessed that arm and its resources, I did not believe it could equip a division of 33,000 troops and provide reinforcements for a war against Germany, especially as during the years 1911 to 1913 I had visited and observed some of the best-equipped corps in the Rhine Valley.

Through years of personal acquaintance I had come to know Colonel Sam Hughes intimately, and I regret to say that this latest evidence of my old friend's optimism, as well as his consummate confidence in the Canadian soldier, caused me to share the general opinion: that his plans of offence on the part of Canada were far beyond the possibility of carrying out.

But he proceeded to carry them into effect with an energy and ability that, at length, brought popular opinion into line with his wonderful optimism. There were wise men by the score to point out the difficulties that he had to face. Among the first were those who pointed out that the infantry of the division must be taught rifle fire. I have a distant recollection of a scene in Colonel Hughes's office during which only the loyal remembrance of an old friend brought me to his assistance; I felt that I was shouldering his own obloquy in taking his part. The question had been brought up, by one of the many critics, as to how 33,000 green young riflemen could be brought to a condition of training in arms (as well as courage) to meet the highly trained Prussian Guard. Strangely enough the man who put the question was Colonel Farquhar[4] of the Duke of Connaught's[5] staff, who subsequently was gazetted to the command of the Princess Pats[6] and later killed accomplishing the very thing he had ridiculed as impossible. Nettled by his tone I assumed the offensive and replied: "Why should not a bullet which will kill a Canadian militiaman similarly exterminate a Prussian Guard?"

Colonel Farquhar was too disgusted at the idea to make any reply.

"That is the way I like to hear men talk," retorted Colonel Sam Hughes.

By that time the Minister of Militia had thoroughly made up his mind to train and send overseas 33,000 Canadian militiamen to assist the British Army. Every Sunday morning at daylight he took me with him in his private car, and we proceeded at a high rate of speed to what later became known as Valcartier training ground. For the first visit or two, our observations saw little progress on the work. On nearly every visit thereafter, however, some slight progress was shown, for a few engineers, ordnance, or other officers of our permanent corps were taken along, and the work was being rushed. The Minister usually remained on the field at Valcartier, Quebec, until sundown, pressing on the work. Switches were built, ordnance and store buildings were prepared for storing equipment, and, finally, rifle butts for the training of the future army commenced to go up. The Minister had had all this work planned beforehand. The contractor was directed to provide ditching machines, and when once these were provided the progress of digging a mile and a half of rifle butts[7] was very rapid. In the same way ditches and wide streets were prepared. Within little

---

4   Lieutenant-Colonel Francis Douglas Farquhar, DSO, was a British officer who was Military Secretary to the Governor General. He obtained permission to name a regiment after the Governor General's daughter, Princess Patricia. Farquhar served as the first commanding officer of the Princess Patricia's Canadian Light Infantry from August 14, 1914, until he was mortally wounded on March 20, 1915.

5   His Royal Highness Prince Arthur, the Duke of Connaught and Strathearn, KG, KT, KP, GCB, GCSI, GCMG, GCIE, GCVO, GBE, VD, TD, ADC(P), PC, was Governor General of Canada from October 13, 1911, to November 11, 1916.

6   Princess Patricia's Canadian Light Infantry.

7   "Rifle butts" are mounds of earth built up to stop bullets in the target area of a rifle range. They were generally constructed by digging a ditch and mounding the excavated earth up on one side in order to form the "butts." Soldiers on a range fire from firing points at targets mounted on frames just in front of the butts.

more than a month after the declaration of war, a magnificent camp was completed that would provide tentage for 33,000 infantry as well as room for excellent drill grounds and targets.

What was accomplished by these battalions of ditch diggers reminded me of a conversation Colonel Hughes had begun in France about a year before. We had taken a party to the autumn manoeuvres and, in his usual manner (which was unfortunately so didactic as to prevent his opinion carrying its full weight), he proceeded to lay down the fact that, if he were commanding the Franco-German War, he would enlist the use of hundreds of mechanical ditch diggers, which would enable him at the outset to build trenches across France. This is exactly as it was subsequently done, but his enunciation of the manner in which the German plans could be met and opposed became a source of amusement to many of the trained soldiers present.

Within a few weeks the rifle practice began, and shortly the remarkable sight of 2,000 yards of rifle trenches, busily occupied by the incipient Canadian Army, could be observed, while the open spaces bordering on the colossal rifle range were used for physical training and small arm drill. The only arm it was impossible to exercise was the medium artillery, but luckily the men had been fairly well trained on artillery of all sizes in Petawawa earlier in the season.

After the third or fourth week, Valcartier had become such a hive of training that it was possible to carry out a really very fine review for His Excellency the Duke of Connaught.

Chapter 2

CANADA'S ARMADA

M eanwhile, Colonel Sam Hughes's energy continued to get things done in spite of opposition. One morning at Headquarters in Ottawa, there appeared some thirty or forty managers and officials of the big American and Canadian ocean liners. Before the day was over it was known that Colonel Sam Hughes—acting really on his own responsibility—had rented thirty-three of the largest liners on the north Atlantic to transport reinforcements for the British Army across the Atlantic to England. The transaction involved a very large amount of planning because many of the steamship companies had to change their mail routes and otherwise make alterations in their methods at very short notice.

This meeting with the steamship authorities was characteristic of the work that was being accomplished, and the manner in which it had been taken in hand. When General Hughes met these gentlemen and explained that he wanted nearly twoscore liners, they at once had as many reasons and a dozen more objections that would make it impossible to devote their vessels to the purpose of taking the Canadian 1st Division to England. It became necessary to impress upon them the fact that a world war was about to occur and that every formal consideration had to go by the board. After their vision had been enlarged, these gentlemen were handed over to a subordinate official and, before evening, the greatest armada that had ever crossed the Atlantic Ocean had been arranged for, irrespective of schedules and mail contracts.

In the course of preparing Canada's first contribution to the War, this sort of mind-broadening process had to be constantly gone through, and it required a man of the vision and character of General Hughes to get the nation moving. Gradually his vision and virility became instilled in the whole country. It was not work that could be done in a gentle or persuasive manner. He had a set formula with which he received every visitor to his office: "Did you come here to fight for your country, or to make money?" This pointed question almost invariably brought a flush to the faces of his visitors, but it saved time and brought them to the point, for it revealed the attitude of the very large majority at that crisis.

With remarkable rapidity the enlistment of men went on all over the Dominion, supervised by the Militia, the Permanent Corps, and (as a result of there being so few related opportunities afforded in the peace-loving country, which had no army and never expected to have one) practically anyone who had picked up a smattering of knowledge about soldiering at training camps or during the North-West Rebellion or the South African War. Gradually thousands of athletic young men were gathered at Valcartier, a few miles outside of the city of Quebec, where a tented city was laid out, its streets lit with electricity. Almost in no time thousands of visitors were going there by train to see the activities and visit the training ground where tens of thousands of civilians, animated by patriotic enthusiasm, were being turned into the first large unit of an army corps. Those who went there to scoff remained to wonder at what was being accomplished. War had been declared on August 4, 1914, and the month of September was not far spent when the Governor General, the Duke of Connaught, was informed that the 1st Division of Canada's army was ready for inspection. On a Sunday afternoon tens of thousands of visiting civilians were thrilled by the sight of over 30,000 mounted, foot, and artillery soldiers ranking past in magnificent order. Veteran soldiers who knew what war meant watched the sight with glistening eyes and felt already the pulse of victory in the wonderful enthusiasm that was turning the young men of a young country sealed in peace into a young army that went abroad, unafraid, for a death grapple with the best-trained and most experienced soldiers of the Old World countries.

On a night of pouring rain in about the last week of September 1914, the 1st Division of the Canadian Army commenced its first march to the port of embarkation at Quebec City. Never did the historic city experience the unfolding of a more wonderful page of history than when that army came pouring through the Stork Nightclub and passed the night saying farewell to their friends and dancing until the dawn, ere they quietly embarked under the shadow of Quebec City's La Citadelle.

Little did those soldiers think that Edinburgh after Flodden[1] would go down into history as but a faint tragedy compared to the history that they were so soon to create, and at such bloody cost to Canada.

One by one the troopships dropped down the Saint Lawrence River under sealed orders, and the first week of October found them rendezvoused in the Bay of Chaleur, whose high, rocky shores concealed them from the view of enemy spies. As the fleet of ocean liners gathered there, four or five comparatively small warships, looking deadly businesslike in their coats of battle grey, took up their stations like watchdogs guarding a flock of sheep. Most of Canada's army had never seen a battleship before, but they realized as these cruisers glided about among the high-decked ocean liners they were to guard that already they were face-to-face with the dangers of war.

Within a week, the Grand Armada was on the ocean and headed for England. It sailed in three columns—thirty-three ocean liners in all, crowded with troops—each column headed and brought up astern by a grim black warship. No Canadian who was aboard that armada will forget the thrilling incident that occurred not far past Newfoundland, when a strange battleship was seen ahead, causing fearful speculation as she headed down upon the fleet. What relief there was as she came down the lane between the lines of troopships, and what an ecstatic whirlwind of cheers burst from the tens of thousands that manned the rails as the Red Cross Ensign of England fluttered from her peak, and the British sailors lining the yards answered cheer for cheer.

There was not one of those tens of thousands who had ever been so glad before that Britain ruled the waves.

A day or two before we sighted England, a wireless message informed us that the city of Antwerp had been captured by the enemy. The best-informed among us believed that much other bad news would render the arrival of the Canadian Armada acceptable. On October 16 another message arrived, cancelling the order that was to take the armada up the English Channel to Southampton, and turning us into the harbour at Plymouth. Notwithstanding the cheering thousands on Plymouth Hoe as our well-trained captains took their ships, without pilots, into the Harbour of Devonport, and though we were heartened by the sight of the old three-decker ships of Nelson's day ablaze with bunting and their yards crowded with men, their lusty roars of welcome served as a reminder that not for the first time was the power and majesty of England being unsuccessfully challenged.

1   A reference to a poem written in the 1800s by William Edmondstoune Aytoun about the 1513 Battle of Flodden between England and Scotland.

Chapter 3

SOME UNPLEASANT THINGS, INCLUDING THE WAR OFFICE AND SALISBURY PLAIN

I t had been the intention to land the Canadian troops at Southampton and have them go into camp in the vicinity of Aldershot, but just before our arrival on October 16, the armada was ordered into Plymouth and we were informed that our destination had been changed to Salisbury Plain, which is the English artillery training area. The fact of the sudden change in the destination of this immense armada was quite sufficient to set aboard rumours that something had happened to render it dangerous to take the armada farther up the English Channel than Plymouth. Such was the case. The German submarines had commenced to show their power. They had actually succeeded in getting into the Channel, and had sunk a powerful cruiser there—or perhaps it would be more correct to say that a powerful cruiser had been sunk, and the admiralty had no evidence as to whether it had been sunk by striking a mine or torpedoed by a submarine. The result in either case was the same, but the British ironclads had not yet suffered sufficiently from the underwater craft for anyone to be sure how deadly they were, nor at what distance from their bases they were dangerous.

On the afternoon of the day of our arrival at Plymouth, the fleet commenced to unload its troops and we were told that the whole force would march to Salisbury Plain, a distance of about twenty miles. One of the first transports to unload was the steamer *Saxonia*,[1] which was loaded with artillery. A most unfortunate episode marked the arrival of those first Canadian troops who were bringing much needed aid to the mother country. It is worth recounting here, if only as one of the lessons of the War: namely, the absolute necessity of a better liaison between the red-taping imperial authorities and the troops from other parts of the Empire. The War was replete with similar incidents, but it can easily be imagined what a bad impression of the mentality (if not of the ordinary courtesy) of the people we had come to help was created by this incident.

As the transport docked, a staff officer arrived on board with written orders that not a man, horse, or gun was to be debarked without written orders from a certain officer of high rank in the port. Moreover, an armed guard in command of an officer was to be posted at the gangway to prevent any communication between the shore and the ship until further orders were received. Shortly after the transport was docked, a naval officer came on board, ignored the Canadian officer in charge of the guard, and proceeded at once to the captain of the transport, and ordered him in a most peremptory manner to have the guns and troops debarked at once. The captain, who was only too anxious to have the horses, guns, and men debarked before darkness set in, quite properly conveyed the order that had been given to the Canadian officer commanding the troops to remain aboard,[2] sent from what appeared to be the senior military officer at the port. The naval officer, instead of facilitating a situation which had apparently been caused by some clashing of authority with his "opposite number" in military rank, flew into a rage and commenced to browbeat the Canadian officer, making some observations to the effect that these half-trained troops did not know their duty, which drew the retort that they knew enough to carry out a written order, and that not a man or gun would leave the ship until the order was rescinded in writing by the officer who had issued it. In the meantime, the Canadian officer offered to send his adjutant to the military authority to report and ask to have the order changed. The naval officer indicated that he did not care a damn what he did, but that within a given time a force of sailors would be sent on board the *Saxonia* to force the guard on the gangway and proceed with the unloading of the ship. In

---

1   RMS *Saxonia* carried most of the 1st Brigade Canadian Field Artillery, along with the unit commanding officer, Lieutenant-Colonel Morrison, and the brigade surgeon and second-in-command, Major John McCrae (who later wrote "In Flanders Fields"). In total, 863 men, 633 horses, nineteen 18-pounder guns, and ninety-one horse-drawn vehicles were on board.

2   Morrison refers to himself in the third person here.

the course of half an hour the adjutant returned with a curt message, again in writing, instructing the Canadian officer to carry out his orders to the letter. By this time an armed party of about two hundred sailors had been drawn up on the deck, and as it would never do to allow a guard to be forced, the guard on the gangway was doubled and the officer in charge instructed that no armed parties were to be allowed to come aboard without the orders of the Commanding Officer.[3]

This was a nice state of affairs to mark the arrival of the first Canadian troops, whose only intention was to assist the mother country in the Great War! The naval gentleman actually went the length of sending to an adjacent dockyard for a party of junior naval officers to take charge of the landing party. Whether he was going to take the risk of bluffing the officer commanding the Canadians[4] is not known, but the situation had reached a very dangerous state when the captain of the *Saxonia* dissuaded the angry Englishman from letting his temper carry him away. Quite late in the evening a cancellation order arrived from the original issuing authority (who regrettably never put in an appearance except by deputy, nor made any explanation or apology for the ugly scrape that he had got the Canadians into with the senior arm of the service). Before the War was over, there had been a sufficient number of more or less similar incidents, not confined to Canadians, and it is to be hoped that before the next "combined manoeuvres" of Imperial[5] and overseas troops takes place, the War Office will draft some instructions governing relations. Because one of the lessons of the War will be that the so-called "Colonials" will not be inclined to put up with so much of this sort of red tape as they used to.

In order to reach Salisbury Plain it was necessary to entrain all the troops and material; they were taken through Devon for five or six hours by trains, cheered on their way by thousands of villagers and countrypeople. The 1st Artillery Brigade, having finished loading by about sundown, reached the detraining station at nearly midnight, and the news was broken to them that they had to proceed on foot to the camping place on Salisbury Plain. This march took all night, and it was near daylight when the marchers found themselves proceeding through the ghostly-looking objects standing beside the road, which turned out to be the Druidical stones at Stonehenge. It was barely sunrise when the very tired marchers, who had disembarked and

---

3   Morrison.

4   Morrison again.

5   Canadians referred to British Army units and formations as "Imperials."

entrained a brigade of field artillery before marching all night, finally threw themselves down in the empty tents and went fast asleep.

When they woke, the lack of preparedness of the camp, as compared with Valcartier, struck them forcibly, and this impression grew as the subsequent days and weeks went by. The Canadians little imagined in the first weeks of October, as they took up their quarters in that partially prepared camp, that nearly six months would elapse before they reached the seat of war. But such was the case, and those six months resulted in one of the most miserable and useless periods of hardship on which many look back. There was no information as to how the War was progressing, owing to the strict censorship prevailing. A cloud of gloom enveloped the towns and cities and every class of inhabitants. It was known that Antwerp and the eastern cities and towns of Belgium were in the hands of the Germans (because nearly every household and farmstead had its quota of Belgian refugees), but the only definite news from the War in the great London dailies like the *Times* and the *Evening Standard* consisted of ghastly casualty lists of two and three columns per day. These named officer casualties only, and were representative of the best regiments in the British Army. I say best not only from a martial standpoint, but as representing in their commissioned ranks the *crème de la crème* of British society: the sort of corps which in former wars had only been employed very sparingly, or in situations of the most serious description.

Another circumstance that affected the Canadians was the absence of British troops. The hoardings in London and elsewhere were flaming with great posters, on which the prominent figure was a recruiting sergeant pointing an accusative finger and backed by a fierce stare. Below him in large type were the words: "JOIN YOUR COUNTRY'S ARMY!" On the other hand the less reputable newspapers were burbling in an unconvincing way that it was "business as usual." Women in mourning appeared much scarcer than one would infer from the heavy casualty lists, until one learned that, by special request, purple had been substituted for black as the badge of mourning. The more the Canadians heard, the more they realized that the public and press of England were doing their utmost to keep a stiff upper lip, and that behind this great curtain of silence some terrible tragedy was being enacted, in which the safety of the Empire was threatened. They saw pale-faced lads in shoddy civilian clothes performing drills in village streets with wooden guns, and without a shred of a greatcoat or raincoat on as the cold of winter set in with rain and slush. When they were informed that this constituted the nucleus of "Kitchener's Army" (which they had only heard of in the newspapers—referred to as an organization of untold divisions of thoroughly equipped and highly trained troops—evidently for Berlin consumption), even the Canadian lads looked at each other askance. Then, as they realized how well-armed, clothed, and equipped they were themselves, and how much better trained and seasoned against hardship in comparison, they wondered why they were being kept month after month in the mud and misery of Salisbury Plain, with their fine horses dying of rot and themselves of spinal meningitis, while Britain's little regular army was filling the paper with casualties. They raved to be unleashed.

The weather that winter was unusually bad. Before Christmas of 1914 it rained for seven consecutive weeks; the sun was never seen, and nor were the occupants of the rotten tents ever dry. The magnificent horses of the Artillery stood in the mud up to their hocks until their hooves actually rotted off. The troops themselves knew that they were well-trained enough when they left Valcartier, and hardened, that they did not require a half-year's experience "under conditions such as an Englishman would not weather a donkey," as some outspoken visitor wrote to a London paper. The spinal meningitis threatened to become epidemic as the year wore its way out, and an undercurrent of desperation excited the Canadians. They demanded to be taken across the Channel to vent their rage upon the bodies of their enemies rather than die of disease in this senseless manner.

The first Canadian units to move for the scene of fighting were the PPCLI[6] and No. 2 Casualty Clearing Station under Colonel A.T. Shillington[7] of Ottawa. The latter left on November 6, 1915, and was the first Canadian unit to depart for France. There were, in addition, a considerable number of medical officers and Canadian nurses who went to assist the English units in handling the wounded of the First Battle of Ypres. The Princess Pats were successfully engaged in the vicinity of St. Eloi. One of the first officers killed was Captain Denzel Newton,[8] nephew of General Lord Dundonald.[9] Finally, fools from the War Office brought down the report that "the Canadians were complaining of their quarters on Salisbury Plain." If the troops were

---

6   Princess Patricia's Canadian Light Infantry

7   Lieutenant-Colonel Adam Tozeland Shillington. It was an army convention to refer to both lieutenant-colonels and colonels as "colonel." Colonel Shillington served in both world wars with the Royal Canadian Army Medical Corps.

8   Captain Denzel Onslow Cochrane Newton, MVO, was killed in action on January 9, 1915.

9   Lieutenant-General D.M.B.H. Cochrane, twelfth Earl of Dundonald, KCB, KCVO. Lord Dundonald was General Officer Commanding the Canadian Militia 1902–1904.

desperate before, they were exasperated beyond measure at this further senselessness. The Corps held indignation meetings and resented the reports as calumnies; all they wanted was to be allowed to go to France. There were many hundreds of surplus officers who were living on the Plain on the chance of getting over to fight; in fact, it was said there were more than enough to make a battalion by themselves. It was largely these gallant fellows, who, carried away by rage and disgust at the many misunderstandings, and not being under close duty or discipline, went up to London and "painted the town," bringing down a broadside of criticism and condemnation on the heads of the long-suffering old 1st Division. It can easily be imagined how, when the news of this made the wires to Canada sizzle, the friends and relatives of the personnel of the 1st Division thought for sure that they had gone to the dogs.

However, sensible Canadians in London soon got to the bottom of the trouble, with the result that in the month of January the Canadian troops were transferred to billets and the horses (what was left of their number) to barns and sheds in the innumerable towns and villages immediately surrounding the Plain, where within a fortnight the horses' coats were sleek and the men shiny as to boots and buttons. After all that had been said in the newspapers about the "carrying on" of the Canadians in London, it was a pleasant surprise to the inhabitants of the villages and country houses to discover what quiet and respectable guests the Canadians were. Not only were they made comfortable, but they were welcome guests; so popular were they that Devizes and Salisbury became that sort of "home from home" of the Canadian Corps during most of the War.

Never will the miseries of the winter of 1914–1915 on Salisbury Plain be forgotten by the survivors of the Old Originals, and it is to be hoped that when the day of appropriate recognition comes, possibly when the Parliament of Canada passes a vote of thanks to the Commander, officers, and men of the Canadian Army Corps, at least some similarly inexpensive recognition will be conveyed to the good people of Devizes and the surrounding villages of the Plain, who took into their hospitable. homes the thousands of muddy, rain-soaked, bronchitic, rheumatic, and weatherbeaten Canadians, and salvaged them from a slough of downheartedness after months of useless suffering. During no winter of the War did the Canadians suffer anything like these useless hardships; in fact, their subsequent transference to the good dry barns with plenty of straw in Flanders seemed a life of luxury in comparison.

Chapter 4

CURRENT EVENTS

Toward the latter part of our stay on Salisbury Plain a number of instructional officers reported from France to convey the latest tips on the new war. Nearly all were officers who had recovered from wounds, and most of their conversation consisted of explanations regarding the new importance of field telephones, shell-proof gun pits, and the absolute necessity of moving into action under cover to prevent annihilation. In a general way we also gathered from these officers the salient features of the campaign to date: the defeat and retreat from Mons, the pursuit of the Germans to the vicinity of Paris, and then how the Allies, in some mysterious way, had routed them and chased them pell-mell back to Belgium.

As a matter of fact the situation in Europe on October 16, 1914, when the Canadian Division arrived at Plymouth, was as follows.

By that date the German Army (having captured Liège, Namur, Brussels, Antwerp, and Bruges) had pushed entirely through Belgium, and the staff officers of the British First Army had enjoyed their view of the North Sea from the pier at Oostende. On the same day the French and British armies, having driven the Germans from the gates of Paris, were engaged in giving them an additional kick at the First Battle of the Aisne. From that fateful date, the German mind, which hitherto had thought of Paris as its objective, turned its attention westward from whence had come "the contemptible little army"[1] which, at Mons, and again in front of Paris, had so

---

1   According to Kaiser Wilhelm.

disarranged the plans of the German General Staff. It is not too much to say that then and there the inspiration was born that it might be well for them to turn their attention to the protection of Berlin.

In conversation with a representative of the American Ambassador's office in Paris at about this time, a German diplomat in Berlin minimized the setbacks that the Fatherland had received and claimed that the Kaiser had so far been successful in all his ambitions except that his troops had not yet captured Calais.

In his book written after the War, General Ludendorff relates that on the evening of the great victory by the Canadians at Amiens, August 8, 1918, he felt for the first time that Germany's defeat was certain. The careful reader of history, with the benefit of the knowledge of subsequent consecutive events, might inform General Ludendorff that a good hindsight would have enabled him to have his premonition four years earlier, when that negligible reinforcement of the "contemptible little army" debarked at Plymouth.

See *The Notebook of an Attaché* by Fisher Wood.

The fact remains that when the Canadians debarked in England they knew practically nothing of the progress or trend of the War. There was little in the English papers except casualty lists, and such alleged news as did escape the censor was rather calculated to deceive rather than enlighten. Personally I got an inkling of the progress of the German Army in Belgium by reading that von Kluck's army staff had taken up its quarters in the hotel in Bruges where I had stayed less than six months before.

A perfect budget of intelligence reached me one dismal, rainy evening on the Plain, when a big touring car squelched through the mud and stopped in front of my tent. It was loaded with friends from Paris, who had been very hospitable and comfortable when I had last dined at their house. That evening the postprandial[2] talk had been kindly directed towards convincing me that the profession of arms was obsolete; the world was consecrated to the making of money and war would soon be no more. It was difficult to realize that though not one year had passed, my hosts were virtually fugitives from Paris and the news they brought was that the Hun was "at their gates" and the French Government had fled to Bordeaux.

Meanwhile two topics were being debated in the camp: when the Canadians were to be rewarded with an invitation to take part in the fighting, and who was to command them in battle. Many names were mentioned, but by no accident was there ever a Canadian held up to their uncritical eye as the man qualified to lead

---

2   During or relating to the period after dinner or lunch.

them to the German lines in France. It may throw some light on the feeling towards the military possibilities of the Canadians at the time to say that when the Princess Pats regiment (which was to be composed entirely of officers and men who had seen active service) was raised, one difficulty to be faced was that of selecting officers with the qualifications necessary to lead such men. In the light of subsequent events, readers can appreciate my feelings when a rumour reached me that my modest friend Lt. Colonel Turner, vc,[3] had been honoured with an offer to command a company in the regiment, and was likely to accept it—chiefly because the bait had been held out to all joining that keen organization that it would be the first corps to leave for the War, and to have the joy of crossing bayonets with the Germans. I telegraphed him to have breakfast with me before he gave his final decision to the gallant commanding officer of the Pats, with the result that the regiment remained short a company commander, and the Canadian Army saved a lieutenant-general.

It is not in any hypercritical spirit that this and other incidents are mentioned. The responsible leaders of greater armies than Canada's inexperienced division were thrown into a frenzy of excitement by the advent of the World War. Government officials and military organizers were forced to prepare for war in a time limit measured by hours, when days were all too short to cope with the innumerable details of preparation.

The provision of a commander for the 1st Canadian Division no doubt overtaxed the exertions of the British War Office and, "tell it not in Gath,"[4] since the untried Canadians had not yet proven themselves in the crucible of Ypres, there was probably no waiting list of ambitious and suitable leaders such as would later have been proud to accept the command of those troops who, once at war, proved themselves the superiors of the Prussian Guard and established a worldwide reputation.

Probably I was one of the first who recognized a strange officer riding about among the tents on the Plain one morning at daylight. His face looked familiar and reminiscent of my South African days. I recognized him as General Alderson,[5] and

---

3   Ultimately Lieutenant-General Sir Richard Ernest William Turner, vc, kcb, kcmg, dso, cd. Turner commanded the 3rd Infantry Brigade from September 29, 1914, to August 11, 1915; 2nd Canadian Division from August 17, 1915, to November 26, 1916; and was then General Officer Commanding Canadian Forces in the British Isles between December 1916 and April 1918, at which point he was named Chief of the General Staff, Overseas Military Forces of Canada until July 31, 1919.

4   Biblical quote, 2 Samuel 1:20: "Proclaim it not in the streets of Ashkelon, lest the daughters of the Phillistines be glad, lest the daughters of the uncircumcised rejoice."

5   Lieutenant-General Sir Edwin Alfred Hervey Alderson, kcb, General Officer Commanding 1st Canadian Division from September 29, 1914, to September 12, 1915, and Canadian Corps September 13, 1915, to May 28, 1916.

was smitten with the intuition (which proved correct) that he had been selected because of his slight connection with the Canadian Forces during the Boer War.

About the time that Lord Roberts[6] had handed over the command of that little affair to Lord Kitchener,[7] Colonel Alderson (as he was then) was commissioned to raise a corps of Canadian Scouts. He had selected Major Gat Howard,[8] an officer whose services as an Indian fighter in our North-West Rebellion, and fondness for fighting in South Africa, rendered him just the man to take charge of such a corps. Colonel Alderson, on Howard's recommendation, was good enough to offer me the second-in-command, but my acquaintance with him was limited to a visit at Pretoria with Major Howard, when we discussed the object and duties of the new corps, a peculiarity of which was that every scout was to have the rank of sergeant. I was most favourably impressed by Colonel Alderson and would have gladly accepted a command under him had it been possible to secure leave by cable in time, even had not Major Howard smilingly thrown out the inducement that the second-in-command would stand a good chance of quick promotion. Another officer who was connected with Colonel Alderson and the Scouts was Major Beatty,[9] a cousin of Admiral Beatty,[10] and a most gallant officer who was with Major Gat Howard when he was killed a month later, and who nearly shared his fate. He also was well acquainted with the Canadians who had been in South Africa. Major Beatty was appointed as Aide-de-Camp to Major-General Alderson when the latter took command of the 1st Canadian Division on Salisbury Plain. Beatty served with great gallantry during the term of the General's command and was very popular with all the ranks. By his helpfulness and efficiency, Major Beatty reconciled human elements in the division who did not always find the manner of his principal congenial.

---

6   Field Marshal Frederick Sleigh Roberts, 1st Earl Roberts, VC, KG, KP, GCB, OM, GCSI, GCIE, KStJ, VD, PC. Commander of British Forces in the Boer War, 1899–1900.

7   Field Marshal Horatio Herbert Kitchener, 1st Earl Kitchener, KG, KP, GCB, OM, GCSI, GCMG, GCIE, PC. Commander of British Forces in the Boer War, 1900–1902. Kitchener was Secretary of State for War from 1914 until his death in 1916.

8   Major Arthur Lochead Howard, killed in action February 17, 1901. He was called "Gat" because he had been a representative of the Gatling Company and brought two Gatling Guns to Canada in 1885 for use in the North-West Rebellion.

9   Major Charles Howard Longfield Beatty, DSO. Died of his wounds May 17, 1917. Charles was in fact Admiral Beatty's older brother, not a cousin as Morrison states.

10   Admiral of the Fleet David Richard Beatty, 1st Earl Beatty, GCB, OM, GCVO, DSO, PC. Commander 1st Battlecruiser Squadron 1914–1916 and Commander-in-Chief of the Grand Fleet 1916–1919.

Chapter 5

THE INTERESTING BUSINESS OF "TAKING OVER"

T he elements of the 1st Division got their orders to move out by rail for Avonmouth during the first week of February 1915, and the orders were received with the greatest enthusiasm. Before departing, the artillery was all tested in shooting on Salisbury Plain. My brigade, the 1st, entrained on the evening of February 7 and the following day embarked on a steamer at Avonmouth and headed south-eastward into the Bay of Biscay, which was carrying on in its usual turbulent manner. The ship was an ordinary freighter, and all on board—officers and crew—could not do too much to make us welcome and comfortable. The officers even insisted on turning out of their staterooms for us.

For three days we tumbled about in the Bay of Biscay. The name of the place we were to land on the Continent was kept a great secret, but it gradually became known that our landing port would be in Saint-Nazaire. As it was the first time we had heard of that port being used, we drew our own conclusions. The submarine had made itself feared, if not actually dreaded.

We were received by a crowd of thousands on the piers at the mouth of the harbour, nearly all of which appeared to be women and children in mourning. This struck us the more forcibly on account of the tacit arrangement in England that purple was to be worn instead of black. The entraining arrangements were under the supervision of Major-General Sir James Asser,[1] and were carried out in the most systematic manner.

Having disembarked early in the afternoon, the whole division was on board trains bound northward by nightfall. In the quaint city of Nantes, where the railway runs along the streets in one of the most populous parts of the city, the buildings' windows and balconies were crowded with ladies waving handkerchiefs; there did not appear to be enough men available in the streets to raise a cheer. The railway itself, its culverts, bridges, and tunnels, were guarded by Territorials in uniforms of blue and red. Both the uniforms and the men inside of them were noticeably old.

The arrangements for feeding the men and horses during the trip were excellent. Huge braziers of charcoal on which the men could do their own cooking were provided at the stations where the train stopped at meal hours, and hot water for tea and coffee was provided from the engine. We were impressed by the absence of any sign of war—notwithstanding the great mass of armed men that had surged down through France from Belgium to the Marne and back again.

On the morning of February 14 the 1st Canadian Division arrived at its destination, an area on the frontier between France and Belgium, just west of Ypres, and between that city and Calais. The division was bedded out after the sealed pattern arrangement it was to follow during its wanderings throughout the War. The infantry and artillery batteries were allocated to a large farm; regiments and brigades to small villages; larger units to small towns; and the division headquarters to the most commodious and centrally located chateau or town hall. The 1st Brigade Canadian Field Artillery was billeted in the village of Méteren, where they saw the first signs of fighting. The old stone church had been more or less knocked about, chiefly by machine gun fire. Little clusters of wooden crosses at different places immediately outside the village limits bore the names of British soldiers who had been killed in a small engagement that had taken place at Méteren about the middle of October, 1914. Peculiarly well-made telephone wire, which had been insulated with what looked like gutta-percha,[2] was stretched along hedges for miles around. This was an ingenious arrangement by which the wire, festooned along the top of high hedges, did not require any other support, and was less likely to be broken or tampered with.

---

1   Ultimately General Sir Joseph John Asser, KCB, KCMG, KCVO, who was at this time serving as General Officer Commanding (GOC) Lines of Communication.

2   A type of latex insulation.

A few Uhlan[3] lances and infantry accoutrements lay among the groups of graves. The crosses, which indicated that they had been erected by British burial parties, certified that the British had retained the field after the engagement. We little knew at the time that the War would last for four years, and that just as one of the first fights had taken place in this little village of Méteren, so—practically four years later to the day—would the last clash take place there, that attrition of two great armies leaving the lovely little village in a heap of ruins, and its inhabitants absolutely dispersed. In the intervening years, it remained untouched by the tide of War.

When the Canadians arrived in France, the race between the armies from the Marne to the sea had left the frontline trenches stretched northward by way of Albert, Arras, Béthune, and Armentières in France and Bizet, Ploegsteert, and Diksmuide in Belgium. No sooner had we settled down in our new area than all arms were moved into the frontline trenches "to be shooted over," and to receive instructions and experience in the new style of trench warfare. On February 17 large contingents of officers, non-coms,[4] and men were marched to the trenches, chiefly in the vicinity of Armentières where a good deal of desultory fighting of a description calculated to be suitable for the instruction of new troops was in progress. Each party remained one week in the trenches. While they were there the British officers and men spared no pains to initiate the Canadians into the grim game, which was largely new to both professionals and amateurs.

The story of the 1st Artillery Brigade will probably prove typical of every other unit. The staff, battery commanders, and a percentage of junior officers and non-coms were marched to Armentières one day in pouring rain and ordered to report to the 24th Brigade Royal Field Artillery, and to his "opposite number." The 24th received them in a most kindly manner and took them about while delivering information and instruction. At that time Armentières had been shelled badly enough to cause practically all its civilians to evacuate, leaving numbers of ideal billets, especially in the shape of chateaux completely filled with furniture and surrounded with well-kept gardens. I may mention *sub rosa*[5] that the tactical layout was such that it was most suitable to have the chateaux for officers' billets and the gardens for the batteries and emplacements.

---

3   German cavalry.

4   Non-commissioned officers (i.e. sergeants and sergeant-majors).

5   Latin, literally meaning "under the rose," as in "in secrecy."

In the morning the grizzled old colonel took the attached officers out for a walk to show them how to construct battery emplacements and how to dodge shells. He pointed out the salient features of the city of Lille, which lay within gunshot, and gave us exhibitions of shooting by each battery as we came to it. We visited every O Pip[6] and continuously talked shop as only gunners can do it. Then we came back for lunch.

After lunch we played Whist, but the War still went on. During the game the old colonel had his cards spread on the mantelpiece beside the field telephone, and the game went something like this:

"I will make it spades." A Bosche[7] shell goes smash into a greenhouse outside in the garden with a tremendous clatter. The old colonel looks provoked and ejaculates: "The damn fellow did the same thing when I made it spades before. I'll make it diamonds." The game proceeds until somebody doubles the colonel, when he takes up the telephone. "Are they leaving the asylum alone this afternoon? Well why don't you strafe[8] them? Give the Quatre Halotz[9] battery three rounds high explosive." At other times, in the middle of a hand, the telephone on the mantelpiece would buzz and the benevolent-looking old colonel would lay down his hand and take the 'phone off its perch: "Yes? Oh, is that you Henry, dear boy? What? The Rue de Bois Battery is shelling you? Certainly, my boy. Give 'em a few rounds. Hope you kill some of those dirty dogs of Germans. Ta-ta." Then he would take up his hand and remark: "I make it three diamonds."

And so it went on until tea was brought in and the discussion switched to the question of the latest War Office outrage in awarding the DSO[10] to a paymaster, when the regulations had hitherto laid down that it was only to be for those in conduct under fire.

Each day had its separate programme and the week ended with a sort of review by a charming old general known as "Rawjah" who made us select battery positions for the defence of the whole city. Having got a tip that he was partial to maps and had an eye for colour, I passed up a Bridge game one afternoon and nearly exhausted

---

6   Observation balloon, pronounced using the phonetic alphabet used by the military at the time (O.P. = "O Pip").

7   French slang term for Germans.

8   Attack repeatedly with bombs or machine gun fire from low flying aircraft.

9   Likely a German Battery position.

10   The Distinguished Service Order.

my paintbox with what a well-remembered commandant of the RMC[11] would call a "pawnarawmaw." It pleased the old general so much that he was quite optimistic as to the probable length of the War when taking leave of us after dinner that night.

And so on February 27 we arrived back in Méteren feeling that we did not care how long the War lasted now that we had been initiated into the science of killing Germans. Of course the initiation was not quite so tame an affair as it might seem. One day, while making an instructional tour, we saw eleven British infantry made into casualties in front of us with a single shell. Our own 1st Infantry Brigade had thirty killed and wounded, and the same experience throughout all the units was the price of the knowledge we acquired.

We were billeted with two nice old French ladies in Méteren, who recounted with terror the incidents of the village's occupation by the Germans. Major John McCrae, whom they called "The Medicine Major," and Captain Cosgrave,[12] who also could speak French, and was known as "The Baby" because he was the youngest officer on the brigade's staff, were particularly popular with the old ladies. The ladies prayed for us every night, and wrote us very charming letters for many months after we left Méteren. I have often wondered what were their ultimate fates, because the village was never molested by the enemy from the time we were there until the last year of the War. But when I visited the place after the Armistice, there was literally not one stone upon another, nor any surviving inhabitants from whom I could get information.

One interesting matter came to my attention on this farewell visit in May 1919. After the instructional tour already described, the four batteries of my brigade were required to construct gun pits similar to the ones we saw at Armentières. The battery commanders were allowed to select, at their discretion, the sites for these battery positions, and did so about half a mile west of the village and to the north of the road. When the Germans made their final push in April 1918, they drove the British through Méteren, and the Artillery, in falling back, found these gun pits, erected by us in 1915, to be in exactly the right position to defend the new front line trench. They placed their field guns in the old pits we had made and stopped the German westward advance, which never reached the village of Caëstre. The place will be

---

11   The Royal Military College of Canada, Kingston.

12   Ultimately Lieutenant-Colonel Lawrence Vincent Moore Cosgrave, DSO, Bar, Croix de Guerre. Cosgrave served on Morrison's staffs for most of the War, being moved up each time Morrison was promoted.

remembered by all the Old Originals, if only on account of the pretty and highly popular barmaid at the inn there.

We were now considered sufficiently experienced to take over a portion of the artillery defence of the line, and were ordered on March 1 to relieve the 22nd Royal Field Artillery Brigade from the village of Fleurbaix. The Canadian 1st Division took over the front line from Neuve-Chapelle to Bois-Grenier, a suburb of Armentières. This brought us into the British First Army, then commanded by General Haig.[13] Before we took over the responsibility of a division frontage, there was a conference between the Canadian officers and those of the division holding the line. The 7th Division was commanded by General Capper,[14] who gave us a very instructive address on our duties and responsibilities, one point of which he stressed in a manner that gave us cause to remember it: namely, that any division that lost its frontline trenches to the enemy was required to counterattack at all costs until it got them back again. Another rather odd suggestion we received was that, when taking over the line, we should pretend to be English troops by calling out to each other: "Hello, Waricks!" or "Right-o, Glosters," and so on. The idea seemed to be that if the Germans thought we were regular English troops they would not be so likely to attack. Whether it was that our men did not feel flattered at the suggestion, or that they were poor imitators of the cockney accent, they had hardly commenced carrying on halloo-ing to the Warickses when a disgusted voice from the enemy's trench, with a strong Buffalo accent, yelled across: "Ah g'wan, when did you leave Yonge Street?" This reminds me that in the early days of the War there appeared to be quite a lot of German-Americans in the enemy's trenches, with whom our men exchanged familiarities.

A contrast to this was the state of things after the repulse of the Prussian Guard at Ypres. A trooper in the 5th Dragoon Guards, in his book *My Fourteen Months at the Front*,[15] writes: "A peculiar thing happened soon after the Canadians so distinguished themselves. A certain English regiment received orders to take some trenches at a given time. The officer of this regiment had the men fix their bayonets and stick

---

13   Ultimately Field Marshal Sir Douglas Haig, 1st Earl Haig, KT, GCB, OM, GCVO, KCIE. Commander-in-Chief of the British Armies in France 1915–1919.

14   Major-General Sir Thompson Capper, KCMG, CB, DSO. General Officer Commanding 7th Division from July 19, 1915, until he died of wounds on September 27, 1915.

15   *My Fourteen Months at the Front: An American Boy's Baptism of Fire* by William Josephus Robinson. Published in Boston by Little, Brown and Company in 1916. Robinson was an American who enlisted in the 5th Dragoon Guards of the British Army.

them over the parapet of the trench several minutes before the attack was to be made. They did so, and kept clashing their bayonets against one another, and making an awful row generally. When the whistle blew, a young subaltern was the first man over the parapet, and he yelled at the top of his voice, 'Come on Canadians.' This got the Germans' goat, and our fellows took three lines of trenches without losing a man. All of which goes to show that the Germans, while they may hate the Canadians, fear them also."[16]

The real object in having us take over the Fleurbaix sector was to get in actual training in the routine of relieving. Officers and non-coms from every unit went in the previous day and spoke with their "opposite number" of the unit they were to relieve. Then the next day they would relieve, piecemeal: first a half-battery would exchange with another half-battery, then a battery by a battery, a brigade by a brigade, and so on, so that there was not an instant during which fire could not be opened in case of an attack. That night being our first relief, and some of the battery positions being awkward to get at, we set up in the billet of Brigade Commander Lieutenant-Colonel Alexander, vc,[17] until nearly midnight, before the telephone wires were tested and the takeover reported O.K.

Colonel Alexander had been in the retreat from Mons and got the vc for saving his guns when his men were charged by German cavalry on a misty morning. He was a pink and white, rather delicate looking man, with a modest, retiring manner, which must have been disappointing to hero worshippers, who seem to have the idea that soldiers bearing the hallmark of bravery should be the uncultured, aggressive, "ready-to-spit-on-your-boots" style of man. The headquarters was in a little French farmhouse chiefly memorable to me for the fact that on the outside wall opposite my bedroom there was an enormous treadwheel, used by an equally enormous dog, in the manner of a squirrel in a cage. This industrious animal began the daily round of churning not long after I turned in, and occasionally varied the monotony and registered his industry by cheering himself with savage yelps. By the time he was finished his duties the whole family would depart for work in the fields with a great deal of noise and argument. Which reminds me: the French peasantry seemed to do all

---

16   *My Fourteen Months at the Front: An American Boy's Baptism of Fire*, page 158–159.

17   Ultimately Major-General Ernest Wright Alexander, vc, cb, cmg. As Battery Commander of the 119th Battery, Royal Field Artillery, he was awarded the Victoria Cross for saving his guns and rescuing a wounded man under heavy fire on August 24, 1914. He was Major-General, Royal Artillery, First Army from April 9, 1918, until the end of the War.

their work either before daylight or in the long evening twilight, so that the first year we were in France the fields were plowed, the crops were sewn, the harvest reaped, and the ripened grain stacked without anyone apparently having been at work in the fields.

The 1st Canadian Division had only one battery of heavy artillery, 6-inch, and as far as could be judged that battery constituted the only heavy guns on the Fleurbaix front.[18] This accounted for the fact that there was a heavy stone tower at a nearby village that overlooked all our line. Prolonged efforts had been made to knock down the tower, but with nothing larger than field guns, the only result heretofore had been to chip pieces off it. One of the first requests was to have Major Magee's[19] Heavy Battery endeavour to destroy the tower, which was about 6,000 yards away. It was a difficult target to hit, but Major Magee brought it down with the second round.[20] This gave our heavy gunners such a reputation that we did not get them back into the Canadian Division for over a year.

---

18   This is a confusing sentence. The 1st Canadian Heavy Battery was equipped with 60-pounder guns. There was one British battery equipped with 6-inch guns on the front at this time. Morrison may be confusing these two batteries in his memory for some reason.

19   The 1st Canadian Heavy Battery was commanded by Major Frank Cormack Magee, DSO, between September 22, 1914, and June 22, 1916. Magee was severely wounded in the head and abdomen in June 1916. He recovered, was promoted to Lieutenant-Colonel, and appointed as Commanding Officer of 2nd Brigade, Canadian Garrison Artillery (2nd Canadian Heavy Artillery Group) until January 1918.

20   The Fromelles church tower was demolished by 1st Canadian Heavy Battery on March 7, 1915.

Chapter 6

ST. PATRICK'S DAY
IN THE MORNING

On March 10 the Battle of Neuve-Chapelle commenced, preceded by a cannonade that was regarded as tremendous for that time of the War. The battle was about five miles west of the Canadians' right flank, and we were required to "make a flank" for the attack, keeping up a continuous cannonade with all our guns on the Aubers Ridge. This was to be followed by an infantry attack in case the battle was successful and the enemy was dislodged along the whole front. For three days in succession our field guns kept up rapid fire for three or four hours at a time, but the battle never developed in such a manner as to create the opportunity for infantry to attack the Ridge. In fact, the battle was fought on a comparatively narrow front, from Bizet to the village of Neuve-Chapelle. From the printed proclamation that was issued to all troops before the battle, it was obvious that the battle was expected to be much more extensive and successful than actually resulted. There was a heavy casualty list, and the British captured a large lot of German prisoners, but from a tactical standpoint the battle was of a featureless character, which began to be common at about that stage of the War, and was duplicated later on at Festubert and Givenchy-en-Gohelle.

The Canadians' share in the Battle of Neuve-Chapelle chiefly consisted of emptying their ammunition echelons, having a few score infantry on their right flank made casualties, and listening for two or three days after the battle to the vindictive fusillade of the Germans immediately opposite Neuve-Chapelle, and "the grumble of cannon far down in the sky," which always characterized the comeback of the ill-tempered Teuton[1] whenever he got his fingers burned.

On the Sunday following the battle, Major John McCrae and I got permission to visit the battlefield. Up to that time we had not had the opportunity to see an up-to-date battle. Lieutenant-General Sir James Willcocks[2] had his headquarters in a farm about a mile north of Bizet, and they were being actively shelled when we called on him. The scene of the engagement was not very inspiring. A number of troops were moving about in a desultory way, as if engaged in fatigues. The majority were units of the Indian Army, and the Germans were methodically sniping them with rifles and field guns. It was a dangerous day such as we came to know only too well before the War was over. The Bosche was taking revenge, and his fire was directed on any men, or groups of men, he might see moving. It was a murderous sort of occupation that the Bosche seemed to enjoy, and in after years that sort of licensed assassination period after an engagement was found to produce more casualties than the engagement itself. On this occasion they spotted McCrae and me as we were crossing a ploughed field, and we had to lie down between the furrows for a quarter of an hour while they endeavoured to murder us with that small type of shell then known as "Pip-Squeaks." As we lay there we discussed the situation, and came to the conclusion that we were fools to run such chances, and would only be ridiculed by our friends if anything should happen to us, and that it was not a square deal to the government that had expended so much money on our education as gunner officers, and that, anyhow, we would never do it again.[3]

We had not been a week on the Fleurbaix front when I was impressed by the fact that while there was a great deal of gunning by the enemy opposite our front, there were seldom any shells came over; nor could we locate any German batteries. That, naturally, was difficult when there were no shells to trace. While closely observing our front one day I was surprised to see a couple of German batteries wheel out from

---

1   Slang for German.

2   Ultimately General Sir James Willcocks, GCB, GCMG, KCSI, DSO. Willcocks was General Officer Commanding the Indian Corps until he resigned in September 1915.

3   Morrison and McCrae were good friends, having served in the Boer War together as Lieutenants in "D" Battery, Royal Canadian Field Artillery 1900–1901. Morrison was awarded the DSO for bravery in South Africa for his actions at the Battle of Leliefontein, November 7, 1900.

behind some brushwood and fire—but the flashes showed that they were not aiming at us, but firing parallel with our front line at our neighbours holding the front to the right and left of us. This solved the mystery, because, as they were not firing at us, we naturally would not be so keen on returning the fire, while it made it very difficult for our neighbours to detect the batteries that were not on their front. This information was passed around in the brigade and all batteries were warned to keep a sharp lookout for these broadside flashes.

The windup, as far as I was concerned, was that on the following day, St. Patrick's Day, Major Britton,[4] commanding the 3rd Battery, reported early in the morning that he had discovered two German batteries on our front engaged in bombarding our neighbours. He asked leave to take them on. I gave the necessary permission and hurried down to the battery to see the fight, which was an exceedingly pretty one. Major Britton caught the clever Bosche with the first salvo and the Germans reciprocated, bouncing their shells on the roofs of our gun pits. One dud, which was picked up, showed that their range in fuse was the same as ours to a second. A lively duel ensued, and when other batteries took a hand the Bosche batteries were soon out of business. On that part of their front there were no trenches; only parapets, which were soon breached by the guns. And as the Germans dashed past these openings they were taken on by our infantry with rifle fire, and a most enjoyable morning was had by all—especially the Infantry. The small battle lasted until noon, and was subsequently remembered as the Battle of St. Patrick's Day.

Well pleased with the morning's work, I hurried back to my headquarters where my orderly officer presented me, long-faced, with an order dated two days previous, though it had only been delivered that morning. It stated that, in future, the expenditure of ammunition would be limited to three rounds per gun per day. We had blown off over four hundred rounds in that one morning. The fact was that in the three-day cannonade of rapid fire, the artillery in the Neuve-Chapelle show had fired all the field gun ammunition available. I did not blame the upper works for lapsing into a fine frenzy when my ammunition return for St. Patrick's Day reached Headquarters, but I don't know yet why they should have sent out a general summons for myself and all my battery commanders to report immediately for a general wigging. Of course I took all the blame, and expressed regret for incommoding the Bosche so much, and

---

4   Ultimately Lieutenant-Colonel Russel Hubert Britton, DSO. Britton was appointed Commanding Officer 5th Brigade, Canadian Field Artillery on September 15, 1916. He was killed in action on May 2, 1917.

enquired of the Divisional Commander[5] whether the Canadian Artillery should sit back and hoard ammunition while the dirty Bosche made a refuge of our front to murder our comrades of the Royal Field Artillery. This near-impertinence got me in wrong, and he grumbled something about insubordination. I maintained, sadly, that I must have misunderstood the attitude of the Canadian Government, and that if he would give me permission I would apply to them for definite information as to what we were over here for. I found that raising this question was not without results—on that as well as other occasions—and we were told to go away and be good boys, or words to that effect.

While we were on the Fleurbaix front, General Lord Dundonald[6] paid my brigade a visit one day and inspected the batteries in their new positions. The men were very glad to see him and cheered him heartily. The word got about that he was to be given command of the 1st Division, but nothing further was heard of it, nor did we see the General again during the course of the war.

---

5   Lieutenant-General Alderson, KCB.

6   Lieutenant-General Douglas Mackinnon Baillie Hamilton Cochrane, twelfth Earl of Dundonald, KCB, KCVO. Formerly General Officer Commanding the Militia of Canada 1902–1904. Around this time Lord Dundonald was Chairman of the Admiralty Committee on Smoke Screens.

Chapter 7

INTRODUCING "WIPERS"

On April 1, 1915, orders were received to march for an unstated destination. The weather was wet, the roads muddy. The march was supposedly in the nature of an instructional route march, and so the division was first rendezvoused at points in rear of the line and then moved off on a day's march, which, by evening, brought us near Cassel. This unusual place is set on a pointed hill, about three or four hundred feet high, rising like a huge potato mound out of an absolutely level agricultural country. On the top of the hill, and around the base, are a considerable number of buildings varying from fine chateaux to casinos and restaurants, a fine old church, and other buildings used as the headquarters of the French Army in the north.

From the casino on the top of the rock a fair view could be obtained of Ypres, Dunkirk, and the Lorette Ridge at Vimy. The country, for many miles in every direction, afforded a very beautiful view, the fields looking like the squares on a checkerboard and the various towns and villages variegating the view for sightseers, for whom the top of the rock was evidently a rendezvous. The buildings on the summit seemed mostly to have been erected for the accommodation of summer visitors. The view from Ypres to the Channel Port passes directly over Cassel. Our columns circulated round the base of the hill and dispersed into the surrounding country where troops were billeted in barns and farmhouses. Our brigade was halted at Oudezeele, a hamlet in a most beautiful country where we spent two or three delightful weeks resting men and horses.

We frequently had long walks in the country, and to the top of the hill at Cassel. There Major McCrae and I had our first view of General Foch, afterwards Generalissimo of the Allied Armies.[1] He was not a particularly impressive figure, attired in a shabby overcoat like that of a private soldier, and had it not been for the large amount of gold on his kepi,[2] he would not have been taken for a general. His face was ascetic and weather-beaten, and he had all the appearance of a tried and capable soldier. He returned our salute in the most courteous and friendly fashion, and there was something in his manner that caused us to ask a young French officer whom we met who he was. He replied that the officer was General Foch, commanding the Iron Division[3] (which was then in front of Ypres), but he said nothing about General Foch being the Victor of the Marne, probably taking it for granted that we knew all about that; though, in fact, we did not. He also very politely pointed out to us the city of Ypres, which could otherwise be identified by a good deal of smoke and the roar of artillery in the vicinity.

The weather and the country were so beautiful that it seemed as though the excitement and terror of war were subsiding and gradually fading away. The country was looking its best and the farmers were busy everywhere seeding their fields. Outside of the General Staff there was so little news that it was difficult to realize that the War was still in progress. On the following Sunday we had a novelty in the shape of a sermon from Major John McCrae. He delivered a very thoughtful address from a pulpit consisting of an ammunition wagon. I impressed on the brigade a lesson of another sort by turning them all out for an hour's route march in heavy marching order. Knowing that, in the circumstances, they would pack the vehicles as lightly as possible, orders were given, as soon as the brigade was clear of its billets, to gather up all equipment that had not been put upon the wagons and turn it in, to store as not necessary to be carried. That evening, the Canadians were inspected by General H.L. Smith-Dorrien,[4] who had commanded most of our troops in South Africa,

---

1   Ultimately Marshal Ferdinand Jean Marie Foch, Commander-in-Chief of Allied Forces from March 26, 1918, until the end of the War.

2   A French military cap with a flat top and a horizontal brim.

3   The French 11th Division, also called La Division de Fer (Iron Division). This division was part of the northern Army Group commanded by Foch at this time.

4   General Sir Horace Lockwood Smith-Dorrien, GCB, GCMG, DSO, ADC. General Officer Commanding British Second Army, December 26, 1914–May 7, 1915.

especially at Paardeberg. He delivered an excellent speech, full of good advice and hints regarding the difference between the Boer War and the present campaign. He praised the appearance of the men and horses very highly.

On the following morning large numbers of French troops came along the roads from the direction of Ypres. They were scuffed and sunburned, but very jaunty and soldier-like, and we were not surprised to hear that they were the men of the Iron Division. Next morning, April 17, the Canadians marched eastward from Cassel and reached Poperinge, the gateway of the Ypres Salient. It was about eight miles from Ypres that the fighting had been going on in a desultory way since the first battle in October 1914. But Poperinge was practically immune from shellfire, and was mainly known then as the last billeting place for troops on their way to Ypres. It may be added that, with the addition of a good many shell holes and an increased number of cabarets, it was still doing business as usual when we marched through it in October 1917. During that two-and-a-half years, the Canadians were more identified with the Ypres Salient than any other troops in the Allied armies. A poem has been written to "The Red, Red Road to Hooge."[5] Without doubt there were more men marched over the road from Poperinge to Ypres who never retraced their steps than ever any other bit of road in the world, and I think it would not be an exaggeration to say that the troops of Canada marched over that road to garrison the Salient oftener during the next four years than any other troops.

April 27, 1915: June 6, 1915: August 28, 1916: October 20, 1917: November 20, 1917.[6]

On the morning of April 18, drafts of officers and non-coms from the batteries and regiments of the Canadian Division proceeded over the road and through the city of Ypres to reconnoitre the positions they were to take up on a division front to the east of the city. The general work of taking over a division front was very much the same as it was in Fleurbaix, with the exception that, for some reason, the artillery was sent into the line in two guns and half an ammunition column per battery at a time. The reason for this was not stated by high authority, but undoubtedly it mixed up the batteries and brigades in a manner that scattered them about a great deal and made them awkward to handle, especially when the surprise of poison gas occurred. For instance, at one such critical moment, some of the brigades were so dispersed

---

5   Author unknown.

6   Here Morrison appears to be listing dates when large units left the Ypres Salient.

that they had part of their guns in Poperinge, part of them on the march to the front, and the remainder in action in the forward trenches, while half of the ammunition columns were with the fighting guns, and the other half were back in Poperinge, or on the road coming up. In addition to that, the Canadians had nothing heavier than field guns or howitzers, their only heavy battery having been detached to the British First Army on leaving Fleurbaix.

On April 19 the advance part of the 1st Field Artillery Brigade went forward to select a position for the second detachment of their guns—the first detachment under Major Maclaren[7] having gone forward the previous day. They scouted the position in the usual way, and were impressed only by the quietness of the sector. Major King, afterwards Brigadier-General King, DSO,[8] had his battery on the extreme left of the line of guns, next to the road that marked the dividing line between the Canadians and the French. It will be recalled that, when the Turcos[9] were gassed and routed, and the German troops swarmed over the parapet and streamed in the thousands past the flank of Major King's battery, he wheeled half the battery to the flank and brought two guns to the front and fired reversed shrapnel at point-blank range into the triumphant enemy. Luckily for the battery there was a tall hedge along the road that ran along that flank, and this obscured the Gunners from view of the charging German Infantry, who, if they had seen them, could have wiped out the gun crews with one volley. Somewhat farther to the rear of the enemy came on half the Ammunition Column of the 1st Brigade, charged by Captain Durkee.[10] The column should never have been in such a place, as it had nothing to defend itself with except a few rifles carried on the footboards of the limbers. However, Captain Durkee determined to save his command, but as soon as he commenced to gallop out of action, the German Infantry, hurrying past the flank, opened fire with their rifles and shot a number of men and horses. Every man had a bandolier of ammunition, and without being in the least daunted by the proximity of an onrushing army corps, the Gunners

---

7   Major Charles Henry Maclaren, Commander of 2nd Battery, Canadian Field Artillery. He was ultimately Brigadier-General C.H. Maclaren, DSO, CRA, General Officer Commanding 4th Divisional Artillery, June 20, 1917–November 28, 1917, when he was sent home due to battle exhaustion.

8   Major William Birchall Macauley King, Commander of 10th Battery, Canadian Field Artillery. He was ultimately Brigadier-General W.B.M. King, CMG, DSO, General Officer Commanding 4th Divisional Artillery November 28, 1917–June 2, 1919.

9   Slang for the Algerian troops who were serving under the French Army.

10 Ultimately Lieutenant-Colonel Adelbert Augustus Durkee, DSO. The Ammunition Column was used to resupply ammunition.

disengaged the rifles from the limbers and opened such a hot and persistent fire that the German Infantry were fairly bluffed, and evidently, not recognizing what sort of a unit it was, sheered off further to the flank. The Ammunition Column got away, inflicting not a little loss on the enemy. There are few, if any, similar instances in the history of the artillery.[11]

Having reverted to the front line as it was on April 20 to scout the battery positions for the 1st Artillery Brigade, the group of officers finished their work by noon without being sniped at or subjected to any of the annoyances that were usual on a lively front. They proceeded to return to Poperinge by the road that runs through St. Julien and Wieltje, and were informed where they would find a very good restaurant still doing business in Ypres. They rode into the northeast corner of the Cloth Hall square and found the city quite peaceful. The restaurant was in the Rue de Lille, just off the square, quite a handsome stone residence. If it interests readers to know what a doomed man has for breakfast before he is hanged, it might interest them to know that we had a most excellent lunch, which we lingered over into the early afternoon.

We had not yet finished luncheon when there was a most thunderous detonation somewhere in the direction of the square, and immediately the little city was in a wild panic. People rushed past in the streets and dived into cellars like rats. Parents ran about looking for their children and carried them, screaming, into the houses. The waiter explained that it was a German shell and went on serving the next course, while our horses, which were in a lane across the street, proceeded to stampede. When they were gathered up by the horse holders our party mounted and rode into the square to have a look at the Cloth Hall and the cathedral; at that date they were only in a semi-mutilated state. The shell that had fallen was the first large one to jar the nerves of the phlegmatic Flemish, but the panic had quickly subsided. Our cavalcade had just ridden across the canal bridge on the road to Poperinge when a second huge shell fell at the northeast end of the square and threw a column of black smoke and debris about a hundred feet in the air. It was as if a volcano had suddenly opened up in the centre of the city, for the buildings were shaken until chimneys, balconies, and other moveable objects crashed into the streets. The shell was one of the 17-inch type with which we became better acquainted before the Second Battle of Ypres was over. It made a hole in the pavé square about fifteen feet in diameter, which remained as a landmark there for several years. We rode back, but not enamoured of Ypres as

---

11   These events occurred on April 22, 1915.

a place of residence. Poperinge was carrying on as usual, excepting that a few long-range shells had been dropped in the suburbs without doing a great deal of damage. The next day, April 21, visitors to Ypres brought back news that the city had been further shelled and a considerable number of the inhabitants killed or wounded: their dismembered bodies plastered up against the fronts of the buildings. Despite this, the bombardment was not of a character to arouse general alarm.

On April 22, at noon, the second detachment of the 1st Brigade had orders to move up to the firing line. It consisted of two batteries and half of the Ammunition Column, and it marched towards Ypres on the Poperinge road at about 3 PM. The weather was beautiful and spring-like, with a strong wind blowing from the east; there was no premonition of an impending battle, and everything was carried out as in the case of routine relief.

TOP Colonel Sam Hughes in his office. WILLIAM OKELL HOLDEN DODDS COLLECTION, UNIVERSITY OF VICTORIA (WOD)

BOTTOM, LEFT *Front row, bottom right-hand corner (L to R):* Lt.-Col. Dodds, Capt. Cosgrove, and Lt.-Col. Morrison, at Valcartier, Quebec, August 31, 1914. (Maj. John McCrae was absent from this photo as he was travelling by ship back from England at this time.) STEVE CLIFFORD, DOING OUR BIT

BOTTOM, RIGHT Lt.-Col. William Dodds and Maj. John McCrae, Valcartier, September 17, 1914. WOD

TOP, LEFT Artillery firing practice, Valcartier, September 1914. WOD

TOP, RIGHT Artillery marching to quay at Quebec City, October 1914. WOD

BOTTOM Artillery and bell tents, Valcartier, September 1914. WOD

TOP, LEFT Hoisting artillery piece aboard ship, Quebec City, October 1914. WOD

TOP, RIGHT Canada's Armada—troopships steaming toward England, October 1914. WOD

BOTTOM Loading artillery, Quebec City, October 1914. WOD

TOP Officers of the 1st Brigade CFA at their Officers Mess, the Bear Hotel, Devizes, England, 1915. *Front row (L to R):* Maj. McCrae, Maj. Sharman, Lt.-Col. Maclaren, Maj. Britton, Lt.-Col. Morrison, Lt.-Col. Dodds, Maj. Ralston, Capt. Durkee, Capt. Cosgrave, Capt. Alderson, Capt. Benson. *Back row (L to R):* Lt. Storms, Lt. Gillies, Capt. White, Lt. Bick, Capt. Goodeve, Lt. Thackray, Lt. Boville, Lt. Smith, Lt. Helmer, Lt. Matthews, Lt. Young, Lt. Craig, Lt. Blue, Lt. Whitely, Lt. Kelly, Capt. Stewart. GUELPH MUSEUMS

BOTTOM, LEFT Poorly ventilated huts that gave rise to the meningitis epidemic, December 1914. STEVE CLIFFORD

BOTTOM, RIGHT *(L to R)* Capt. Lawrence Cosgrave, Lt.-Col. Edward Morrison, and Maj. John McCrae at the Ark, Devizes, England, 1915. GUELPH MUSEUMS

TOP 16th Battalion Canadian Scottish in trenches, Fleurbaix, France, March 1915. STEVE CLIFFORD

BOTTOM, LEFT 16th Battalion Canadian Scottish in snowy trenches, March 19, 1915. STEVE CLIFFORD

BOTTOM, RIGHT General Ferdinand Foch, Cassel, France, April 1915. DINGE EN GOETE BLOG, SOUTH AFRICA

TOP 16th Canadian Scottish survivors of Battle of Kitcheners, Wood, April 26, 1915.
STEVE CLIFFORD

MIDDLE, LEFT Cloth Hall and Grand Place, Ypres, Belgium 1914. WOD

MIDDLE, RIGHT Yser Canal, Ypres, Belgium, April 1915. STEVE CLIFFORD

BOTTOM, LEFT Chlorine gas cylinders, April 22, 1915. SOURCE UNKNOWN

BOTTOM, RIGHT Yser Dyke "spoilbank," April 1915. STEVE CLIFFORD

Chapter 8

THE GAS ATTACK AT YPRES

For many years to come, the events of the spring of 1915 will be remembered with grief and pride, for it was then that the raw, untrained Canadian troops, unsupported, and in the face of deadly poisonous gas, withstood the onset of the Prussian Guard and other of the Kaiser's most dreaded troops, and saved the Channel Ports. In the first great fight in which they were called upon to show their mettle, they were pitted against the best-trained and best-armed troops in Europe—and came off victoriously. The poison gas had dispersed tens of thousands of Allied troops, and the 1st Canadian Division was left half-surrounded and practically alone, but, with a valour almost unequalled in the history of modern warfare, it stood its ground for days and nights until it was decimated several times over, yet "saved the day" for the Allies.

Already the demand is being made that, while the details are fresh in the minds of survivors, and before the lapse of time has dimmed the recollection of these stirring events, the story of this wonderful feat should be put on record. Years may elapse before a full account of this glorious accomplishment may be written. But it is still possible for eyewitnesses to bring home to their countrymen a partial description of those heroic deeds, some inspiration for their children's children to cherish, which roused the emulation of the finest troops who took part in the Armageddon of the Great War.

The troops of Canada had arrived in France during the first week in February 1915, and had been attached to British troops in the trenches, from whom they had learned the salient points in the new art of fighting which marked the commencement of the World War. After a period of several weeks in various parts of the trench line, they were marched north to an area around Cassel, some miles west of the city of Ypres, and were held ready to strengthen the line that defended the Channel Ports, the possession of which would practically decide the World War. To facilitate their movements and reinforcements, the Canadian Division of four brigades of infantry,[1] with a brigade of field artillery attached to each, was billeted between Cassel and Ypres, and during the third week of April was moved forward by units to the line of battle east of Ypres where they relieved the Iron Division commanded by General Foch.

The city of Ypres had been shelled severely, but in a desultory way, for some months previous; but on April 19, while the city was still occupied by some fifteen thousand inhabitants, chiefly women and children, the Germans increased the bombardment to a terrible extent. The Canadian officers who went forward beyond the city to reconnoitre positions for their field guns were actual witnesses of the descent upon the city of shells seventeen inches in diameter, which created panic among the inhabitants and sent them scurrying about the streets seeking shelter in the cellars and wherever protection might be found. One of these mammoth shells fell in the Grand Place near the Cloth Hall, and the mark of it is there to this day. All the following day the terrible projectiles fell at intervals, and great crowds of fugitives began to flee from the city. On foot and in vehicles, they fled towards Poperinge.

On April 21 large detachments of infantry, each with the necessary proportion of artillery to support it in case of battle, were moved forward from Poperinge to the battle line east of Ypres city. One third of the 1st Brigade's Artillery, including half of the Ammunition Column, was dispatched to this position beyond Ypres on April 21, and on April 22 half of the brigade was ordered forward along the Ypres–Poperinge road to be ready for the impending battle.[2] That there would be a battle was now anticipated with certainty, for infantry fighting had broken out on Hill 60, to the south of Ypres, and the city was continually being bombarded.

---

1   There were only three brigades of infantry in 1st Canadian Division. An ad-hoc British brigade was attached to the Canadian Division during the battle. Morrison may be referring to this British brigade here, although it was not yet attached.

2   Only a quarter of the brigade moved forward on April 21, with the remainder moving forward on April 22.

It was a beautiful April day, bright and sunny, with a brisk but balmy breeze from the east. This breeze later became an important factor in the attack, which was impending. The second half of the artillery brigade previously mentioned was marching along the road to go through Ypres and get into position beyond, but there was no particular apprehension among either the troops or the populace until the head of the Ammunition Column reached a point about one mile west of Ypres, when a violent cannonade was heard beyond the city and to the north of it. The cannonade increased in violence until it attained the proportions of a battle. At the same time, over the trees to the northeast of Ypres, there appeared what looked like a huge cloud of dust, driven before the wind, and attracting our attention by a greenish tinge that gave it an unusual appearance. The Ammunition Column was halted while the officer in charge[3] rode forward to reconnoitre, and he had not progressed far when, out of the woods and keeping ahead of the dust cloud, came a terrible rout[4] composed chiefly of French troops. Some of them were mounted on horses that still had their artillery harnesses lashing around their heels; others were on gun limbers in large numbers—driving across country through barbed wire fences and over ditches while the horses were beaten with sticks to make them go at their highest speed. Turcos and other uniformed troops were running beside these artillery wagons, while ambulances filled with unwounded men bounced and bounded over tree trunks, through ditches, and over swampy places. As the rout was coming obliquely towards the Canadians' Ammunition Column on the road, all the mounted men of the brigade were ordered to the front and formed a wedge to ride off this panic-stricken rabble. The rout had the appearance of being pursued by the enemy, which were still concealed by the woods. But though no shots were fired, members of the fugitives, without apparent cause, began dropping off the horses and falling from the wagons and out of the ambulances, and lay curled up on the ground where they fell, struggling and foaming at the mouth, and breathing stertorously.

In order not to be taken by surprise, the Canadian Brigade wheeled off and unlimbered two sections beside the road, ready in case the enemy should appear following the Turcos. The officer in command of the Canadian Artillery[5] rode forward

---

3   An officer from either the 2nd or 3rd Battery, CFA.

4   A disorderly retreat of defeated troops.

5   Brigadier-General Henry Edward ("Harry") Burstall. General Officer Commanding 1st Divisional Artillery. Burstall later became the first GOC Royal Artillery Canadian Corps (September 13, 1915–December 14, 1916) and then GOC 2nd Canadian Division December 15, 1916–May 22, 1919. He ended the War as Major-General Sir H.E. Burstall, KCB, KCMG.

to find out what was the matter and whether he could open fire to clear his front before the enemy appeared. At the White Chateau, where the causeway enters Ypres, he met a British staff officer who was watching the wild panic with an expression of bewilderment. To the Canadian officer, seeking information, he said that the enemy had broken through our lines beyond Wieltje, that they were expected to follow up the fugitives in a few minutes, and that the proper thing to do would be to deploy all available guns to obstruct their advance and hold on. In answer to the cause of the line breaking and the panic, he stared at the interrogator through his eyeglasses and snapped: "Gas." Then he wiped his eyeglasses with his handkerchief, and with delightful coolness strolled back into the chateau, of which he appeared to be the only occupant at the time.

As this was the first time that the word "gas" had ever been heard on a modern battlefield, it did not convey much information, though it was indeed the key to the day's happenings. Later in the night it was definitely stated that several miles of French native troops had been driven out of their trenches by a discharge of poison gas. In fact, the troops thus driven out of the line were equal to a frontage of two divisions.

It was the steadfastness of the Canadians, who refused to recoil before the lethal gas, and the promptness and dash with which their reserves came forward that closed the road to Calais. The stand they made was one of the most gallant and courageous deeds in the history of war, and the advance of their reserves was a magnificent sight that will never be forgotten by those who witnessed it.

Following the discharge of the gas and the rout of the French divisions, the German Artillery redoubled its fire on the city of Ypres, and hundreds of the inhabitants left the city and came pouring down the road towards Poperinge, exhibiting a dreadful spectacle of the horrors of war. The fugitives consisted almost entirely of women, children, and old and feeble folk. Many of the unfortunates were delicate and cultured women, with feet bleeding and torn from the attrition on the cobblestones, and with little children clinging to their skirts. Hundreds of old and decrepit men and women were on hay wagons drawn by small boys, goats, crippled old horses, and any beasts of burden that could be made use of. The old women and young children wailed and screamed with fright as every few minutes a new 17-inch shell landed in the midst of the burning city, causing a deafening detonation and projecting a cloud of sparks and burning brands high in the air. Random shells from beyond Ypres and from the fight in progress at Hill 60 added to the refugees' terror, and it seemed only a question of time until the heartless Germans would switch their fire upon the screaming fugitives on the high road. Added to all this was the roar of the battle beyond, and cheers and counter-cheers as the conflict ebbed and flowed. The Canadian and German cheers could be distinguished from each other, and the listeners keenly endeavoured to draw an inference from the cheering as to how the battle was going.

The incoming wounded had some time before this given an idea of the extent and nature of the catastrophe, and urged that the timely arrival of reinforcements must eventually decide the day. With the city blazing before them, and with swarms of fearsome fugitives choking the highway, the spectators by the roadside listened eagerly for signs of the reinforcements that were to turn the scale of battle. Thousands of French troops were mingled with the fugitives from the city on the pavé road, and it became a serious question whether those in flight would impede the progress of the reinforcements, and so gain precious time for the enemy.

Darkness had just settled down when the sound of the approaching troops was heard. Instead of anything dramatic, as the occasion seemed to call for, on the night air rang the whistled strains of the well-known tune "It's a Long Way to Tipperary," and as the two Canadian infantry regiments surged by, the whistling changed into a roaring chorus. They locked their arms and surveyed with nonchalance the scene before them, filling the air with a full-throated roar of the old, familiar song. The artillery drivers stood erect upon their saddles and screamed in pure ecstasy at the sight. Even the women seemed to take heart. A gassed Turco lying in the road of the column raised himself on his hands, and with glazing eyes shrieked something in Arabic, before he reeled out of the way of the column and fell dead. It was a dreadful choice the reinforcements had to make—whether to plunge into the burning city and find a way through to the battle raging beyond (after stemming the torrent of that ghastly rabble of terror-stricken inhabitants pouring out of Ypres), or to shoulder their way through the wailing, dying Turcos: the tangible evidence of the havoc of poisonous gas. But the Boyle and Birchall regiments of General Mercer's[6] 1st Canadian Brigade[7] made their choice and, through the suffering troops, shouted their way into battle to hold back an army.

---

6   Later Major-General Malcolm Smith Mercer, CB. He commanded the 1st Brigade from September 29, 1914, until November 21, 1915. He was then appointed GOC 3rd Canadian Division from December 24, 1915. He was killed in action on June 3, 1916.

7   In fact, these units were the 1st Canadian Infantry Battalion commanded by Lieutenant-Colonel F.W. Hill and the 4th Canadian Infantry Battalion commanded by Lieutenant-Colonel A.P. Birchall. Lieutenant-Colonel Russell Lambert Boyle was Commanding Officer of the 10th Canadian Infantry Battalion, which was already in action on the front lines at this point in time. Lieutenant-Colonel R.L. Boyle died of wounds on April 25, 1915.

An hour elapsed and dawn was commencing to break when the order arrived for the Artillery to advance at the gallop and support these regiments, which in the meantime had crossed the canal by footbridges and taken up a position a mile north of Ypres, opposite the wide gap left by the gassed French, and through which, by this time, an army corps of Germans was pouring so as to extend the rout into the heart of the British Army's territory.

When the Gunners came up two thin lines of infantry were extended on the ground. They busily dug themselves in, in preparation of charging the hordes of Germans who, having fought their way past the left flank of the main portion of the Canadian Division during the night, could be seen on the high land about Wieltje. It was an awful moment, but the infantrymen were in the best of spirits and good humour. As the leader of the Artillery[8] galloped through them to pick out a position for his batteries, brave old General Mercer came out of his headquarters in an *estaminet.*[9] where the road from Brielen to Wieltje crosses the canal, and rapidly explained that he proposed to stop the oncoming Germans by charging them with two regiments supported by the guns which only numbered two sections, and ordered that they be brought into position for that purpose. As the gunner officer rode forward to select his position, he found himself among the Infantry. His horse was well-known, and as he rode through the infantry line he was saluted with a chorus of good-natured chaff,[10] which included exhortations to "leave some of the Heinies for us." Only a few minutes sufficed to get the guns into action, and as their shells went screaming over, the gallant regiments sent up a cheer so hearty that it must have inspired the Germans with the idea that twice the actual number of attackers awaited them. As the guns made targets of the masses of Germans on the redoubt, which crowned the ridge north of Wieltje, the Infantry cheered, encouraging the Gunners with intimate yells of "Good old Petawawa!" and then charged.

Too little attention has been given to that splendid charge in which these regiments,[11] supported only by two weak batteries, never stopped until they reached

---

8   Likely a reference to Major W.B.M. King. See chapter 7, footnote 8.

9   A small cafe in France that sells food and alcoholic drinks.

10   Light-hearted teasing or joking.

11   The 1st and 4th Battalions attacked on the morning of April 23, 1915. The 1st Battalion lost 404 soldiers of all ranks and the 4th Battalion lost 454 soldiers of all ranks, including Lieutenant-Colonel Arthur Percival Birchall. Lieutenant-Colonel Frederick William Hill survived. He was ultimately Brigadier-General F.W. Hill, CB, CMG, DSO, General Officer Commanding 9th Infantry Brigade June 7, 1916–May 25, 1918.

the German trenches—though they were almost annihilated, for they literally charged an army. Both their commanding officers, Colonel Boyle and Colonel Birchall, were killed,[12] but their brave fellows never stopped until they had reached their objective, and it is the opinion of many, based largely on statements of the enemy, that but for the sacrifice by General Mercer of half his brigade, nothing would have prevented the swarming enemy from pouring down through the gas-broken line and passing the canal on the north side of Ypres, which would have ensured the fall of that city.

About 6 PM in the afternoon infantry reinforcements arrived, consisting of the 13th British Infantry Brigade, commanded by General Wanless O'Gowan,[13] and nothing would satisfy this officer but that his brigade must charge in support of General Mercer's two regiments of Canadians. In the meantime, an adequate artillery support had come up in the afternoon of April 23 and taken positions on the west side of the canal. It was a brilliant effort, and the brigade again reached the objectives aimed at by the two regiments of General Mercer in the morning, but the 13th British Brigade was also almost annihilated, and the survivors brought back the report that all they had found in the front line trenches were the dead and wounded Canadians of the morning attack, and that those that were left of them were out of ammunition. The great historic fact is that for sixteen days and nights the Canadian Artillery, which was subsequently reinforced by three other Canadian brigades and several corps of French Infantry and Canadian Engineers, never allowed the Germans to push through the gap that the gas had made in the line to flank the city.

It is a matter also of general interest that Major John McCrae was the surgeon of the 1st Canadian Artillery Brigade at that time, continuing in action from April 22 to May 9, and that it was during this period that he wrote the poem "In Flanders Fields," the inspiration for which came from his active participation in these exciting episodes. I write this with the intention of bringing to the minds of the readers the conditions under which this wonderful poem was written, but also with a vivid realization that no attempt has been made to describe fully the equally stirring and glorious exploits of the Canadian troops in other areas of that great battle. McCrae

---

12   Lieutenant-Colonel Russell Lambert Boyle. Died of wounds April 25, 1915, after leading the 10th Battalion attack on Kitcheners' Wood on April 22.

13   Major General Robert Wanless O'Gowan, CB, CMG, GOC 13th Brigade of 5th British Division February 8, 1915, to August 21, 1915. He was then promoted and appointed as GOC 31st British Division on August 24, 1915, to March 21, 1918.

had served with me in the South African War, and when the war with Germany broke out, McCrae obtained the position of surgeon in my brigade and served with great gallantry during the first year of the War, being qualified both as a surgeon and as an officer. At the Second Battle of Ypres, when the brigade advanced, its headquarters were established and entrenched in a "spoil bank"[14] on the canal, which afforded a fine field of fire. Major McCrae located his dressing station in a cave dug into the west side of this spoil bank, and so numerous were the casualties during the first day that many wounded rolled down the spoil bank into his dressing station. During the heavy shelling of the batteries he exposed himself so bravely that he was recommended for Mention in Dispatches. McCrae was an enthusiastic artilleryman, and when not otherwise employed was on the "bridge" watching the phases of the battle and judging the effectiveness with which the artillery was being handled. As an overwhelming attack from the Germans was expected every morning at sunrise, he always rose early and joined his former comrades in the headquarters trench on the top of a hillock, known as the "bridge," and there they stood watching together until the dangerous period was over. It was during these periods that the poet was impressed by hearing the larks singing their songs, heedless of the enemy's fire, which was smashing the trees around them, and by watching an adjacent French brigade burying its dead of the past night, planting their "crosses, row on row."

---

14   A bank of excavated refuse or waste earth.

Chapter 9

BEING MOSTLY ILLUMINATING
OBSERVATIONS AND ASIDES

At the end of the Second Battle of Ypres, all the units of the Canadian Division were at once transferred to other fields of usefulness, and, it may be added, of hard fighting. The Field Artillery relieved British batteries at Ploegsteert, Bizet, and other portions of the front north of Armentières, where they remained for three or four weeks before joining the Infantry, which had been ordered into a big fight at Festubert, and later on at Givenchy.

The Festubert fight was in the nature of a blister in need of lancing to reduce the activity of the Bosche in the vicinity of Ypres. Matters had reached a peculiar phase at that period of the War. It is not too much to say that in the terrific cannonade that lasted several days at Neuve-Chapelle, the British Army practically exhausted its supply of field gun ammunition and especially everything in the shape of high-explosive. General Sir John French, Commander-in-Chief,[1] was brought to a realization that the War would be won by the nation that could make the most ammunition and keep their rapid-fire artillery most constantly in action. The divisions of the

---

1   Ultimately Field Marshal Sir John Denton Pinkstone French, 1st Earl of Ypres, KP, GCB, OM, GCVO, KCMG, ADC, PC. Sir John was Commander-in-Chief of the British Expeditionary Force from August 5, 1914, to December 19, 1915. He was then Commander-in-Chief of Home Forces December 19, 1915–May 30, 1916.

new Kitchener's[2] Army were also commencing to arrive in May 1915, but there was nothing to do with them further than man the parallel lines of trenches facing the Germans, and so a situation was created which lasted at least two years or more.

All previous wars, and the beginning of this one, had been wars of movement, but for the time being movement ceased and the troops took up positions in the trenches facing each other across No Man's Land. The real situation was that a sort of military stalemate ensued. There was no precedent for it, and the leaders on both sides were in a quandary as to how to push on the War. As already said, the Battle of Festubert was a big frontal attack, pressed heavily, with the idea of alarming the Germans farther north in fear that the British would break through. Save for the casualty list, it did not differ much from the Battle of Neuve-Chapelle, except that we commenced to hear from a few British heavies,[3] which were only then beginning to make themselves felt; the effect of their arrival may be judged when it is reported that the noise of the first few heavy shells coming over the British troops on their way to the enemy was such a welcome novelty that the British infantry cheered every time they heard one.

There was a feature of fighting of that period which was no novelty, and elicited no cheers from the Infantry. That was the ghastly casualty lists resulting from frontal attacks on the entrenched machine guns. Up to that time, the barrage had not come into use, and at the Festubert period, the Artillery had just about enough ammunition to cut the wire in front of the German trenches. To do that at Festubert with sufficient economy of shells, we had to go into action about 800 yards from the trenches.

The Germans appeared to be more prolific in dispensing big shells then than during any period since the commencement of the War. On one fine June afternoon—June 2—Ottawa Battery, having rendered itself conspicuously offensive near the Quinque Road, drew upon itself the exclusive attention of German artillery for an hour and a half, during which nearly two hundred shells were sent to its address, of which nearly ninety were 8-inch or bigger. On that occasion I adopted as a precedent a manoeuvre that, according to the traditions of the service, would have brought me anything but praise or approval. When I recognized by the signs that the battery

---

2   Named for Field Marshal Horatio Herbert Kitchener, 1st Earl Kitchener, KG, KP, GCB, OM, GCSI, GCMG, GCIE, PC. Lord Kitchener was Secretary of State for War 1914 until he was killed in the sinking of the HMS *Hampshire*, which struck a mine on June 5, 1916.

3   Heavy artillery.

was in for a "blacksmithing" I ordered all the personnel to double off to a flank and take shelter in a disused trench several hundred yards away, a decision that meant they could comfortably view the practical annihilation of the material of their battery, but which acquired no casualty list of any size.

When the battery was refitted, its morale was unimpaired (though a great deal of its moveable equipment, such as blankets, buckets, and camp kettles, had blown up among the branches of the neighbouring trees). The traditions of the service would have demanded that the men should stand beside their guns until they were blown into the trees themselves, but so many traditions of the service were ignored in the last War that this one was unanimously voted out of date, and it was never regretted.

The terrain about Festubert was very flat and without distinguishing features—the same characteristics of the country in the whole vicinity of La Bassée. Not only was the country flat, but it was intersected in every direction by deep ditches, about a dozen feet wide and filled with water, the edges of which were marked by lines of heavy willow stumps, which had been so closely "bobbed" that they showed no semblance of a tree. For all the fighting ground in that vicinity, the engineers, for the first and last time during the War, got out field maps, which had two peculiarities: one, that the top of the map was to the south,[4] and the other that the featureless nature of the country was corrected by covering the map with little circles like fish bubbles, each one identified by a letter and a number. To a certain extent this made up for the absence of natural objects. For instance, instead of a clump of willows as the objective of an attack, it would be set down as "M.6." In this way an area of fierce fighting became known as "K.5.," and so forth. As usual, the Germans had the only observation point on the whole field of battle, and that was the strong, square, stone tower of La Basseé's church, on the opposite ridge. Whereas the only O Pip on our side was a brewery on the Rue Quinque, strongly built of brick reinforced with steel girders.

The Canadian Division spent the latter weeks of May cropping a sparse harvest of glory and acquiring many thousands of casualties, besides an apprenticeship in trench warfare, until June 7, when our artillery followed our infantry down to the front of Givenchy, where the frontal attack manoeuvre was repeated until it commenced to pall. So much so, that we began to infuse some novelties into what had become a predictable form of slaughter. For instance, our predecessors had a set

---

4   The top of a military map usually portrays north.

method of strafing.[5] When the Infantry were about to attack the first line trenches, they would "prepare," in the good old style, by showering the front line with shrapnel until the Germans were all driven out of it, and the going would be good. The Germans would take their cue that an attack was imminent, and would retire to their second- or third-line trench, where they would remain under cover until the attackers appeared, at which point they would kneel, still under cover of the third-line trench, and shoot a deadly and well-aimed fire into the British as they came over the top in front.

By careful observation we got on to the methodical habits of the Bosche so that we first strafed the front line trench, and when the German defenders crowded back to the third line, we suddenly lifted our line of fire and spoiled the game of the cunning Bosche. Then the Bosche changed his tactics, and after we had shelled the front line and also got the crowd in the back trenches, he adopted the trick of leaving his back trenches and crowding into the front to await the attackers with bayonets and bombs. He was so sure of fooling us at this game that he would sometimes indulge in jeers and catcalls, until one day, when there was no attack on, we shelled his back trenches until some hundreds of them swarmed down into the front line trench, and then we suddenly pulled back our barrage on the front line trench. This was followed by wails and shrieks of agony, above which came a yell in a decidedly Chicago accent: "What are yez ***** dubs tryin' to do?" These little incidents served to prevent the time becoming monotonous.

One afternoon a Victoria Cross was splendidly earned. An English soldier had been wounded and fell outside the parapet among the barbed wire, and lay all day in the broiling June sun. He was in full sight of both armies, and when he pleaded with the Bosche to throw him over a canteen of water, they threw hand grenades at him, which only increased his suffering without killing him. About 4 PM the English could stand it no longer, and a big soldier jumped over the parapet, rushed across No Man's Land, and, shouldering the wounded man, carried him back to safety, only sustaining some slight wounds.[6]

---

5   Slang term for bombarding the enemy.

6   This probably refers to Lance-Corporal William Angus, VC. On June 12, 1915, he went into No Man's Land at Givenchy under heavy fire to rescue a wounded officer, Lieutenant James Martin. Angus was wounded several times and lost his left eye in this action.

Chapter 10

THE DEBACLE OF GIVENCHY

O n June 15 it became noised about that the Canadians were to make another frontal attack on the Germans. By this time the Canadians were getting rather fed up with frontal attacks and heavy losses, and especially frontal attacks of which the enemy had warning several days in advance.

One in particular the men heard talked about in the cabarets of Bethune; two days before the zero hour every barmaid in that city was gossiping about the attack and questioning the men and so forth. It was more than usually well-advertised because an English company of engineers had dug under No Man's Land and put a mine under the German trench at a well-known point called "the Duck's Bill," and this had made a good deal of talk because there was doubt as to whether the mine was in fact under the German trench or had not gotten that far. This doubt created still more discussion until the talk was so rife that the senior Canadian officers got worked up about it and made representations regarding it. The 1st Battalion of the 1st Canadian Infantry Brigade was to make the assault, and Brigadier-General Mercer, one of our best and bravest officers, was courageous enough to have it out with the senior army authorities. He told them point-blank that just because the Canadians were first-class fighting troops and that fact had been discovered at Ypres was no reason why they should be frittered away in senseless frontal attacks that did not get them anywhere. He assured them that his men would do the work all right, but he wanted those in authority distinctly to understand that this was the last time that they were going in under such foolish conditions. He was an old friend of mine, but I had never seen him so worked up and determined to stop what he considered a senseless waste of the lives of brave men. He even discussed the advisability of refusing to obey the order, or at least of warning the authorities that he would disobey the next order of that kind. Though he had the moral courage to discuss the advisability of disobeying the order, he was just the sort of soldier who would never for a moment seriously consider such a measure.

It was decided that the assault should be made at 5:45 PM, in broad daylight, and that, in order to help out the assaulting party, the Artillery would put two field guns into the front line trench to clear the way. Careful scouting located several machine guns in the parapet of the enemy's trench, and the gun crews made the necessary preparations to smash these with the first round. The operation was difficult in every way because opposite the Duck's Bill in No Man's Land was a shallow point which left little room to assemble the storming party, so that before the Field Artillery could open fire, the parapet in front of them would have to be torn down, at once sounding the alarm, and the gun crews might be wiped out with one volley before they could get into action. Besides, it was no easy job dragging field guns and limbers up the hill to Givenchy without alarming the enemy, let alone keeping them in rapid fire at point-blank range of entrenched infantry. It was arranged that the Artillery should open rapid fire at zero hour, knock down the enemy's parapet, destroy his machine guns, and then cease firing, which would be the signal for the mine to be sprung and the assaulting force to charge across. The Artillery were assured that absolutely bulletproof shelters, invented by a staff officer and made from specially prepared Gillette steel, would protect the gun crews. But not having absolute confidence in all the promises, the 1st Brigade detailed two officers in charge of its gun so as to provide against casualties. The noise of the guns' wheels was muted by the attachment of rubber motor tires over them.

As premonition had only too truly foretold, the whole affair was one of the heroic tragedies of the War. Officers and men did all that troops could do, but everything that could go wrong went wrong. At the given signal, the Gunners, assisted by the Infantry, tore down the parapet in front of the Duck's Bill for about 100 yards, and the moment the front was cleared the 18-pounder opened a rapid and accurate fire against the German trench, the first half-dozen shots sending the shattered machine guns flying up into the air. They raised a cloud of dust that almost blinded the enemy's riflemen, who sprang up and kneeled along the parapet, ready to repulse the storming column that came pouring out of the adjacent dugouts with rifles and bombs in their hands and across No Man's Land. They had almost traversed it when the mine was sprung. As had been feared, it was too close, and instead of blowing up the Bosche trench, it blew the head off the Canadian storming column. But the column was only checked for a minute, and picking up new armfuls of bombs, the survivors came rushing on, only to be met with a shower of debris from a premature mine, which in turn exploded the store of bombs that had been prepared for the assault, and again caused temporary demoralization. A third time the column pressed on, and their furious onrush carried them to the third or fourth line of German trenches, only to find that arrangements had not been made to protect their flanks, and they were being enfiladed[1] from the south at every line of trenches. For over an hour they held onto the fourth line of trenches, but it was only a question of time until they would be annihilated. So, slowly and reluctantly, they retreated from trench line to trench line, and the only surviving officer left to command the remnant was shot through the heart as he jumped over our own parapet.

Of the eight hundred men who charged, and so valiantly followed their officers, an hour before, only two hundred, mostly wounded, survived this gallant but futile attack.[2] One of the last large shells fired that evening burst just in front of the 18-pounder field gun. Its splinters went through the so-called bulletproof shield as if it had been plate glass, and every officer and man on the gun was killed or wounded, including Lt. Craig and Lt. Kelly.[3]

The surviving infantry were requested to see that the field gun was run down into the trench where it would be out of sight of the enemy when day dawned. Unfortunately, in the dark and confusion succeeding the attack, the gun was run back but, instead of being hidden behind the parapet, it was on top of a knoll in full view of the enemy across No Man's Land. This was the condition it was in when I visited the Duck's Bill the next morning, just as the mist was rising. The place was a regular shambles. The wounded and dying who had survived the charge were lying about, and the communication trenches were literally choked with wounded who had been

---

1   Were the target of a volley of gunfire directed along a line from end to end.

2   The 1st Battalion's casualties in the attack were: 68 killed, 226 wounded, and 84 missing (378 men in total).

3   Both officers were wounded, and Gunners William Bamford and Thomas McDonald were killed. An unidentified gunner was also wounded.

taken down and had died on the way. In the middle of a mass of wounded who were patiently waiting for stretchers stood the field gun, on a piece of rising ground and in full view of the enemy, and as the morning mist rose the Germans commenced firing on it with rifles. It was still very early, and it was only a question of time until they would bring up heavier ordnance and smash the gun to pieces.

I had only my groom with me, and though we tried to move it, it was impossible. I did not have the heart to ask any of the several hundred poor wounded chaps lying about to give me a hand, and was sorrowfully departing from the place when a sergeant scrambled to his feet and asked me: "Do you want to take the gun down, Mister?" I said that I did, but did not like to ask the wounded men as the gun was already under fire of the Germans opposite. The sergeant replied: "That's all right, but what do you want done with it?" I explained briefly, and the poor wounded fellows lay about watching me as I explained what was wanted and how it should be done to get the gun under cover. The sergeant said quietly: "Come on, boys," and immediately a score or so scrambled to their feet and climbed up to the gun, where they lifted up the pole and manned the wheels. They were in full view of the opposite parapet and immediately the Bosche opened fire. Their lack of knowledge in handling guns caused the limber to cramp on the gun trail, and they did not know what to do with it. They were an easy target for the Bosche, and the shots commenced to take effect, one poor chap being shot in the side, but the rest of them still continued the effort to move the gun. I ordered them down from the exposed position and told them I would bring up a squad of gunners, but they did not seem at all satisfied, and as I walked away the sergeant and several of the men came after me to assure me that if I would show them how to do it, they would be very glad to get the gun down for me. Partly because I did not want to be killed myself, and certainly because I did not want to let these brave fellows sacrifice themselves, I went away, and a fatigue party got the gun off later in the day. One of the officers killed that night was Major Becher[4] of London, who had particularly distinguished himself at Ypres.

Some idea of the tremendous power of the German high-explosive shells was gained when we examined the so-called bulletproof shields on the gun. The shell had broken into small pieces weighing a few ounces each, and every piece that struck the shield had gone completely through it, leaving a hole the same shape as the bit of projectile. The shields were half an inch thick, specially made of Gillette razor steel.

---

4   Major Henry Campbell Becher, Second-in-Command, 1st Canadian Infantry Battalion, was killed in action June 15, 1915. When Morrison says "that night" he means during the attack previously described.

As a test I fired several .303 bullets from an ordinary rifle at the shield, but so far from piercing it, the bullets barely produced a slight nodule on the inner side at point-blank range. Yet these comparatively small pieces of high-explosive shell went clean through in over a score of places.

Lieutenants Craig and Kelly were severely wounded in the chest, but entirely recovered. They received no decoration, nor even a mention, for the splendid risk they took. It was Craig's third wound in as many weeks and as many battles: at Ypres, Festubert, and Givenchy; two in the head and one in the lungs.[5] Perhaps the most fortunate result of this unhappy evening was that the Canadian Division was withdrawn from the line and marched north to a quiet sector in Neuve-Église in Belgium. There they spent the rest of the year in inventing and carrying out the system of raiding that was subsequently adopted throughout the whole army.

---

5   Lieutenant Charles Stewart Craig. His third wound was to the chest. He was in fact later awarded the Military Cross as a result of this action, on August 25, 1915, while recovering in hospital. Morrison was also in hospital with pneumonia from July 28 to September 9, 1915, and was clearly never made aware that Craig had received the MC. Craig ended the War as a Major with the DSO, MC, and the Croix de Guerre.

    Lieutenant Lawrence St. George Kelly was actually wounded in his right arm and leg. He was not decorated for this action. He also ended the War as a Major and was awarded the Military Cross in 1918.

Chapter 11

THE SHELL SHORTAGE

After having fought on nearly every part of the British front from Ypres to La Bassée, the 1st Canadian Division was moved to a new area on and behind Hill 63, where their position extended south from southwest of Messines to Ploegsteert. Most of their marching was done at night so that German aeroplanes would not spot the movement of troops. They arrived at their destination on the evening of June 29, after three nightmarches.

The troops marched to the chorus of "Bella's basting belly bands for Belgians," a parody on the "Sister Susie" musical atrocity.[1] But the first eighteen miles of their journey was done on a bleak, rainy night, when the poor exhausted infantrymen fell out by the score. The march took seven-and-a-half hours, and was extremely hard on the men, who had had a gruelling fortnight in the trenches, especially as a proportion of them were just out of hospital. Even for mounted troops it was tiring, and towards the end of the night the Infantry were completely done up.

As the Artillery passed, shadowy forms slept in rows beside the route, or in the streaming gutters of the towns we passed through. At one place I threw the light of my electric torch on something that startled my horse, and there were two tired lads asleep on a pile of crushed stones. At the last halt they had probably sat on this by no

---

1   "Sister Susie's Sewing Shirts for Soldiers," a First World War–era song that tells about a young girl sewing shirts for soldiers fighting abroad.

means downy resting place thinking to keep awake, but they had been "gassed by Morpheus" and lay huddled together on the stone heaps in the pouring rain. Their rifles dropped from their hands, and from "the pure lips" of one hung the sodden end of a cigarette—his last solace. All the worn out men who fell out had to struggle along the next day in the broiling sun till they caught up with their column, and then march with their unit again at dusk.

After the first rain the weather was beautiful, and the highly cultivated country-side was like a garden: but it would have scarcely comforted the Canadians if they had known that they were to remain in Ploegsteert, engaged in desultory trench war-fare, from June 30, 1915, to February of the following year.

In September 1915, the 2nd Canadian Division of Infantry began to arrive, and the command of it was taken over by Major-General Turner, CB, VC.[2] In October I myself was promoted to Command of the 2nd Divisional Artillery, with the rank of Brigadier-General, and Lt. Colonel C.H. Maclaren[3] was promoted to the command of my old brigade, the 1st Canadian Field Artillery Brigade.

I was under orders to proceed at once to Westenhanger in Kent, England, to organize and train the new division, which consisted of only men and horses. They had no guns, and little, if any, equipment. When I received command, instruc-tions were to train the division in the shortest possible time and return with it to France, ready to take the fields. Every facility was afforded by officials at the War Office and elsewhere with the result that early in October the 2nd Division was drilling with handmade dummy guns. On December 15 the Corps was ready for inspection by General Drake,[4] Inspector of Field and Horse Artillery, and pro-ceeded the next day to Salisbury Plain for its test in gunnery and inspection in manoeuvre. During the first week in January 1916, it was reported as the best divi-sional artillery among some fifty divisions inspected by General Drake during the preceding year.

During that period of training, the 2nd Division had a disastrous visit from a squadron of German dirigibles[5] on the night October 13, when it lost forty men and twice as many horses from bombs. The railways were officially warned of the approach of the dirigibles, but in the case of the great training camps at Otterpool

---

2   See chapter 4, footnote 3.

3   See chapter 7, footnote 7.

4   Brigadier-General B.F. Drake, Royal Horse Artillery.

5   Airships; zeppelins.

and Westenhanger, with their several miles of brightly illuminated tents, the matter was evidently treated as an "official secret," with a result that might have been expected.

The test firing was carried out on Salisbury Plain under most tempestuous conditions of snow and sleet. It was, incidentally, a test of the soundness of the methods of artillery training carried out by that arm in Canada, and elicited expressions of admiration, not unmixed with awe, from veteran British Gunners. A large percentage of the horses came direct from the Canadian northwest, and some had never had shoes, let alone riders, previous to the first parade of some brigades. The result was that a considerable number of recruits went (not uncheerfully) into hospital. On the evening of January 17 the 2nd Canadian Division Artillery entrained for France, sailing from Southampton for Le Havre, and marching by Abbeville and Cassel.

The 1st Division, under General A.W. Currie,[6] was quartered at Saint-Jans-Cappel, and the 2nd Division, under General Turner,[7] was in the vicinity of Dranoutre. The 1st Division Artillery was out at rest and was relieved by the 2nd Canadian Division Artillery.[8] The 3rd Division, under General Mercer,[9] a former Commander of the 1st Infantry Brigade, then stood on the main road between Ypres and Cassel, where the Prince of Wales[10] was introduced for the first time. He was then a blushing youth whose diffidence of bearing was quite out of keeping with his weather-stained uniform, for he had already been in the field for about a year. There was snow on the ground, and the troops of all arms reported putting in an uncomfortable but rather quiet winter.

The practice of raiding the German lines had been brought to a high state of efficiency, and the 2nd CDA[11] had scarcely reported to the 1st Division when they were required to put on a box barrage to cooperate in an infantry raid of considerable importance. The affair was very successful from all points of view, the Gunners coming in for many kudos from the Infantry. Unfortunately the officer commanding the

---

6   Lieutenant-General Sir Arthur William Currie, GCMG, KCB, General Officer Commanding Canadian Corps, 1917–1919.

7   See chapter 4, footnote 3.

8   The relief occurred from February 4 to 6, 1916. The 2nd Division Artillery remained in the line supporting the 1st Division until March 12, 1916.

9   See chapter 8, footnote 6.

10   Later Edward VIII.

11   2nd Canadian Division Artillery.

raid, Major George Richardson of Kingston,[12] a well-known and highly respected officer, was killed during the hand-to-hand fighting.

On our arrival in France we found the ammunition situation worse than ever. The responsibility for the shell shortage had been passed along from the Government via the contractors and manufacturers to the British workmen. The Government blamed the contractors, and the contractors the manufacturers, and the manufacturers the drunkenness of the British workman. So like the nursery rhyme—"The stick commenced to beat the dog; the dog commenced to worry the cat, etc."[13]—and the net result was that Tommy Atkins[14] had his one tot of rum per week cut off, though later information showed that the workmen had only been made the scapegoat for incompetence higher up.

The *Times of London* had made a political issue of the shortage of ammunition by attacking its government, and the nation had adopted an ostrich-like policy by burning copies of the *Times* on the floor of the Stock Exchange. The only effect of this, so far as the Gunners could see, was the issue of the most stringent orders regarding the expenditure of ammunition, actually limiting field artillery to "two rounds per gun, per day, perhaps." Shortly after, the situation became such that there was a further restriction explaining that the order referred only to shrapnel. As for high explosive, not a single high-explosive shell was to be fired without divisional authority.

Whenever the question arose of restricting the use of ammunition, I seemed fated to get in wrong. On one occasion I had received grievous complaints from our infantry at the number of casualties they were suffering from snipers on the left of the line near the Messines road. By careful scouting they had located the rascals who were sniping at them—in a small house within German lines—which they had named "Sniper House." The field telephones reported that, on the following Sunday morning, if I could spare the time, a small committee of infantry would meet me near Barrel House on Hill 63 and exactly point out Sniper House with a view to having it destroyed. They appreciated the importance of not wasting ammunition on the wrong house. Such courtesy and consideration of our limitations by the Infantry could not be ignored by the Gunners, and anyway, it was generally known that the Sabbath morning was my favourite morning for visiting down front. The 2nd Ottawa

---

12   Major George Taylor Richardson, Chevalier of the Legion of Honour, 2nd Canadian Infantry Battalion, killed in action February 9, 1916.

13   A misquote of the song "The House That Jack Built."

14   Slang for British soldier.

Battery of the 1st Brigade and Commanding Officer Major Donnie White[15] had a high shooting reputation, and in fact had been foxily suggested to me by the Infantry as sure to do the trick without wasting the precious ammunition. So with my orderly officer, Capt. Moore Cosgrave,[16] we made an appointment with Major White and our infantry friends near the Barrel House for the Sabbath morning. The Infantry showed a pathetic readiness to point out a small house, just within the enemy's lines, with a high-pitched roof and gable windows as the proposed target.

The battery was called up by phone and given as its target the gable windows in the roof, as well as a reminder that the ammunition allowance of two rounds per gun, and no "perhaps" connected with it, was not to be exceeded. Then we all watched while Major White gave the order to fire. The result was a beautiful line shot for the dormer window, but it landed a few feet short of the front doorstep. Observations and corrections were made, and the second shell went on its way just on a level with the dormer, but a few feet to the right so that it cleared the south end of the house. A correction of a few feet to the right and on the same level would take the next shell right in the dormer window and blow the back out of the house. Then some of the anxious artillery officers had a brain wave: "Why not make your third shot a high explosive and pop it in the dormer window so as to entirely ruin the interior and make a good job of it?" It was a great temptation; but there was the order that no high explosive was to be fired without written permission from Headquarters. Everybody had tempting arguments why the order should be ignored. It was a ridiculous order anyway: the idea of starting in a war with artillery ammunition, the firing of which had to be authorized round by round. And anyway, if we did not report firing it, who would be any the wiser? This capped the climax. Major White was going on leave to London as soon as he could get back to his headquarters and mount his horse; his adjutant would neglect to report the expenditure of one high-explosive shell; and if any enquiries were to be made, the Major would be away on leave. All this was so plausible and the shooting looked so good that I weakly consented. Accordingly the battery loaded with high explosive and what I was satisfied would occur happened. There was not a breath of wind, and the gun was laid just right according to the

---

15   Major Donald Alexander White. The 2nd Battery was part of the 1st CDA and was back in the line relieving elements of the 2nd CDA from March 9 to March 10. This firing occurred on Sunday, March 12, 1916, just before Morrison handed artillery command authority for the front back to GOC 1st CDA Brigadier-General H.C. Thacker, CB, CMG, DSO.

16   See chapter 5, footnote 12.

sighting shots, with the result that the high explosive, dispatched with deadly accuracy, went straight into the dormer window and exploded as it struck the back wall of the interior. The back wall collapsed with a clatter of falling bricks, and a cloudlet of dust, drifting drowsily in the summer air, was all that was left of Sniper House. Major White scarcely waited to accept the handshakes and well-earned congratulations before he skipped down the hillside, mounted the horse his orderly held, and galloped off to catch the leave train for London.

Then everything commenced to go wrong, as I might have expected. The adjutant, busily intent upon taking over his new-found responsibility, carefully put "One high-explosive shell" into the ammunition return. Myself and Capt. Cosgrave rode across country to Brigade Headquarters and, lunch just being ready, we sat down to a mess full of enthusiasm at the destruction of Sniper House, and so full of elation about it that the mess table buzzed with conversation. The office clerk, who had just received the ammunition return, did not want to interrupt our enjoyment by handing in the return for my O.K., so he did what he had never done before in a blue moon, and sent it to the signallers to be dispatched to Divisional Headquarters.

Then things began to happen with an appalling promptitude. A telegram arrived: "M.S.G.[17] not understood. What do you mean by firing one H.E. without authority?" I should have had a premonition that I was in the wrong, and badly. But instead of that I made things worse by endeavouring to treat the matter lightly. That was all that was necessary to make Divisional Headquarters ferocious and demand "prompt and complete explanations." Then I made explanations prompt and complete, but the cold and calculating reply would have convinced a halfwit that a Field General Court Martial, with an unlimited number of witnesses, could not commence to make it prompt and complete enough to satisfy Divisional Headquarters. When it became obvious that they were determined to find me guilty of deliberate and intentional refusal to obey an important written order, I took another tack. I expatiated on the importance of destroying Sniper House, and on the impossibility of waiting for permission to use the shell, because the wind might change, the atmospheric conditions frustrating the accuracy of the fire of the shell and preventing my carrying out the highly important task called for by the Infantry.

It was all in vain. Headquarters was determined that no one should use a high explosive, and to demonstrate that there was not a high explosive to use anyhow.

---

17   Message.

The telegraphic correspondence went on, day after day, until it became ridiculous in quantity and idiotic in quality, at least in my conception. I gathered up a bundle of it and sent it to my friend, John McCrae, and he enjoyed the joke. But my superior officers could not commence to see the jest, let alone enjoy it, until finally my own sense of humour became threadbare. Then I stopped putting anything further on paper. Instead I rode to Corps Headquarters and dropped a hint, with a gallus[18] air, that I was about to ship all the correspondence to London as an illustration for the use of the newspapers, who were being told by the War Office that the Army was not at all pressed for artillery ammunition. After this, as I walked out of Headquarters, I heard a pained voice say: "Those Canadian fellows are liable to do anything." That was the last I heard of the incident.

18   Slang for "cocky."

Chapter 12

THE ST. ELOI CRATERS, 1916

T he spring of 1916 opened early in April with warm rains and sunshine. The 2nd Canadian Division, with its artillery, was ordered to relieve the 3rd British Division, which had been holding St. Eloi and the southern area of the Ypres Salient. On April 7, the 2nd CDA moved north from near Bailleul to the small village of Reningelst in preparation to make the relief.

The Commander of the British Division[1] had mined the large mound that dominated St. Eloi, and wished to blow the mines before withdrawing his troops, and then have General Turner and the 2nd Canadian Division take over. General Turner demurred; he was willing that his division should blow the mines, consolidate the craters, and seize the position thereafter, but he properly objected to having the British blow the craters and the Canadians take over the front in the hullabaloo that must instantly ensue.

However, after a lot of negotiation and argument, the British general had his way, and all the foreseen losses ensued. It had been pointed out that the scheme involved the British inflicting the blow on the enemy and securing the kudos, leaving the Canadians to "hold the bear by the tail" while the 3rd British Division withdrew; that was exactly what happened.

---

1   Major-General (later General) Sir James Aylmer Lowthorpe Haldane, GCMG, KCB, DSO. GOC 3rd British Division November 21, 1914–August 7, 1916. He went on to command the VI British Corps.

The mines on the mound were all fired at one moment before dawn on a beautiful spring morning. A large number of staff officers had gathered on the hill, not far from Kemmel Hill, known as the Scherpenberg. Promptly at the zero hour, what looked like five colossal toadstools of burning peat rose into the air above the mound, remained standing for several seconds, then disintegrated with a deafening detonation and drifted off leeward in a mass of friable debris in which hundreds of human bodies, as well as arms and equipment, were visible. At least 250 Germans were killed in the explosion of the mines and the artillery bombardment that immediately ensued. Hundreds of guns opened fire from concealed gun pits immediately after the explosion, and it looked, from the top of the Scherpenberg, as if the country below was swarming with fireflies.[2]

Exactly what happened after the blowing of the craters was the subject of much acrimonious discussion and endeavour to place blame. The explosion destroyed the trenches and most of the defensive work of the mound. With the coming of daylight, German artillery hammered the mound dreadfully, and by about noon the situation was that the English had departed without being relieved in the trenches and without consolidating the five large craters on the summit of the mound. The Canadian Infantry alleged that they found no British to relieve, and no consolidated craters to take over. They did find a good many Germans, who had launched a counterattack and consolidated trenches of their own. So that, all afternoon and far into the rainy, dark night, wild fighting continued for the possession of what remained of the St. Eloi mound.

The next day the weather changed. It was a beautiful sunlit morning. What was left of St. Eloi Mound stood out, an abomination of desolation, on which there did not seem to be a living soul. Where the mound had been there was only mud and rubbish. The explosion had thrown the wet clay about in huge lumps where it mingled with wrecked houses, shattered wagons, torn uniforms, and broken equipment—such a medley of debris as, luckily for some people, made it impossible to reach the base on foot. I say "luckily" advisedly, because the impression prevailed that the top of the sombre, squalid-looking mound was held by our Canadians, and in the early morning, Capt. Cosgrave, along with my orderly officer and myself, undertook to climb the mound to examine the condition of the craters. But we failed to reach the top on account of the heavy going. And when later in the day it was found that the top of the mound was held by the Germans, we were quite reconciled.

---

2   Six mines were detonated at 4:15 AM on March 27, 1916. Mine number six was slightly behind the other five when viewed from the area of Kemmel, so only five blast clouds were seen.

The consolidation of the craters involved several days and nights of hand-to-hand fighting, under more or less constant German shellfire. Many days afterwards, awful looking objects crawled up to our wire, nearly dead from gangrene, and proclaimed themselves casualties from the craters. There was one instance of a pigeon arriving in Poperinge, nearly a fortnight later, with a message from a non-com who had been sent out with a party to the craters, saying that all were dead, but he had remained to tend the wounded until they were dead or able to move. The captor of the carrier pigeon sent in the note with a report from himself telling when and where the pigeon arrived, and expressing the opinion that, as it had evidently been detained in transit, it would be too late to do anything for the parties of wounded or dying. However, we sent out a rescue party and found the heroic surviving non-com, but he was in such a condition that he could only be sent to hospital to die. About the same time a German who apparently could not speak much English shoved his head over the parapet of our trench and bowed ingratiatingly to the sentry in the trench, exclaiming: "Scoose me. Good morning." His condition indicated that he had been wandering about, suffering from gangrene.

What became known as "The Affair of the St. Eloi Craters" gave rise to much suffering and loss of life. The bad feature of the affair was that the new troops, who went in for the relief, had no opportunity to reconnoitre the position in advance, and found it impossible to consolidate owing to the confusion caused by the explosion and their lack of knowledge of the situation, especially after the explosion entirely changed the appearance of the mound. Undoubtedly those who were to take over the mound should have been the ones to blow it up. The truth is that, until the Canadian troops had made a world reputation, there was a tendency to impose on them by influential British officers who never lost an opportunity of dealing with them as though they were green and inferior troops. General Sir Julian Byng, now Lord Byng of Vimy,[3] assumed command of the Canadian Corps early in June 1916, just at the time when it was suffering from another bad mauling at what was known as the June Ypres,[4] but it retrieved itself, and never again, under his leadership, failed to cover itself with glory. Lord Byng's success was due in part to his own personality, and also to the fact that he held the troops of Canada at their true value. From first to last, he

---

3   Lieutenant-General (later Field Marshal) Julian Hedworth George Byng, 1st Viscount Byng of Vimy, GCB, GCMG, MVO, replaced Lieutenant-General Alderson (see chapter 4, footnote 5) as GOC Canadian Corps on May 28, 1916.

4   Now called the Battle of Mount Sorrel, June 2–13, 1916.

never allowed them to be interfered with, or their leaders browbeaten and the troops under them mishandled, as in the case above recorded.

The explanation of the St. Eloi affair is that the politically influential general who made the whole trouble forced his junior, the British officer at that time entrusted with the command of the Canadians,[5] to adopt his obviously ridiculous plan *against* the protests of General Turner, Commander of the 2nd Canadian Division.[6] When the situation became so unfortunate from the Canadian standpoint, and explanations became necessary, it was obviously impossible to lay the blame on the Commander of the 3rd British Division when that division was publicly acclaimed as the heroes of St. Eloi, and General Turner absolutely declined to allow anyone of his subordinates to be made the goat, even when he himself was threatened with that unhappy fate. The upshot was that General Alderson was himself recalled, and General Byng became Commander of the Canadian Corps.[7]

After the fight at St. Eloi, the 3rd Canadian Division, commanded by General Mercer, prolonged the line of the 2nd Canadian Division to the northeast of the Salient, its infantry being supported by the Lahore Artillery,[8] pending the arrival of its own gunners from Canada. They took over the trenches that other troops had been holding in the Salient during the winter, and found them in very bad condition. In some places the water and mud was such that the parapets had sunk into the ground and the trenches were full of water. The line ran from the 2nd Canadian Division in a north-easterly direction, by way of Zillebeke Lake, Sanctuary Wood, and the Menin Road east of Ypres, near Hooge.

---

5   Lieutenant-General Alderson.

6   Major-General Haldane was the first cousin of Lord Richard Burdon Haldane, 1st Viscount Haldane, Secretary of State for War 1905–1912, and Lord Chancellor 1912–1915. Morrison is saying that Lieutenant-General Alderson was the social junior of Major-General Haldane, and so felt that he could not overrule him.

7   Relieving officers who were seen to have failed in battle was common between the British and Canadian Armies during the Great War. It should be noted that Lieutenant-General Sir Hew Dalrymple Fanshawe, KCB, KCMG, GOC, V British Corps, was also relieved due to this battle.

8   The 3rd Indian (Lahore) Divisional Artillery was left in France when the infantry divisions of the Indian Corps were deployed to Mesopotamia in November 1915. The Lahore Artillery supported the 2nd, 3rd, and 4th Canadian Divisions in succession while the Canadian Divisional Artilleries were formed 1916–1917. It was renamed the Reserve Divisional Artillery in 1917. It left the Canadian Corps in June 1917.

Chapter 13

THE JUNE YPRES

Sir Julian Byng had not yet taken over his command when there took place another of those ghastly engagements which made history and filled the casualty lists with the names of Canada's dead. On June 2 was fought the battle of the June Ypres.

After the fight at St. Eloi the 3rd Canadian Division under General Mercer, one of the heroes of Ypres, took over a line of trenches in the northeast of the Salient that ran, by way of Zillebeke Lake, Sanctuary Wood, and the Menin Road, to the east of Ypres, near Hooge. In many places the trenches' parapets had broken down, and no effort had been made to drain them. General Byng, with characteristic thoroughness, at once decided to make a personal inspection of his line, and with Divisional Commander General Mercer and Brigade Commander General Victor Williams set out on the very morning that the Germans had chosen for a violent assault on that part of the Salient.

The enemy opened its attack with a tremendous cannonade that smashed the eastern wall of the city of Ypres and practically obliterated the trenches from Menin Road south through Sanctuary Wood, Maple Copse, and Zillebeke Bund. Curiously enough the atmospheric conditions were such that not a sound of the heavy bombardment was heard at Reningelst, less than three miles from the battlefield, and the 3rd Division sent no cry for help. All morning the enemy kept up a devastating fire on the trenches and gun positions of the division and then, about noon, burst upon them with an infantry attack which overran the position almost to the eastern wall of the city of Ypres.

The infantry of the 3rd Division put up a most heroic resistance in the deadly hand-to-hand fighting of that afternoon. On one place were found twelve dead Germans who evidently had all fallen victim to the bayonet thrusts of a huge sergeant-major of the Mounted Rifles and two brave members of the Princess Pats Regiment. General Mercer refused to surrender and was killed by the enemy.[1] General Williams[2] was severely wounded and taken prisoner. Officers and men died in their trenches, and only 350 unwounded prisoners, according to official German claims at the time, were captured. In Maple Copse the dead lay very close together; in Sanctuary Wood it was the same.[3]

The Artillery, too, had suffered. The Lahore gun positions, most of which were in front of the moat in Ypres, were destroyed. The 1st Divisional Artillery, whose guns were in Sanctuary Wood and south from the Zillebeke Bund, were in some cases overrun, though none of them were captured. Officers and men fought to the last. Lieutenant Matthews,[4] a forward observation officer, remained at his post and was killed. Lieutenant Cotton,[5] whose guns had been firing parallel to our line, enfilading German trenches some miles to our right, could not turn his 18-pounders towards the enemy's front, but caught them on the side as they went past. The two guns were almost buried in empty cartridge cases, and when the position was recaptured on June 13 by the 1st Division Infantry, Lieutenant Cotton and his gunners were found lying about their guns where they had died. Only two escaped.[6] One was wounded early in the engagement; the other seized a bit of scantling[7] and felled a German who attacked him with his bayonet, and ultimately escaped, wounded, to the rear.

Many brave deeds were done that day. One wounded Canadian, who had been taken prisoner by the enemy, drank the coffee the Württembergers (xiii Royal

---

1   General Mercer was killed by artillery fire on June 3, 1916.

2   Major-General Victor Arthur Seymour Williams. GOC of 8th Infantry Brigade December 28, 1915–June 2, 1916, when he was wounded and captured.

3   The 4th Canadian Mounted Rifles suffered 89 percent casualties in this action.

4   Lieutenant Harold Stratton Matthews, 1st Brigade CFA, killed in action June 3, 1916.

5   Lieutenant Charles Penner Cotton, 2nd Brigade CFA, killed in action June 2, 1916.

6   This was the only instance during the Great War when Canadian guns were captured by the enemy.

7   A small piece of lumber.

Württemberg Corps) offered him then slipped away unnoticed into the woods. Again he was taken prisoner, and again he escaped and reported back to our lines. An Ottawa officer named Bruce Hill[8] distinguished himself by remaining in his forward observing position after the Germans had charged past, and keeping up communications with his battery till the wire was cut by shellfire. He waited until dusk, then made his way back, carrying his telephone instruments with him. Unfortunately he was wounded the next day.

It was a terrible battle from the commencement. Officers and men made a splendid stand. The Princess Pats had been forced to give ground slightly, but Colonel Buller[9] called on them to charge. His men followed him with such a rush that he found himself in their way and sprang up on the bank out of their way. He was running forward, cheering on his men, when he was shot through the heart. Not only he but nearly every battalion commander was killed or wounded in that first assault.

During the whole of that bright June day, the Württembergers and the 3rd Canadian Division fought their duel, it might be said, alone. There was no interference from either side, in the sense that the Canadian Division received no reinforcements, and the Württembergers might have been well on the way to the Channel Ports by sundown if the success of the morning had been followed up. As it was, the Germans never set foot in the city of Ypres, though there was nothing to prevent them from doing so. It was reported at the time that the officer commanding the German Forces was relieved because of his failure to follow up his success. The truth seems to be that the attacking force had been so severely punished that they were not aware of their success, and had got all the fighting they could stomach.

The 3rd Division did not have, possibly, the careful training the two previous divisions had received, but in the surprise attack the men fought with a bravery and determination, and their officers led them with a confidence and readiness of sacrifice, that surprised and pleased the veterans of the two other divisions, who had already survived half a dozen battles, and nearly two years of war. By the time the day's fight was over there was only a portion of the 9th Canadian Infantry Brigade that could not be moved, and the survivors of the rest of the 3rd Division had rallied around their officers, firmly determined to renew the fight. During the night reinforcements

---

8   Lieutenant Clarence Bruce Hill, 4th Battery, 1st Brigade CFA. He finished the War as a Major with the Military Cross with bar.

9   Lieutenant-Colonel Herbert Cecil Buller, Commanding Officer PPCLI, was killed in action June 2, 1916.

were brought up and a counterattack was made that recovered a large portion of the ground lost. One of the brilliant features of the counterattack was a bayonet charge by the 49th Battalion, led by Colonel (now Senator) Billy Griesbach.[10] The regiment went in 900 strong and returned with only 350. Colonel Baker, MP,[11] the only member of the Canadian House of Commons to be killed in the Great War, fell in this assault. At such costs to Canada her right to nationhood was won.

This battle was General Byng's first experience of the Canadian Corps, and he showed his genius by the prompt and vigorous measures he took to secure Ypres and the Channel Ports, once more placed in jeopardy. The 9th Infantry Brigade and the survivors of the 3rd Division were left in their positions in the field, as immovable as their heaps of dead around them, while the General extended a line of guns from the Menin Road to St. Eloi. I was given the honour of commanding this Artillery. It was a great responsibility, and day and night I patrolled the line of batteries whose barrage, supporting that thin line of determined infantry, was all—if the German Army had known it—that barred the road to Calais.

General Byng had determined to throw in the grand old 1st Division, with an artillery barrage in front of it, and retake the position and make all right again. The men of the "old red patch" were taken out for ten days of rest and preparation, and the artillery put up a box barrage around Lieutenant Cotton's guns[12] to prevent them being taken away. The counterattack was set for midnight of June 13. The night turned out to be stormy and blusterous and black as the pit, but at zero hour the 1st Division Infantry went over with a magnificent dash and before morning had recaptured all the ground lost to the Württembergers, including Maple Copse, Mount Sorrel, Zillenbeke Bund, Sanctuary Wood, and our two guns. Enemy losses were very heavy; in front of Lieutenant Cotton's guns their dead lay heaped, one on the other. Both attack and defence had been a very costly business.

During the summer of 1916 important changes took place in the methods of organizing and fighting the Artillery in the British service. In 1915 the head of

---

10   Lieutenant-General William Antrobus Griesbach. As Brigadier-General W.A. Griesbach, CB, CMG, DSO, he commanded the 1st Infantry Brigade from February 14, 1917, until February 25, 1919. He was Inspector-General for Western Canada as a Major-General during the Second World War, retiring in 1943. He served as a Senator from 1921 until his death in 1945.

11   Lieutenant-Colonel George Harold Baker, Commanding Officer 5th Canadian Mounted Rifles, was killed in action June 2, 1916. He was MP for Brome, Quebec, from 1911 until his death.

12   The guns were captured on June 2, 1916.

artillery was known as the Artillery Advisor, and his duties were what his name implied; namely, to advise the Divisional Commanders what to do with their artillery. Sometimes the Artillery Advisor's advice had been taken in 1915, and sometimes it had not. So, in the following year, the Artillery Advisor was succeeded by a more authoritative person known as the General Officer Commanding Royal Artillery. To this officer was now given the command of all artillery and the responsibility of organizing it and arranging for counter-battery work against the enemy. Naturally it took some time for the new organization to solve the problems thrust upon it. For instance, when the 2nd Division took up its position for the first time after its arrival in France, even though its batteries were well protected by the high ground of Hill 63, it was immediately subjected to severe and systematic strafing by enemy guns. Whereupon I called up the senior artillery authority aforementioned and requested that the German batteries be silenced. The counter-battery authorities very politely answered that if I could tell them where the German batteries were, they would comply with my request. I replied that if I knew where the German batteries that were shooting at us were, I would soon shut them up myself. This brought on a "conference" at which the General Officer, in an indulgent tone, wanted to know how he was to discover and silence said German batteries. When I innocently told him that he should send up aeroplanes to discover them and then stop them, he immediately made the triumphant retort: "But if I send up aeroplanes the German batteries will at once stop firing." To which I replied: "The next time they strafe my batteries for two or three hours, for goodness sake send up an aeroplane." Thus was discovered the initial feature of what subsequently became the most involved and difficult but successful system of counter-batterying.[13]

Another difficulty was solved in the spring of 1916. The Germans had plenty of ammunition and used it lavishly in annoying our infantry in the trenches. Naturally the Infantry, when they were being strafed, put up an "exceeding bitter cry" for retaliation on the part of their own Artillery. But we had not enough ammunition to properly retaliate, and our efforts at retaliation did little more than aggravate the situation. A new system was required. So orders were issued to save up the ammunition for guns of all calibres until a large stock was on hand. Of course the first effect of this was a series of grievous complaints from the Infantry that they were getting no support from their Artillery. But, in the meantime, I had personally reconnoitred

---

13   This is a conversation between Brigadier-General Burstall and Morrison.

the enemy's lines and picked out a half a dozen spots in different parts of the German lines where there were large clusters of hutments (small huts) for infantry. These spots were marked and laid down on maps, and a new system of strafing organized. It was explained to the Infantry that when the Germans shelled them a good deal and they wanted retaliation, they were to call up the Gunners when they considered it desirable to hand the enemy a jolt to the solar plexus. A certain number of batteries would then be warned to lay their guns on one of these selected vulnerable points, and would simultaneously commence a ten-minute strafe on the point mentioned, absolutely obliterating it from the earth. At the end of ten minutes the strafe would cease with the same suddenness it began. If the German annoyance did not cease, the batteries would load again, and at the end of ten minutes would open a second strafe on another selected point.

The result was most successful. The next time the Germans, insolent in the possession of much artillery ammunition, were annoying our people in the trenches, and retaliation was called for, an order went out to prepare for a "Number nine strafe on point 'A' at the zero moment." A tremendous devastation descended on the selected spot. The Germans were taken by surprise, and even more so at the end of ten minutes when, as suddenly as it began, our strafe ceased. Our gunners were ordered to stand by to repeat the operation, but there was never any need, and thereafter our infantry had no cause to grumble about lack of retaliation.

So effective was the system that General Plumer,[14] commanding the Second Army, delegated Major-General Franks[15] and Major-General Harington[16] to observe the workings of one of these crashes. On their report, the system was promptly adopted by the whole Second Army.

In August the Corps was visited by His Majesty who got a most enthusiastic welcome from the troops, though his visit was intended to be quite "informal." On the morning of August 14, His Majesty witnessed an artillery demonstration on the Corps front, of which I had the honour to be given command. Not to attract undue

---

14   General (later Field Marshal) Herbert Charles Onslow Plumer, 1st Viscount Plumer, GCB, GCMG, GCVO, GBE. Commander, Second Army May 7, 1917–November 9, 1917.

15   Major-General George Franks, Major-General Royal Artillery, Second Army (the senior Artillery Officer in Second Army).

16   This name was left blank by Morrison. It was most likely Major-General C.H. Harington, Major-General General Staff (senior staff officer), Second Army. He had just been promoted from Brigadier-General, General Staff Canadian Corps.

attention, only seven officers, including my Brigade Major[17] and ADC,[18] were allowed on the Scherpenberg Hill from which His Majesty watched the "shoot." His Majesty remained for over an hour. A few minutes after his arrival, a heavy rain squall came on, obscuring observation, but the Sailor King glanced at the sky in true nautical fashion and remarked that the squall would soon blow over, and he would wait. My Aide-de-Camp, Lieutenant Fripp, got an armchair from a neighbouring farmhouse with a nice soft cushion for His Majesty, and had it placed on the grass. We were a good deal amused when an old Officer of the Royal Staff, who had evidently been much fatigued climbing the hill, calmly took the chair intended for the King. His Majesty smiled and walked over and sat down on a log.

A telephone line had been laid in the long grass only forty feet away, and I knelt in the grass between the royal group and the telephonists and received orders for the operation, nominally, direct from the King, through the Chief of Artillery for the Army.[19] The batteries, which were in some cases several miles away, turned on their fire simultaneously, fifteen seconds after the order was given. It was a very fine spectacle. The Prince of Wales arrived in time to see the end of the affair.

Later on, all the general officers of the Army Corps were received by the King near the 2nd Divisional Headquarters. Wherever His Majesty appeared the troops spontaneously rushed in masses to line the roads and raise cheer after cheer for Britain's king. In no hearts in France did there burn a more passionate love for the Empire's ruler than in the stout Canadian sons who saw him pass so quietly here and there among his troops.

---

17   Major Charles Francis Constantine, Brigade Major, 2nd Canadian Divisional Artillery July 29, 1915–February 16, 1917. He ended the War as Lieutenant-Colonel and was awarded the DSO.

18   Aide-de-Camp (personal staff officer). Lieutenant (later Captain) Herbert Downing Fripp, who served as Morrison's ADC 1916–1917 and on Corps Artillery Staff in 1918.

19   Major-General Franks. See chapter 13, footnote 15.

Chapter 14

THE BLOODBATH IN THE SOMME

From the time the 1st Division left Valcartier the Canadian Corps had steadily grown in strength until four full divisions, with the necessary troops, were trained and in the field by the summer of 1916. The old 1st Division was commanded by Major-General A.W. Currie; the 2nd Division by Major-General R.E.W. Turner, vc; the 3rd by Major-General Lipsett;[1] and the 4th by Major-General David Watson.[2]

Since April 1915, the Corps had spent practically all its time in the Ypres Salient. The older divisions had been through some of the heaviest fighting of the War and had suffered severely, but they were able to hand on to the younger units the proud tradition that they had never lost a gun or a single yard of trench that had not been recovered.

In July of 1916, the Imperial Forces plunged into the "bloodbath" of the Somme. Little information had come to the troops about the course of events there, but it was understood that the "big push" had not been as successful as had been hoped. Early in August it was rumoured that the Canadians were due for a turn on the new

---

1   Major-General Louis James Lipsett, cb, cmg. goc 3rd Canadian Division June 16, 1916–September 2, 1918. Major-General Lipsett was killed in action October 14, 1918, while commanding the 4th British Division.

2   Major-General Sir David Watson, kcb, cmg. goc 4th Canadian Division April 25, 1916–June 23, 1919.

battlefront. The rumour was shortly confirmed. Colonel Fotheringham,[3] Chief Medical Officer of the 2nd Division, and I were ordered to proceed at once to the Somme area to inspect the battlefield and lay plans to overcome the obstacles that would be presented to our respective branches of the service.

We left Reningelst by motor on August 19, and on the morning of Sunday 20 reached Albert, the headquarters of the Australian Division covering the front from Pozières to near Thiepval. The town of Albert had been badly shelled even previous to the Somme operations, and very few buildings in it were inhabitable. The most striking feature in the place was the statue of the Virgin, stood with arms extended and holding the Child, its hand uplifted in an attitude of supplication for suffering humanity. But as the tower of the church had crumbled under shellfire, the heavy metal statue had bent over with its own weight, until the extended arms of the Child, instead of being lifted to Heaven, seemed spread out in a protecting gesture over the city. There was a tradition among the citizens that as long as the figure held, the city would not be taken.

The country about Albert is rolling country with occasional patches of woods. Originally it had been dotted with villages, but Ovillers-la-Boisselle, Contalmaison, Fricourt, Mametz, Pozières, Montauban, Thiepval, and others of those places were only to be distinguished by ruins that looked like the ashes of an old campfire. Looking at the celebrated village of Pozières, from a point half a mile down the road from the village, all one could see was an unkempt fringe of broken, tortured trees on the skyline, with two or three brown humps of debris. Contalmaison, from a distance, was just a black and grey splash. Closer up, the splash resolved itself into a piece of ground, half a dozen acres in extent, littered with broken bricks, with here and there a larger heap where a church or some public building had stood.

So far as the former German front line system was concerned, the word "trenches" was a misnomer. Originally there had been a line of redoubts or ramparts, deeply undermined in some cases, and as much as three storeys deep. But the original line of ramparts had been pounded till it appeared as a series of chalk mounds, thirty or forty feet high, and in some places fifty yards wide. These mounds, with their casemates and galleries, could be described only as fortresses, and they constituted the most serious problem in the whole offensive.

During an artillery bombardment, the Germans took refuge within these casemates and remained there, allowing the storming parties to sweep past. Then, when

---

3   Later Major-General John Taylor Fotheringham, KStJ, CMG, MD.

our troops had pushed far within their lines, the garrisons in these fortresses would issue in swarms and attack from the rear. The troops that pushed through without first taking and destroying these fortifications could not be reinforced or fed, and ultimately had to fall back on their old positions.

The German scheme of defence was plain. As long as these fortresses (inadequately named "strong points") held out, our troops could not push between them for any considerable distance; meantime, the delay occasioned by the taking of these forts would allow the enemy to withdraw a large proportion of their artillery to their second line of defence, and also bring up the necessary reinforcements to make that second line almost as impregnable as the first. It gave the enemy time and opportunity, too, to organize counterattacks on a large scale on any particular part of the front.

Yet the advantages of observation were with us. The British Infantry held the skyline; British aeroplanes held the air; and in the immediate hinterland British troops enjoyed life, liberty, and the pursuit of happiness, tempered only by sprinkles of unobserved fire.

In the Ypres Salient, it was not so. There the all-seeing eyes of the enemy looked down upon us from Wytschaete, and one could never get away from the discomforting feeling that, if the Bosche had not actually got a mortgage on your life, you existed at best only on sufferance. On the Pozières–Longueval front that was not the case. On that Sunday afternoon, battalions were marching in column of route within 1,000 yards of the front line trenches, horsemen and motors were moving, and pioneers[4] were working in the streets of Montauban, comically ignoring the fact that a heavy barrage of 8-inch shells was pounding away on the edge of Bernafay Wood, only 500 yards to the east of them. If a German F.O.O.[5] could have overlooked the area for one minute, he would have hopped that barrage 500 yards to his right, and the results would have been sanguinary. In the same way, the road to Pozières was thronged with troops, and the Bosche was industriously lobbing shells, first on one side of the road and then on the other, as ineffectively as a blind man hurling rocks over a fence. The advantage to us was not alone that the enemy's shooting was blind shooting; it was also that he was forced to keep his guns as far to the rear as possible, and that his morale suffered from the accuracy of our fire.

As soon as the generals commanding the Canadian divisions had completed and coordinated their plans, some of the Canadian troops were withdrawn for rest and

4   A soldier employed to perform engineering and construction tasks.

5   Forward Observation Officer, i.e., an artillery officer directing artillery fire.

instruction. They were glad to leave Ypres, and were calm; confident that nothing they would meet on the front they were going to take over would be worse than what they had endured in Flanders. But by the second week of September, they were deep in the heavy fighting of the Somme.

On the morning of September 10, Headquarters went forward from Ruprembre to the battlefield. There was a general shuffling about of units on September 11, so that the 1st Division Infantry was supported by the Lahore Artillery and the 2nd Division Infantry by the Artillery of the old 1st Division, while the 2nd Division Artillery supported the 3rd Division Infantry. The Artillery of the 3rd Division was still in Ypres supporting the 4th Division Infantry.

On the morning of September 15, the 2nd and 3rd Divisions attacked east and north. It was a beautiful morning, and in addition to our corps, the 3rd British Corps on the right and the 2nd British Corps on the left also attacked. The three corps put on a cooperative barrage of a most intricate description on a front of nearly fifteen miles following the convolutions of the trenches.

In order to ensure exact cooperation in this artillery attack (which was probably one of the greatest combined artillery operations in the history of the War), watches had to be synchronized throughout the two armies. The signal officers all took the army-time over the wires and then sent our orderlies with watches from staff to staff, showing the right time. Then the staffs telephoned correct time to the brigades, and the brigades to the batteries. It seemed that for forty-eight hours everyone went about comparing watches, so anxious were they that the mammoth barrage should be absolutely successful.

On this occasion everything worked like a charm. General Lipsett and I went up on a hill where we could get a good general view of the country. It was a magnificent morning, and the sky overhead was thick with aeroplanes. The great battlefield happened to be unusually quiet; usually lively shelling continued day and night. We watched the hands of our watches while they almost imperceptibly neared the zero minute, and, exactly to the second, with one prolonged roar, about a thousand guns opened fire, and in an instant a streak of bursting shells appeared across the scenery literally from one horizon to the other.

For one minute that fifteen-mile line of smoke and bursting shells lay like a thread across ridge and valley; then the whole line moved forward 100 yards and rested on the enemy's trenches for five minutes. At "Zero Six"[6] it lifted again, and

---

6   Zero hour plus six minutes, i.e., six minutes after the attack had started.

myriad little figures could be seen scampering into the dense smoke left by the five-minute barrage. Those were our infantry attacking, and the closer they could keep to our line of shells the less they would suffer from the enemy's fire. From all fronts came telephone reports that the barrage was perfect and that the Infantry had lost almost nothing in getting into the enemy's trenches. For about thirty minutes this barrage crept on, ahead of our infantry in little jumps of 100 yards, and it is difficult to imagine the accuracy of the workings of this tremendous aggregation of artillery as the shells from nearly a thousand guns all made their little hops together along this front of nearly fifteen miles. Never before had anything on the same scale been attempted, and it was thoroughly successful.

General Turner's division, the 2nd, went forward with a splendid rush on a line with and to the north of the Bapaume Road, attacking lines of trenches one after the other and finally capturing the village of Courcelette. I walked along "Taffy Trench" after the battle. The infantry of the 2nd Division had paid off their scores for St. Eloi. The trench was three quarters of a mile long, and throughout its length and in front and behind it was a continuous litter of German dead. After two years of war on the British front, I had never before seen either German or our own dead "in heaps" until I reached Taffy Trench. Not only was the ground thick with Germans; in five different places I saw heaps of four or more piled on top of each other.

Written on the ground was a tale of many tragedies and curious happenings. Out to the front of the trench in one place there was a row of three big Germans, about 20 yards apart, in a line in the direction that our infantry had charged. Each German had a gaping bayonet wound in his breast, a wound that is never to be confounded with a rifle bullet or a piece of shell. In a line with these Germans, and near the lip of the trench, was a little Canadian crumpled up on his face, with his rifle under him and his legs drawn up, showing that he had been killed in the act of running forward. The bayonet of his rifle was covered with blood, and it was quite apparent that as he had charged forward he had bayoneted the three Bosches in succession before he was dropped.

At another point, a shell hole had been made into a small trench. There was a dead German in the bottom of it and one of our men, who had died in the act of crawling out, was on his hands and knees with his head fallen forward. Neither the Bosche nor the Canadian had arms beside them, but had evidently been wounded before they crawled into the same shell hole. From the appearance of the ground and the attitude of the bodies, it looked as if these two wounded men had fought with their bare hands, and that the Canadian had done in the Bosche, and was crawling out of the hole when he died, exhausted, on the edge.

On the evening of September 16, MacDonnell's 7th Brigade of the 3rd Division formed in the sunken road leading northeast into Courcelette to the celebrated Mouquet Farm. It was a fine bit of work and the commencement of a series of advances towards the north.

On the afternoon of September 17 I went forward to reconnoitre new positions in the territory we had captured. The dead were lying very thick everywhere, and the wounded were being brought in. Most of the Germans had been killed by shellfire. The Bosche was evidently in a bad humour, and was hopping barrages of heavy shells from one point to another over the captured area. It was lively work dodging them. I met Captain Cosgrave in the thick of it and he was acting as liaison officer with the Infantry, and as he and I were standing talking on the parapet of a trench with a signal officer, a Bosche shell nearly made a direct hit on us, exploding twenty feet past us. As it went by we unanimously rolled down into the bottom of the deep trench and landed in a heap, covered with chalk and dirt, but nobody hurt.

A little farther on I saw a curious sight. Along the top of a ridge, in full view of the German Artillery, our stretcher-bearers were coming along in Indian file, carrying wounded. In front of each stretcher was a man with a long pole on which was a white flag about half the size of a handkerchief. They constantly waved the poles as they advanced, and the Germans did not fire on them. They put heavy barrages in front of them and on either side of them, but carefully respected the line of wounded. I was told that this had been going on all day.

The fortitude of our wounded was a splendid thing to see. I never heard a cry or a groan out of one of them, though the going was very rough over shell holes and broken ground. My ADC[7] told me that he was at one of the forward dressing stations where a large number of Germans and our men were waiting their turn to have their wounds dressed. One German officer was making a great to-do and "yelped like a dog" while he waited. Next to him was a Canadian Kiltie[8] who laughed at and "joshed" the German officer, and the rest of our wounded stood by or lay about on the ground not saying a word. When their turn came to have their wounds dressed, it was found that the Kiltie was far worse hurt than the German officer, being wounded in three places severely.

---

7   Lieutenant Herbert Downing Fripp.

8   Soldier in a Highland or Kilted regiment.

As I went along I came upon many of our wounded who had received first aid and who were planted out in shell holes to protect them from the German barrages. In addition to their wounds, they were liable at any moment to be wiped out by a shell, but they were as quiet and unmoved as though they were already in the comfortable hospital beds at Cliveden. The Signal Officer had a few cigarettes, and we put one in the mouth of a fine-looking lad and lit it for him. He thanked us quite politely and was more self-possessed and unperturbed than many people have been seen suffering from a sprained ankle—so much so that I was tempted to ask him where he was hurt. "Through the stomach, sir," he answered, quite simply.

On the outskirts and in the village of Courcelette the enemy dead were very thick. In one bit of sunken road, about 500 yards long, there had evidently been a fierce infantry fight at close quarters. The dead lay sprawled about, in places literally in heaps: one hideous hurley-burley of death, Germans and Canadians mixed together, though mostly Germans. And this was only one little corner of the field.

In another place I passed I saw a lonely soldier kneeling upright in a trench. The butt of his rifle rested on the ground, and his head was bowed forward on his hands where they clutched the barrel of his rifle. He looked as if he might be praying or had fallen asleep in that position from sheer exhaustion. His cap was off, and his glossy black hair shone in the sunlight. I walked over to see if I could do anything for him. The top of his head was caved in level with his eyebrows.

The main trenches were heavily manned by our indomitable infantry, who sat or lay about asleep among the dead, not "grim looking and unafraid" as a fictionist might describe them, but silent and calm-eyed, as if it was the most natural thing in the world that they should be there in such surroundings and were ready with the same cold, unswerving air of determination to hold on or advance as they were required.

On the evening of September 17, the 7th and 9th Infantry Brigades on the left, and the 2nd Division on the right, again attacked. The objective of the 3rd Division was the Zollern Graben,[9] the Zollern Redoubt, and Mouquet Farm. The idea was for the right of the 3rd Division to make a half-wheel to the left so as to bring its flanks on the Zollern and Fabeck Graben, and advance westward about 1,000 yards, being reinforced as it proceeded by the 9th Brigade from the south, and then wheeling northwest to capture the Zollern Redoubt.

---

9   *Graben:* German for "trench."

It was a most complicated movement, as the attacking force would need to describe almost a letter *S* in its advance. The result was that when it had traversed the first curve of the *S*, the enemy took it heavily on the flank with machine gun and rifle fire, and the advance did not go on any further.

Meanwhile, however, our troops in front of Mouquet Farm, while waiting for the main body of the attack to reach the second loop of the *S*, assaulted Mouquet Farm—or rather raided it—and took it.

This mysterious stronghold (one of the fortresses already described) had gained a sinister reputation from having been assaulted five or six times by the Australians without any permanent success. At least twice they had taken it, but strange things had happened. On one occasion they had captured the farm, which was nothing more than a heap of wreckage on a slope, and had put a small garrison in it. Next morning, so the story went, the Bosche were again in possession, and the garrison had mysteriously disappeared—whether taken prisoner or slaughtered, none were left to say.

Again the Australians attacked the place, and to be sure, went beyond it and dug in. While they were so engaged, the Germans suddenly reappeared behind them and turned machine guns on them from the rear, killing or driving them all off.

When we arrived there, Mouquet Farm was supposed to be one of the hardest nuts we had to crack. It was supposed that the Germans had a tunnel from Thiepval, nearly a mile away, and were able to reinforce or withdraw the garrison through this tunnel. On September 11, I reconnoitred the position myself, and had Colonel King[10] put one of his justly celebrated howitzers in a select position 1,500 yards from Mouquet Farm, which was a mile and half nearer than any other battery at that time. A few days later, the whole battery was put forward and with the usual luck, never had a single casualty while it remained in that position.

I made it the business of that battery to continually shell Mouquet Farm when it was not otherwise employed. After forty-eight hours we ceased to observe any signs of life at Mouquet Farm, except that twice a Red Cross flag was put up so we stopped firing but recommenced as soon as it was taken down. Our infantry found that they could walk over to the immediate vicinity of the farm without even being shot at, and gradually they dug a sort of horseshoe trench around three sides of the farm. This was the situation on the afternoon of September 16.

---

10   Lieutenant-Colonel W.B.M. King, who was now commanding the 6th Brigade, CFA, under Morrison. The howitzers were from the 22nd Battery, commanded by Major J.K. MacKay, DSO.

As part of the artillery scheme of the attack already referred to, Colonel King put a hundred howitzer shells into Mouquet Farm without ever hitting our own trenches, within 50 yards of it on three sides. When the shelling stopped, the Infantry crept forward from their trenches and took possession of the farm, finding only a few prisoners among the ruins. The Infantry Commander, a Major Foster,[11] was a clever officer, and after searching the farm he withdrew his men outside it and kept watch. The story is that after some time the watchers saw some Germans coming out of a tunnel that had an iron door on it. Our men rushed into the farm, but the Germans slammed the door and they could not batter it down. They withdrew again to their trenches, but left some men with large Stokes bombs stationed near the mouth of the tunnel. Thinking all our men had withdrawn, the Bosche carefully opened the door again, whereupon the guards outside threw in a Stokes bomb. Four or five more bombs were thrown down the tunnel, with the result that the end of it was blown in and closed up, and our people occupied the stronghold in peace.

A week later, our infantry turned it over to the Imperials, and when the next battle occurred on September 26, the British advanced from the farm, leaving it behind them, whereupon the Bosche suddenly reappeared out of the tunnel with machine guns and fired into their rear as they had done before. This time the British returned and mopped up the place thoroughly, capturing sixty-three prisoners. The secret of the place was that the Bosche had a tunnel about 400 yards long, one end of which was in the farm and the other was on the brow of the hill to the north of it.

---

11 Major William Wasbrough Foster, Officer Commanding C Company, 52nd Infantry Battalion. He was later promoted to lieutenant-colonel and commanded the 52nd Battalion. He ended the War as Major-General William Wasbrough Foster, DSO, CMG, VD with two bars, and the Croix de Guerre. Prior to the War he had been Deputy Minister of Public Works for the province of British Columbia.

Chapter 15

REGINA TRENCH

On September 26 there was another battle in which the 1st and 2nd Canadian Divisions attacked northward, the objective being the Zollern and Hessian trenches, with the hope of going on 500 yards farther to Regina Trench. It was arranged that we should barrage in front of the Infantry as on September 15, and that after they had captured the second trench, there should be a halt while patrols were sent forward to see if there were entanglements in front of Regina Trench. Zero hour was at 12:35 PM and a second zero hour was to be given late in the afternoon if the first two objectives were reached and it was found possible to assault Regina.

The capture of the Zollern and Hessian trenches behind our barrages proved comparatively easy, but considerable time elapsed before any definite information could be obtained regarding the state of Regina Trench. The result was that the third objective was not attempted that afternoon, and the capture of Regina Trench was postponed four days to allow the Artillery to cut the wire. As a matter of fact, very little wire could be seen.

By September 29, the 2nd Division had extended its front nearly 1,000 yards to the northeast, capturing what was known as the Practice Trenches, and got its right flank on the Bapaume Road another 500 yards farther east.

On October 1, the 2nd and 3rd Divisions assaulted Regina Trench and the Bosche territory to the northeast. The 2nd Division went forward up the Bapaume Road, almost to Le Sars, and also got a foothold in Regina Trench. The 3rd Division also got into the latter trench in a number of places, and held on until early the following morning, when it was driven out by repeated counterattacks delivered by German Marines, a new force that had just been brought down to the front and that fought with great spirit.

During the battle of October 1 the Artillery was much hampered by the fact that the aeroplanes could not find out where our troops had got in and where they were not. The assaulting Infantry were supposed to send up red flares when they saw our scouting 'planes over them, but they either had no flares or neglected to send them up. In the same way, when they were counterattacked next morning, no S.O.S. rockets were sent up. The net result, so far as the 3rd Division was concerned, was that on the morning of October 2 they were out of Regina Trench, but held Kenora, the trench that ran forward north-westerly from near Courcelette to a junction with the Regina. Again the 2nd Division pushed its line north-eastward for 500 yards. It was relieved a few days later by the 1st Division.

On October 8 another try was made for Regina Trench by the 1st and 3rd Divisions. The weather had been bad in the meantime, and the Bosche had worked hard in strengthening their position and putting out wire, so that Regina was a dangerous position to attack. The attack was launched at 4:50 AM, and, the morning being dark and rainy, it was not daylight at the time. The regulation barrages were put on and reported to be perfect, but matters did not go right. In the 3rd Division one battalion got astray in the darkness, and did not reach its objective.[1] Part of another attack was held up by wire, which had been put out in lanes, but in the darkness and excitement the assaulting Infantry could not pick out the lanes. In addition to this, blinding rain and heavy mud generally retarded the attack, and made information hard to obtain by runners.

As late as 1 PM, the situation was not cleared up. It was known that both divisions held the enemy's trench in spots, but the reports were conflicting as to where it was held and where it was not. At 12:30 PM General Byng personally ordered me to resume shelling Regina Trench, but as soon as the Infantry Brigade commanders heard this they all asked that it not be done, as they could not tell whether their men were in it or not. General Byng commented on the slowness with which information had been received regarding the progress of the Infantry and their whereabouts. Several of my officers went forward themselves and sent back reports that later were

---

1   The 49th Battalion.

shown to be entirely accurate; however, in the absence of any verifying information through the Infantry channels, progress was paralyzed.

By 2 PM it was fairly certain that all the 3rd Division Infantry were out of Regina and back in Kenora Trench. At 2:35 PM, an S.O.S.[2] call came in, and we shelled Regina Trench heavily and got a column of enemy reinforcements coming from the north, apparently to counterattack, and smashed them up.

About the same time the Germans counterattacked the 1st Division, who had succeeded in getting a portion of Regina Trench and a very strongly entrenched position called the Quadrilateral, about a mile northeast of Courcelette; the upshot being that the 1st Division were driven out late in the afternoon, and by the night of October 8, both divisions were "as you were."

After this fight there was a good deal of criticism flying about, the Infantry alleging that the Heavy Artillery had not done enough smashing of the trench, and that the Field Artillery had not cut the wire sufficiently. There was also a general impression that our infantry, after the heavy losses of the past month (only a portion of which had been made up by reinforcements), needed a rest. It was agreed on all hands that during the night preceding the assault, the Germans had thrown a lot of concertina wire over the parapet where the Artillery had already cut it, but at no point on the front of the Corps was there any evidence that the wire had proved a real obstacle. The weather and the mud and the darkness had contributed a good deal to retard the advance. Some of the Infantry said that they had been so exhausted after an advance of 500 yards through it that they simply fell into the Bosche trench. It would appear that the Heavy Artillery preparation had been insufficient, because not only was Regina Trench not "done in," but there were many machine guns in it and in some old gun pits in front of it, which inflicted heavy casualties during the assault and prevented our reinforcements from getting into the trench.

It was not until October 21 that Regina Trench was finally taken.[3] In the meantime the 18th Imperial Division took over from the 3rd Canadian Division, and the 4th Canadian Division took over from the 1st Canadian Division, the 1st and 3rd going out of the line. There was then a peculiar mix-up of fighting units. The 2nd

---

2   S.O.S.'s were targets chosen to be fired on as quickly as possible. Guns were aimed at their assigned S.O.S. target when they were not otherwise firing.

3   Most of Regina Trench was captured on October 29, 1916. The remaining portion was blocked by the Germans and essentially became part of Desire Trench. The 49th Battalion attack on the portion remaining in German hands was defeated on October 25. It finally fell to the 4th Division on November 11, 1916.

Canadian Division had gone to Vimy Ridge and were there supported by the Lahore Artillery; the 2nd Canadian Artillery Division supported the 18th Imperial Division under General Maxse;[4] the 1st and 3rd Canadian Artillery Divisions supported the 4th Canadian Infantry Division, whose artillery was still in England. General Burstall, GOC, RA, Canadian Artillery, handed over his command to General Lawrie, GOC, RA, II Corps.[5]

It was decided to attack Regina Trench at 12:06 PM on October 21, on a front of 5,000 yards. The 18th Division, supported by my 2nd Canadian Divisional Artillery (to which were attached the 2nd and 3rd Brigades of the 1st Canadian Divisional Artillery), had the chief role. On our right, the 4th Canadian Division, supported by a brigade of the 1st and 3rd Canadian Divisional Artillery, threw forward a defensive flank on a front of 500 yards at Regina Trench. To our left, the 11th and 25th Divisions prolonged the line.

The weather was bright and cold and a heavy barrage was put on by the Artillery. On our particular front, it differed from previous barrages very materially. At zero I opened a triple-barrage that consisted of five batteries about 50 yards short of Regina Trench, ten batteries on the trench, and three batteries searching and sweeping in rear of the trench. Previous to this we had a succession of "sealed pattern" barrages, which usually commenced 100 yards short of the trench, where they remained a minute or two, then hopped onto the trench, and after three or four minutes hopped forward in hundred-yard barrages.

The Bosche had become wise to this, and it was reported that he'd placed infantry, and even machine guns, in shell holes about 50 yards in front of his parapet; also that a considerable number of Bosche had time between the opening of the forward barrage and the lifting of it onto the trench to get into dugouts or to run back to hide in shell holes behind the trench. The result of these manoeuvres was that when our hundred-yard barrage opened in front of the trench, it was a warning for those in the trench to get under cover, or for those behind to get into shell holes. When the barrage was lifted 100 yards onto the trench it missed those out in the shell holes in front, and when it lifted 100 yards off the trench it missed those in the shell holes in rear.

General Maxse having asked me to suggest a barrage, I made mine open 50 yards in front the trench and on the trench and 50 yards in rear of the trench at

---

4   General Sir Frederick Ivor Maxse, KCB, CVO, DSO. GOC 18th British Division until 1917, then GOC XVIII Corps.

5   Brigadier-General C.E. Lawrie, GOC, RA, II Corps December 26, 1915–February 19, 1917.

the same time. After five minutes, the eighteen batteries continued on as one barrage in 50-yard lifts, thoroughly combing out the ground for 500 yards in rear. The effect seemed to have been excellent, as practically every Bosche in Regina Trench was killed or captured. The infantry of the 18th Division expressed themselves "delighted" with the Artillery support. They went into the trench 20 yards behind the barrage with scarcely any casualties at all, and practically all the surviving Germans surrendered.

I inspected the trench on the following day, and was very interested to discover the number of dead Germans in the shell holes, about 40 yards in front of the trench. At one point there were six dead on a front of 50 yards, each man simply dug in. The trench itself, and its vicinity, was a shambles. As already stated, every Bosche on a three-mile front was killed or captured. Twenty-four hours afterwards, we continued picking up stray Bosches who had run away and hidden in shell holes and were unable to retreat through our barrage.

Though the 18th Division had the chief role in the show, the other divisions did almost equally well. The prisoners captured were 1,100, including sixteen officers. The total losses of the four divisions were less than 1,200. While this would rank as a minor operation compared to the gigantic offensive on the Somme, it is noteworthy that the British force engaged was larger than the whole original British Expeditionary Force that came to France in August 1914. The number of infantry divisions was the same, but the Artillery was very much stronger.

The British Infantry appear to have been extremely pleased with the shooting of the 2nd Canadian Divisional Artillery. Lieutenant-General Gough,[6] commanding the Reserve Army, came to my headquarters to personally compliment me on the support given to the 18th Division. He was most complimentary, stating that from the descriptions he had received from the Infantry, our barrages were perfect, and that the 18th Division ascribed to the accuracy of this fire the small losses they had suffered. Major-General Maxse, after visiting the infantrymen who had taken part in the assault, also telephoned in equally laudatory language.

On the day following the capture of Regina Trench, I went forward to examine it, with special reference to the complaints of the 8th Infantry Brigade, 3rd Canadian Division, during the two previous attacks. It being rather foggy, I was able to walk

---

6   General Sir Hubert de la Poer Gough, GCB, GCMG, KCVO. Gough was relieved of command of the Fifth
     Army as a result of the German Spring Offensive in 1918.

along the parapet of Regina Trench and thoroughly inspect it from one end to the other. I particularly examined the wire, which the 8th Brigade patrols had reported as having held up their attack at one place, and as "very strong" practically along the whole front. As the dead of the 3rd Canadian Division were lying just where they fell, and as the 18th British Division had scarcely any casualties at all, it was possible to see exactly what had happened in the two previous assaults, especially on our left front.

In the first place the wire was little more than a myth. On long stretches there was no wire and had never been any wire. At a few points there was just a "show" of wire, produced by a single line of stakes with a few strands on them. Just west of Twenty-three Road in the angle made by Regina Trench where it runs southwest from the road, there was a small bunch of wire covering only a few hundred feet, but what the Infantry patrols had reported as "thick and heavy wire" were clumps of dried weeds. What wire there was would scarcely have presented any obstacle, but even that had been efficiently cut before the 8th Brigade attacked on October 1. This was proven by the fact that the only three men who had reached the wire were not hung up on it but had been killed in the passages through it. The remainder had never reached the wire, but there had evidently been a heavy machine gun fire brought to bear on them 100 yards short of it, as there the dead lay thick. It was also certain that the wire had been cut as we saw it before the 8th Brigade assault, because the bodies of the men who had reached the wire had not subsequently been mutilated by shellfire as they would have been had the wire been cut after they fell. There was also evidence, judging from the number of their dead facing in that direction, that in the early morning attack our infantry had lost their way and had swung around and attacked their own Kenora Trench from the northeast.

All these things had not been the fault of the men, but of a lack of supervision by the brigade staff and by some of the battalion commanders. It was inevitable that, in spite of the most thoughtful preparations, things should now and then go wrong. The strength of the enemy, the location of his machine guns, and the power of his artillery, the condition of his trenches, and even the state of the weather were all uncertain questions. Repeatedly when arrangements had been made for battle, and orders were out for the attack, rain fell and continued falling for days, making movement impossible, dislocating plans, and causing confusion. Then, too, battalion commanders and brigade staffs were dependent upon their signal services for knowledge of the movement of their troops. A single shell fragment might cut a wire and sever connections for an hour. Runners died with their messages undelivered and only the utmost courage enabled any push to succeed. It happened at times that brigade staffs did not exercise proper supervision, and that battalion commanders failed their men in an emergency. But it was rarely that the blame of failure could be thrust upon the men, for their coolness, their courage, their endurance, and their will to conquer never failed them. Never once did the troops fail their leaders unless their leaders had first failed them.

Chapter 16

THE END OF THE SOMME OFFENSIVE

After the capture of Regina Trench on October 21, the line was thickened up with artillery, and preparations were made for a more ambitious operation on the part of the Reserve Army, now known as the Fifth Army. Three divisions of artillery were placed in support of the 18th Infantry Division, the 2nd Canadian Divisional Artillery, the 11th Divisional Artillery, and the 25th Divisional Artillery, the latter two commanded by Brigadier-General Lamont[1] and Brigadier-General Kincaid-Smith.[2] The 1st and 3rd CDA supported the 4th Canadian Division on our right, and the 32nd Imperial Infantry Division was in reserve at Albert. It was proposed that the 4th Canadian Division should attack to the north to capture Miraumont; the 39th on its left to capture Grandcourt; and the 19th to keep touch along the south bank of the River Amore.[3]

This in itself promised to be a good day's work, but the secondary phase provided that it should be accomplished by noon, and that the 32nd Divisional Infantry were to follow up the success by crossing the rear of the 18th Division and moving to the attack of the villages of Pys, Irles, and Achiet-le-Grand, the 4th Canadian Division continuing its role of flank guard on the right. This meant that, at an hour to be

---

1   Brigadier-General J.W.F. Lamont.
2   Brigadier-General K.J. Kincaid-Smith.
3   Likely a small tributary of the Somme or L'Ancre, probably misnamed.

named, my division was to switch from the support of the 18th and I would auto-matically become CRA of the 32nd Division and barrage the latter division into Pys and Irles.

Then followed a period of alternating good and bad weather. The mud became so bad that all ammunition had to be taken up on pack horses. When the weather conditions improved, we would prepare to carry out the operation, which would take several days—and just as the zero hour was to be fixed, stormy weather would set in again. Many such postponements took place, and the deferred fight commenced to make the troops rather sick, especially as they were living under summer conditions, in the open, though it was now winter.

Finally, on November 13, an attack was made by the V Corps to the north, and the 19th and 39th Divisions of the II Corps, while the Artillery of the 18th and the 4th Canadian Divisions put up a heavy barrage to distract attention preceding an attack of the Ancre, which was quite successful, except in spots. Beaumont-Hamel was captured, but Serre held out. The 19th and 39th Divisions moved forward without much difficulty so as to keep abreast of the advance and connect on the right with the 18th. Nearly seven thousand prisoners were taken, but the casualties where the attack was held up were rather heavy. The old 3rd Imperial Division, for some reason, did not get out of their trenches in time to follow the barrage closely, and were repulsed with machine gun fire.

As the weather continued fine and frosty, another operation was ordered for November 18. The 4th Canadian Division took over 1,000 yards of front to its left, and was supported by the three Canadian Artillery Divisions: the 18th narrowed its front and took over a bit from the 39th, which was to attack on its left, with the 19th to the west of that again, its left flank resting on the River Ancre. It was rather a tentative operation. The Canadians were to attack the Desire and Desire Support Trenches, and, if the going was good, the Grandcourt Trench 1,000 yards farther on. Similarly, the 18th Division prolonged the objectives to the left, and the 29th behind that. All these divisions were facing north, while on the extreme left the 19th Division faced nearly east.

If all had gone well, it was the intention to take Grandcourt and Miraumont. What happened was that, while the 4th Canadian Division and the 18th Division got their first objectives at the double, the 19th Division failed to get forward at all on account of the heavy machine gun fire, thus preventing the 39th next to it from getting very far, and in turn, the 18th had to draw back its flank to maintain touch with the 39th. The Canadians not only got their objective, but one battalion (the 87th) took Desire and Desire Support Trench, and then continued on 1,000 yards farther and took a portion of Grandcourt Trench on its front, together with 120 prisoners. The whole division took over seven hundred prisoners.

Though the previous days had been fine and cold, on the morning of this attack the weather had changed and there was a snowstorm at dawn. The ground was frozen hard, and visibility was very bad. This became worse about 8:00 AM when the snow changed to rain and hail with mist. When the 87th Canadian Battalion overran its objective, it disappeared into the mist, and a period of great anxiety ensued for several hours. Even its own battalion headquarters could not tell our liaison officers where the battalion had disappeared to, and this had a paralyzing effect on the Artillery because we were unable to barrage forward for fear of getting our own troops. At the request of the GOC 4th Canadian Division, I undertook to have the battalion found, as our Forward Observing Officers had been sending in nearly all the information as to what was going on at the front. Each of the three Artillery groups sent forward one of its best-observing officers to find the missing link to the line. Lieutenant Oliver was killed,[4] Lieutenant Hammond was wounded in the arm,[5] but Lieutenant Carmichael[6] got through and brought back the information that the 87th were in Grandcourt Trench taking numerous prisoners. Apparently they had been too busy to send back word. It was subsequently learned that in the mist a portion of this battalion had actually penetrated to the church in Miraumont without serious opposition.

The question now arose as to whether the rest of the line should advance to Grandcourt Trench and join up with the 87th, or that the 87th should retire to its proper objective in Desire Support Trench. The failure of the 19th Division to get on at all settled the question, and it was decided to withdraw the 87th during the following night. They came back very reluctantly, bringing their prisoners with them. On our extreme right we had a slight check on about 500 yards of line. There was a small

---

4   Lieutenant Allen Oliver, MC, 7th Brigade, CFA, was killed in action November 18, 1916. He was awarded the MC just prior to this battle.

5   Lieutenant (later Captain) Herbert Renwick Hammond, MC (awarded for this action), 6th Brigade, CFA. He was wounded in the left arm in this battle. He was severely wounded again in 1917 and discharged as medically unfit for further duty.

6   Lieutenant (later Captain) Eoghan Kenneth Carmichael, MC (awarded for this action), 6th Brigade, CFA. Carmichael had been wounded in October 1916, but stayed at duty until December.

isolated plateau, a few hundred yards in extent, which was swept with machine guns. The Canadian Right Brigade failed to make this good, but the latter was of little importance as it was on the refused flank where our line turned south to connect with the III Corps.

Certain peculiar conditions surrounded these latter operations of the II Corps from a strategic standpoint: Grandcourt, Miraumont, Pys, and Irles are down in a hollow, some of which is submerged by the Ancre during the winter. This depression is under complete view from the Bapaume Ridge. The capture of Bapaume was the immediate business of the III Corps on our right, and until Bapaume was in our hands, the Miraumont–Irles position would be under complete observation for the enemy's artillery. In other words, if we took these places, they would have to be held all winter under the fire of the German Artillery around Bapaume. On the other hand, if we retained the ground we had already taken, the Germans in these places would have to winter under our observation and the fire of our guns. The III Corps on our right made several strong attempts to get forward in the direction of Bapaume, and got within 4,000 yards of it, but could get no farther, so that there was no great eagerness on our part to take up such an undesirable position as Miraumont, Pys, and Irles, except in conjunction with a united operation that would include Bapaume.

On November 21, the 4th Canadian Division, and the 1st, 2nd, and 3rd Canadian Artillery Divisions received orders to move out by the 28th inst.[7]

For more than twelve weeks the Canadian Corps had been engaged in battle. Considered in the aggregate, their losses had been heavy; but when the gains they made are considered, and the conditions in which they fought are taken into account, their losses were relatively few. Day and night the struggle went on: heavy shelling, continual shrapnel, high explosive, gas. The enemy put as many as five hundred gas shells into one area between midnight and dawn. Nightly his aeroplanes bombed our lines.

Early one morning he dropped some tremendous explosive, whether a large bomb or an 8-inch shell there was no one left to say, on the 22nd Howitzer Battery. Where No. 4 Gun had been, there was a crater sixty feet in diameter, and twenty-five feet deep; the mangled remains of a two and a half ton howitzer had been hurled 120 feet through the air, and lay piled up in a tangled mass out in front of the aiming posts. A portion of the remains of the gun crew were discovered a quarter of a mile

---

7   November 28.

away. All of No. 3 Gun Crew was also either killed or wounded. There was no one left to throw any light on the tragedy. As soon as news of the 22nd's misfortune reached me, I hurried down to the battery position to give my sympathy to the commanding officer and his men. When I arrived, the Gunners were busily manufacturing a huge camouflage net of rope ends and torn sandbags to spread over the crater so that the Bosche aeroplane scouts could not see how the poor 22nd had been done in. Such was their pride. And such the stuff they were made of.[8]

If our men suffered, so did the enemy. For the first time there was ammunition enough—and to spare. The Gunners had got such mastery of the barrage—an artillery manoeuvre that the Germans never mastered, even by the end of the War—that our infantry could move in line 20 yards behind our barrage. In one part of the Somme advance it was found that a certain gun was shooting 20 yards short. For a short time the Infantry felt themselves threatened by their own guns, but the short-range gun continued to shoot, true to form, always 20 yards short, so that the Infantry respected his idiosyncrasies and followed him in as securely as the others. Now and then it was possible to introduce a little humour into the situation; to provide the enemy with guessing contests as to what terrible trick that deadly annihilating barrage would do next. Anyway, when the barrage had done its work, even the redoubtable fortresses that the Bosche believed to be impregnable fell prey to our infantry.

Their gains were such that the enemy was forced to retire to the Hindenburg Line, and leave in our hands all the area in between.

---

8   This incident occurred on November 10, 1916. One howitzer was destroyed and one was damaged. Five men were killed and three were wounded.

Chapter 17

VIMY RIDGE

The Canadian Army marched north from the Somme, and early in December of 1916 settled down in the Lens–Arras sector. This part of the front was to be their battleground—with the exception of a month at Ypres, again, in 1917—until August of 1918 when the last stage of the War was reached. Just as Poperinge will never be forgotten by the Old Originals, so the villages of Bully-Grenay, Barlin, Bouvigny-Boyeffles, and Aix-Noulette will always be remembered by those who did not see the first stages of the great conflict.

On December 16 I was relieved of the command of the 2nd Divisional Artillery and was promoted to be General Officer Commanding Royal Artillery, of all the Canadian Corps. On the day after Christmas I took over my new responsibilities. For a few days I was absent in England on duty, and returned on January 6 to take command of artillery preparations for the expected capture of Vimy Ridge.

Corps Headquarters at Rebreuve-Ranchicourt was already busy. A general order for the capture of Vimy had reached us from the Second Army in the latter part of December, and early in the New Year active preparations were commenced. The work that was ahead of both staff and units was immense. The operation was the most extensive that had been undertaken by an army corps up to that time, and, in certain respects, remains the greatest effort of the whole War. The staff preparations leading up to it covered a period of over three months and were on an elaborate scale that left nothing to chance where military skill could foresee and adjust.

All ranks shared in the work of preparation. I was early informed that I would have under my command for the operation at least 480 of our 18-pounder guns, 126 howitzers, and 275 heavy and siege guns. Never before had there been so much artillery massed for one attack. But as the greater of this artillery would not be available until shortly before the preliminary bombardment, the work of digging gun emplacements and filling them with ammunition fell upon the Canadian Corps Heavy Artillery and the four divisional artilleries already on the ground. The magnitude of the task may be estimated when it is considered that every 18-pounder in the two Right Divisions was supplied with 1,500 rounds in the gunpit, and that, in addition, reserve dumps with tens of thousands of shells were established to the rear.

The weather during January and February was unusually severe. The continual snow and abnormal cold put out of action several hundred motor lorries that had been depended on to bring forward this immense amount of ammunition and other materials needed for the action. Nevertheless the work went on, in spite of the weather and the heavy fire of the enemy. The Gunners did wonders with the little material they had to hand, and in conditions that were appalling. In March the weather broke, and as the frost came out of the ground the roads became impassable for heavy traffic. The ammunition for the guns was brought up on pack horses. Always a dread business in the best of conditions, under the heavy fire of the enemy it exacted a heavy toll of both men and animals. The extreme weather of that winter had been hard on the Artillery horses. Nearly all had been picketed in the open and the issue of forage had been reduced to a minimum. Steadily the horses had been reduced to skeletons, but it speaks well both for the stamina of the animals themselves and for the care their drivers gave them that they got the necessary ammunition in place and recovered their condition in time to take the guns forward during the great advance after the battle.

The four attacking Canadian divisions were spread out on a front 6,700 yards long. The XVII Corps on their right was to attack in front of Arras, and the I Corps on their left was to put on a feint barrage in front of Lens. As the action was to cover a depth of 4,500 yards, it was a task of considerable magnitude to evolve a workable barrage that would suit the local needs of each divisional front. East Division was asked for a draft barrage for its own front; then, after several conferences on particular points, Major A.F. Brooke, DSO,[1] Artillery Staff Officer of the Corps, worked out a barrage which met all the demands of the Infantry and at the same time satisfied the requirements of the section as a whole.

That barrage made possible the splendid successes of our infantry. First, there was a rolling barrage immediately in front of the Infantry, put on by about 320 eighteen-pounders firing shrapnel, and each gun covering a front of only 30 yards. Second, there was a jumping barrage put on by 126 of our 4.5-inch howitzers and the remaining 160 eighteen-pounders that dealt with the enemy's trenches. Each gun covered a front of 60 yards, and kept 200 yards ahead of our infantry. Third, there was a barrage of heavier howitzers to deal with specific trenches and strong points. The 6-inch howitzers covered a 60-yard front each, and kept 300 yards in advance of the Infantry. The heavier guns had a front of 200 yards each, and kept a distance of 400 yards ahead of the attacking force. It was arranged as well that as soon as the Infantry had advanced beyond the range of certain guns, those guns would drop out and advance into the open while other guns carried on the barrage.

The wire cutting that was always preliminary to an infantry attack was done on the front and support lines by 18-pounder guns and trench mortars. The heavy howitzers were used on the rear portions of the enemy's areas. For the first time the No. 106 Fuze[2] was extensively used, and with great success. This fuze was one of the most deadly inventions of the War. The ordinary contact fuze required a heavy blow to detonate it, and shells often sank a considerable distance into the ground before exploding. In soft ground they might thus be rendered harmless a few feet away. But the 106 Fuze was so delicate that it would detonate if it struck so much as a leaf in flight. Its instantaneous action resulted in the shell bursting the instant it touched the ground, making a very small crater and distributing its splinters with deadly force along the surface of the ground for hundreds of yards. The troops called them "grass cutters." It is sufficient to say here that the wire cutting was most effective. In the subsequent attack, the Infantry experienced no difficulty from wire throughout the large area they covered.

---

1   Major Alan Francis Brooke, later Field Marshal Sir Alan Francis Brooke, 1st Viscount Alan Brooke, KG, GCB, OM, GCVO, DSO and bar. Chief of the Imperial General Staff December 25, 1941–June 25, 1946.

2   The first British instantaneous percussion artillery fuze.

The counter-battery work was under the direction of Lieut. Colonel Andrew McNaughton,[3] to whom three groups[4] were allotted. He worked in close cooperation with the Artillery Reconnaissance Officer, Lieut. Colonel J.L.R. Parsons.[5]

Meetings were continually held at which the representatives of all these sections coordinated their information as to the location of the enemy's batteries. A map was constructed with the enemy's batteries placed on it and numbered, and so accurately was this done that on comparing the map with the ground after the battle, almost every battery was found to have been correctly plotted.

The method employed in the counter-battery work, which commenced five weeks before the battle, was to take on each day, when visibility permitted, all those enemy batteries most difficult to locate, leaving the better-known and more easily dealt with units to the last. The sound ranging section was found very valuable during these weeks, being able to pick up batteries within 50 yards of their actual positions. Later on, as the volume of artillery fire became greater, this method could not always be depended on as the instruments were "jammed" when a number of the enemy's guns fired at the same time.

Most of the work against the enemy's concealed batteries was carried out with the help of observation from the Royal Flying Corps. The RFC Artillery Observers became very expert in ranging batteries from the air, but unfortunately as the day of battle approached, enemy planes were heavily reinforced and a number of our best observers were shot down while engaged in this work.

The Corps Artillery Reconnaissance Officer, Major Cosgrave, spent the weeks preceding the battle in examining the ground, studying aerial photographs, examining *rapatriés* (returnees) and sifting out the statements of prisoners in order to secure full information regarding the top and reverse slopes of the Ridge. He succeeded in placing on a special map the location of the enemy's battalion and brigade headquarters, as well as ammunition stores, telephone exchanges, etc. In addition to this, the paths

3   Andrew George Latta McNaughton, who ended the War as a Brigadier-General GOC Canadian Corps Heavy Artillery. During the Second World War he became General A.G.L. McNaughton, CH, CB, CMG, DSO, CD, PC. He was Commander First Canadian Army 1942–1943. He was replaced as Army Commander in part due to criticism of his performance by Alan Brooke, and served the remainder of the Second World War as Minister of National Defence.

4   Three heavy artillery groups.

5   This officer could not be identified, but presumably was a staff officer in the First Army Artillery Headquarters.

and the road most used at night by enemy ration parties and reliefs were studied by the examination of snow photographs, taken early in the morning by the RFC so as to reveal the freshest tracks. The enemy's observation posts were carefully scouted for noted down, together with all other information that would provide useful targets for the guns.[6]

These targets were roughly divided into two classes: one for immediate demolition, and the other for the harassing night fire, which was kept up from February 14 until the day of the battle. The object of constantly harassing the enemy was to wear down his morale, keep him from obtaining his rations and supplies of ammunition, and worry his reliefs at night. Subsequent reports from prisoners showed that this night firing contributed greatly to disorganize and reduce their fighting efficiency.

In the scheme of demolition it was arranged that the telephone exchanges, enemy OPs,[7] and battalion headquarters should be left until the last, and then destroyed shortly before or at zero hour so as to spread demoralization among the enemy; those that could not be readily destroyed would be neutralized by gas and smoke shells. The reason for leaving them to the last was that the enemy would not have the opportunity to re-establish his means of hearing and sight before the attack developed.

Generals commanding divisions were requested to send in the special strong points, machine gun emplacements, trenches, villages, and buildings that were likely to be obstacles to the advance of their Infantry. All of these targets were laid on a map, and divided into tasks to be dealt with by the several types of guns. Six days before the attack, two 15-inch howitzers and six 12-inch howitzers, under the control of the Army, were placed at the disposal of the Corps for special work, such as battering villages and those strong lines of deep dugouts in the sunken roads.

As the period for commencement of the demolition bombardment approached, the Canadian Corps Heavy Artillery, under Brigadier-General R.H. Massie,[8] was continually augmented by additional batteries, until fifty-six batteries had reported. These were divided into four double-groups for purposes of demolition, and three groups under the Corps Counter-Battery Staff Officer, to get the enemy's guns under

---

6   McNaughton is often incorrectly credited with this work by Cosgrave.

7   Observation Posts.

8   A British Artillery officer, Brigadier-General Roger Henry Massie, CB, CMG, was General Officer Commanding Canadian Corps Heavy Artillery January 22, 1917–October 21, 1918. He was succeeded by Andrew McNaughton.

control.[9] When all the demolition targets had been obtained, a daily bombardment programme was issued, and the results were reported each evening, either by direct or aeroplane observation. As the demolition progressed the trenches, strong points, and other targets "done in" were blocked out on a map so that the progress of the work and the amount remaining to be done could be read at a glance every day.

The harassing night fire commenced on February 14, and the routine work of the guns gradually increased from that day onwards, but it was not until March 28 that the artillery programme can be said to have commenced, and it did not reach its height until April 3. The 31st, 5th, 63rd, and 2nd Imperial Divisional Artilleries reinforced the fronts of the 1st, 2nd, 3rd, and 4th Canadian Divisions respectively, together with a number of artillery brigades.

The four Canadian infantry divisions, in order from right to left, and supported by the 5th Imperial Division (in reserve five miles to the rear), were to carry out the attack. The right two divisions had to advance on a front averaging one mile in width and a depth of nearly three, while the left two divisions advanced on about the same front to a depth of about a mile. The 2nd Division, which had to attack the villages of Les Tilleuls, Thelus, and Farbus, was supposed to have the hardest task, and the 4th Division the easiest. As it turned out, the 2nd Division had the easiest task of all, thanks to the success of the artillery preparations, while the 4th Division, which had a much smaller but rougher area, had the hardest task.

The morale of all branches was excellent. Throughout the winter so many local raids had been carried out and so many prisoners captured, that the Infantry had ceased to regard going over their own and the enemy's parapets as anything more than an exciting recreation. The Artillery had barraged these raids until they had attained the greatest proficiency and accuracy, at the same time earning the absolute confidence of the Infantry whom they supported. While it was expected that the capture of such a stronghold could only be accomplished with considerable losses (the Medical Corps had provided for twenty thousand casualties), the utmost confidence existed that the positions could be taken, and all ranks were eager for "Z Day," and the "Zero Hour," as the day and hour were officially denominated.

---

9   Heavy Artillery Groups (later to be renamed Brigades of Garrison Artillery) were units commanded by lieutenant-colonels with a variable number of heavy batteries (usually four to six). They were the heavy artillery equivalent of the field brigades. A double group was a joining of two groups under the command of the senior lieutenant-colonel in order to better control the fire of all of the batteries.

Owing to the prevalence of alternate fog and snowstorms, the preliminary bombardment did not reach the maximum until "Z-Minus-Four," four days before April 8, which was the original date fixed for the attack. On account of this unfavourable weather, Z Day was advanced to April 9, somewhat to the disappointment of Lieutenant-General Sir Julian Byng and the whole corps. As it turned out, Easter Sunday, April 8, was a beautiful warm spring day, the first during the operation, whereas the day of the assault [Monday, April 9, 1917] opened gloomy and cold with snow squalls, but brightened up during the afternoon. However, there was great satisfaction when at last the Zero Hour was named and the die was cast.

The strategic situation was briefly this: about ten days previously (on March 26) the German line in front of the 4th and 5th Armies in the Somme area had commenced a deliberate retirement to what was known as the Hindenburg Line, pursued as rapidly as the weather and bad roads would permit by the British troops on that front and the French farther south. Considerable excitement was caused on March 28 when the German retirement extended up to a point in the southeastern suburbs of Arras. The Canadian Corps launched numerous raids along its front to discover whether the retirement of the enemy was about to include Vimy Ridge, but it soon became evident that the enemy had no intention of relinquishing this stronghold, and that it was being held as the hinge on which the long line to the south was being swung. The discovery greatly accentuated the importance of the capture of the position, as it was evident that such a success would seriously interfere with the strategic situation from the enemy's standpoint.

At 5:30 AM on the morning of April 9 our barrage opened, and was extended by the Third Army to the south, which was also attacking, and by the feint barrage of the 1 Corps to the north. Owing to the overcast weather, it was still quite dusk when the first wave of Canadian Infantry went over the parapet on a front of 7,000 yards. From that moment the whole programme of the battle as planned proceeded on the right-hand two-division front without a hitch. The routine of the 3rd Division attack was somewhat interfered with by a nest of machine guns in the rear of the advancing Infantry after the first wave had passed; that of the 4th Division by the desperate resistance of the enemy in the rough ground known as Hill 145; and the interference of machine guns from the lower hill to the north known as "The Pimple," which was not included in the attack and was to have been neutralized by the 1 British Corps, commanded by General Holland.[10]

---

10   Lieutenant-General Sir Arthur Edward Aveling Holland, KCB, KCMG, DSO, MVO. GOC 1 Corps February
        19, 1917–September 19, 1918.

With the above exceptions the battle might almost be termed featureless so far as any departure from the plans of the Corps Commander was concerned. The barrage climbed the slope of the Ridge with scientific precision; the enemy's artillery was duly neutralized by our counter-batteries; our lines of infantry followed the barrage, fighting those who would fight and accepting the surrenders of those who had no fight left in them. The prisoners commenced to arrive at the cages in the hundreds—rapidly mounting into thousands—and almost to a minute of the time laid down in the barrage table, our infantry stood triumphant on the farther side of the Ridge, looking over the great expanse of the Douai Plain. The enemy's guns along the edges of Farbus Wood, Station Wood,[11] Goulot Wood, and Bois de Bonval were in our hands. Our casualties were light.

For the left two divisions the programme did not work so smoothly. The 3rd Division was hampered by the nest of machine guns, which developed its presence after the front lines had unknowingly passed it in the rough ground. Several hundreds of the enemy made a fierce stand there, but were overcome later in the day and all killed or captured. By evening the division had made good its final objective.

Somewhat unexpectedly, the hardest fighting fell to the 4th Division. It was not until after dark[12] that the stubborn resistance of the enemy around Hill 145 was overcome and that portion of the Ridge cleared. It had been arranged, but for this unforeseen delay, that the 4th Division should, at dusk on the evening of April 10, attack and capture The Pimple to the north, which was the last feature of the Vimy Ridge still in the enemy's hands. The preparation of this attack made it necessary to postpone the operation twenty-four hours, but in a blinding snowstorm in the early hours of April 12, the 4th Division triumphantly accomplished this further task, and finally drove the enemy from his last holding on Vimy Ridge with considerable slaughter.

The examination of the battlefield showed with what completeness the work of the Artillery had been carried out. At no point had the Infantry been held up by wire. The trenches had been so thoroughly done in that over large areas it was quite impossible to distinguish them among the shell holes. The villages of Les Tilleuls and Thelus had been demolished even to the cellars, and there was no cover from which the enemy could delay the advance. Neither was it in any sense an indiscriminate bombardment. In sections where there were no trenches to be demolished, there was not a shell crater. For instance, in the area east of the Nine Elms, the ground was

---

11   Likely a temporary name of the time and that battle.

12   On April 10.

so untouched that, as a staff officer remarked, you could have laid down a cricket pitch anywhere; three of the communication trenches which crossed the portion were absolutely done in.

However, speaking generally, the whole Ridge presented a picture of devastation. It could scarcely be said to be pockmarked with craters, because the ground where trenches had been was simply churned up; not only had the trenches disappeared, but most of the wire as well. Machine gun emplacements and dugouts had nearly all been destroyed or buried from sight.

Among the finest bits of work was the destruction of two extensive belts of wire, each one and a half miles long and 30 yards wide, on the eastern side of the top of the Ridge, which had been made perfectly passable for the Infantry by the heavy howitzers, using the 106 Fuze, and shooting from the map (i.e., without being able to see it). Before the battle, considerable anxiety existed as to whether this wire had been cut out, as its existence might have been fatal to the attack's success in its later stages.

Owing to the state of the weather, no aeroplane observation or photographs could be obtained of this wire up to forty-eight hours before the assault. On April 7 an aeroplane scout flew over it, under very trying conditions and at a considerable height, returning with the disappointing intelligence that he could not locate it. It was vital that the condition of this wire should be known before the attack was launched, and on the following day, under better weather conditions and protected by a heavy barrage of machine gun fire, another scout flew up and down the whole length of the wire several times, and returned with the welcome information that the wire had been done in so well that over large stretches it had entirely disappeared. As he described it, the ground where the wire had been looked as if it had been gone over with a giant harrow.

The Infantry were loud in their praises of the barrage, which was carried out with scientific accuracy and complete effect. It was at once the most extensive, complicated, and successful artillery work of that description the Army had ever attempted. The lifts were 100 yards each, and at the deepest point were forty-three in number.

The counter-battery work may also be said to have reached the highest point of efficiency. There was not a battery position that had not been discovered and successfully dealt with. Even the heavy concrete gun emplacements had in numerous cases been smashed, as had a large proportion of the guns.

When on the morning of April 10 the Canadian Corps looked down from the Vimy Ridge towards the east, they saw a vast plain extending to the horizon, dotted with small villages, and bounded in the north by the Lens Ridge, covered with mine buildings and steel latticework towers, called *fosses*, which mark the entrance to coal mine shafts. Close below and opposite the centre of the Ridge lay the small town of Vimy, and a few hundred yards beyond that quite a large block of brick buildings, known as Vimy Station. At a distance of half a mile from the foot of the Ridge, a railway line runs north and south in the direction of Lens, on quite a high embankment.

All these points were still held by the enemy, the railway embankment forming a natural fortification for the protection of their infantry and guns. Under cover of heavy fire from batteries farther out on the plain and on the Lens Ridge, the enemy attempted to remove the guns at the foot of the Ridge, from Vimy, and from the vicinity of the railway embankment. At the same time there was evidence of an attempt to mobilize their infantry at the foot of the Ridge for a counterattack.

On the day of the battle, as soon as it was evident that we had gained the Ridge, several brigades of field artillery were ordered forward onto the Ridge. The roads were in desperate condition, and across the former No Man's Land they had ceased to exist altogether. Notwithstanding this, the elements of four Canadian Artillery Brigades succeeded in reaching positions well up on the Ridge.

When, on the morning of April 10, observers commenced to report parties of enemy infantry on Douai Plain attempting to remove the guns, a heavy harassing fire was opened by all guns that could reach the Plain, including those of the field batteries mentioned. That this was successful was evidenced later by the number of abandoned limbers and dead artillerymen that were found littering the plain below the Ridge when Vimy and the railway embankment were captured. In numerous cases, guns had been partly removed and then abandoned and artillery stores and debris covered the ground.

The 60-pounder batteries dealt with the enemy infantry and broke up their formations long before they were able to reinforce the railway embankment or assemble for a counterattack. Apparently, throughout the day, the greatest disorganization prevailed among the enemy. Isolated parties of fifty to several hundred men were moving about the Plain in all directions, seemingly not knowing what to do or where to go, and continually harassed by shellfire. Finally they gave up all idea of a counterattack.

On the following day the town of Petit-Vimy, the railway embankment, and other points below the Ridge were bombarded by our heavy guns, with the result that on April 13 the enemy evacuated these positions and retired east to the Arleux–Acheville–Avion Line, leaving behind them sixty-six guns of all calibres, from 77s[13] to 8-inches, besides large numbers of machine guns and trench mortars.

---

13   7.7 cm field guns.

The state of the ground at this time made it extremely difficult to get either Field or Heavy Artillery forward, let alone the ammunition necessary to continue the pursuit. It was not until April 28 that the Artillery preparation for the capture of Arleux could be made, when this village—together with the trenches to the north of it known as the Arleux Loop—was taken by the Infantry.

On May 3 the village of Fresnoy was bombarded and captured after heavy hand-to-hand fighting, together with trenches for a mile to the north of it in the vicinity of Acheville. On each occasion about four hundred prisoners were taken, making a total of over five thousand.

On the night of May 5–6, the 1st Canadian Division, on whom had fallen the chief brunt of the fighting since April 9, were withdrawn for a rest, their place being taken by the 5th Division of the XIII Corps. This concluded the first phase of the operations of the campaign, and the Canadian Corps rested pending the advance of the long British line to the south, which now, in its turn, hinged on Vimy Ridge.

In General Byng's own office at Headquarters there hung a poster with this legend: "THE BYNG BOYS ARE HERE."

Not only was the great soldier proud to have the men under his command known by his name, but he liked their Canadian slang and chuckled over it, repeating it to himself whenever he found it expressive. At the height of this great battle, when I got the report that we had taken the Ridge, I went to him and said: "General, everything is Jake. We are shelling the retiring Bosches."

He sprung his jolly smile and answered me in equally atrocious slang: "Morrison, go to it."

Later, he issued his congratulations to the Canadian Corps in a proclamation that is historic in its significance.

G.O.C., P.A.

NO. 347

4 May 1917

Canadian Corps

The brilliant operations during the last month, culminating in the capture of Arleux and Fresnoy, seem to give me the opportunity of expressing to all ranks the pride I feel in commanding the Canadian Corps.

Since the 9th April, when the offensive against the VIMY RIDGE began, till the morning of May 3rd, when Fresnoy was captured and consolidated, it has been one series of successes only obtained by troops whose courage, discipline and initiative stand pre-eminent. Nine villages have passed into our hands. Eight German Divisions have been met and defeated. Over 5,000 prisoners have been captured, and booty comprising some 64 guns and howitzers, 106 trench mortars, and 126 machine guns are now the trophies of the Canadians.

The training undergone during the winter has borne its fruit and it is this training coupled with the zeal and gallantry which are so conspicuous in all ranks of the Corps, that will continue to gain results as potent and far-reaching as those which began with the capture of the VIMY RIDGE.

(Signed) J. Byng
LIEUTENANT GENERAL
COMMANDING CANADIAN CORPS

Chapter 18

IN DEFENCE OF ENGLAND

After the capture of Fresnoy on May 3, the Canadian Corps front underwent a slight change. The line of villages, Willerval, Arleux, and Fresnoy, which had been successfully captured by the 1st Canadian Division between April 13 and May 3, were handed over to the XIII Army Corps to the south, and the Canadian Corps's left flank rested on the Souchez River in the north. The line extended across the Douai Plain from just north of Fresnoy, in front of Acheville, thence northwest to the eastern end of the Hirondelle Ridge. In front of Méricourt the lines were about 1,200 yards apart, the enemy keeping close to that village while our trenches were far out on the Plain and coming closer to the enemy again opposite Avion, quite adjacent from the end of the Hirondelle Ridge to the Souchez River.

This condition prevailed in a general way until June 19. In the meantime the artillery on both sides had been constantly at work, and casualties to guns and personnel constituted a steady drain on both the Heavy and Field. The enemy had good observation from the high mine towers, particularly in Méricourt and from a hill about a mile southwest of Lens, on the top of which was the city reservoir. Méricourt overlooked every part of the Plain, from Fresnoy to Hirondelle Ridge, and the Reservoir Hill looked down the Souchez Valley. It was consequently very difficult to get batteries forward or secure positions in advance on the Plain, where there was no cover from view. The field brigades, however, were pushed out into Willerval, along the railway embankment to Vimy Station and into Vimy itself, while a couple of brigades were retained on the Vimy Ridge. The artillery division on the left got fairly good cover in the Souchez Valley, northeast of the town of that name.

During the latter part of May more than half our Heavy batteries were moved off to Ypres to take part in the preparation of the attack on the Messines–Wytschaete Ridge. Not only was this the case, but the order was that all the best guns should be selected to be sent away. It may be interpolated here that, while during previous campaigns the question had only been one of ammunition, now we had abundance of ammunition, but the guns were becoming worn out and were difficult to replace.

This was partly owing to the increasing strength of our armies, which necessitated large numbers of additional guns, and partly to the fact that the workmen were on strike, literally in tens of thousands, at the Woolwich Arsenal and other gun-making plants. The condition was so serious that it was kept out of the papers for a considerable time, and eventually the British Government had to arrest seven of the strike's ringleaders on charges that were never definitely laid out but which would have amounted to treason. As a matter of fact, the arrest of these men brought about a settlement, and they were released within forty-eight hours without being brought to trial.

Meantime, the commanders of the Artillery Corps were called together and confidentially informed of the conditions prevailing, and cautioned to do their best to prolong the lives of the guns in each corps. The allotments of ammunition were not reduced, lest it should cause talk, but it was put up to General Officers Commanding Artillery Corps to keep the shooting down to a minimum. The "lives" of the guns, as represented by the total of rounds fired, were carefully computed, and the guns were sorted out, as far as possible, in batteries, the guns of which had relatively the same "life." These batteries were to be used as little as possible, and most of the shooting was to be done with the newer guns, so as to equalize their condition.

On the other hand orders were issued for the continual harassment of the enemy by night bombardments, wire cutting, trench demolition, and periodical raids, all of which provided for a large amount of continual shooting. The coordination of these two policies required considerable finesse on the part of the commanders, especially as the enemy came back on the Vimy front with quite strenuous bombardments, to which our own artillery were supposed to reply in still more strenuous terms. It was largely a case of putting the blind eye to the telescope, and making sure that we killed more Bosches than they did of us.

Our infantry since Vimy were in great fighting trim, and their eagerness to raid the enemy's front was difficult, and indeed undesirable, to repress—especially on the left flank where the lines came in close contact. During the latter part of May the Electric Generating Works, a group of steel girder buildings a few hundred yards east of the Hirondelle Ridge, became a bone of contention, and was finally taken and held by the 4th Canadian Division.[1]

On the left of the Souchez River the 46th Division I Corps were gradually gaining ground towards Lens, but scarcely fast enough to suit our people, who on several occasions crossed the Souchez River and captured enemy posts that were annoying them with flanking fire and handed them over to the Imperial troops. By June I our line ran from the Souchez River southeast, just short of the Electric Works, to the village of Coulotte on the Lens–Arras Road, and thence to Acheville and Fresnoy.

The zero hour for the attack on Messines and Wytschaete was approaching, and in order to keep the Bosche busy on our front the 4th Division put on quite a stiff attack and succeeded in getting the Electric Works, but failed to enter Coulotte. The casualties were rather heavy, as our infantry would not be denied, though a heavy concentration of enemy artillery in different parts of the line was brought to bear on this isolated effort.

On June 7 news arrived that the Second Army had captured the Messines–Wytschaete Ridge and achieved a victory comparable only in extent to the capture of Vimy Ridge up to that point of the War. The Canadian Corps had been very keen to take part in the operations to the north, as they considered that they had a preferential claim on the key to the Ypres Salient, but this could not be arranged. Their activity found vent in constant raiding and harassing of the Bosche in the direction of Lens and Avion. In the absence of a distinctly aggressive policy on our front, they (under the guise of raids) captured long sections of the enemy's front, killed or captured everybody in the trenches, and then returned to their own lines before morning.

Following the victory of the Battle of Messines, the general trend of operations underwent a change. From the knowledge at this time available, two factors apparently dictated this course:

The grand offensive by the French in the middle of April, for which great preparations had been made and of which great things had been expected, turned out to

---

1   On June 4, 1917.

be only a moderate success that bordered on failure, and as late as June 1 the French armies, despite heavy desultory fighting, had failed to get on.

The United States had declared War[2] and decided to send a division of regular troops to France, which was expected to be available about midsummer. Admiral Sims,[3] with a flotilla of destroyers, and General Pershing,[4] accompanied by a large staff of American army officers, had come over, and were actually in London, staying respectively at the Carlton and Savoy Hotels, when the enemy launched a series of destructive aeroplane raids on the city of London. The raid of June 13 was the most deadly blow that had yet been struck by the enemy's airmen. Some of the bombs fell within a mile of the Savoy Hotel, and the casualty list reached nearly six hundred, a large proportion of which were children. Two weeks before, Folkestone had suffered heavy casualties, and public opinion throughout Great Britain became very exasperated.

The fact that the raids were carried out in broad daylight, by less than a score of aeroplanes, pointed to the possibility of even more disastrous raids, though the British aviators along the coast of Kent and over at Dunkirk intercepted the raiders on more than one occasion and inflicted severe casualties on them. There was a strong outcry for reprisals on German cities, such as Cologne and Düsseldorf. Our airmen had previously confined their raids to military centres in Belgium, but these obviously did not effect the population of Germany, who received the news of the bombing of London with every demonstration of joy. In this connection it is important to hark back to the history of events on the continental side of the Channel. In 1915 Germany had been able to seize Zeebrugge, Ostend, and the whole Belgian coast north of Diksmuide, and her desperate and continuous efforts for the capture of Ypres had as their object the seizing of Calais, and probably Boulogne, which would have gravely endangered the safety of England. Failing in this, the enemy, during 1915 and 1916, had been quietly turning Zeebrugge into a fortified base for directly harassing England by sea and air. It was not until early in 1917 that the British naval authorities were brought to a realization of the growth of the menace by repeated and daring incursions by German destroyer flotillas into the Channel, and actually into the mouth of the Thames itself, where they bombarded Margate. These marine raiders usually operated at night and escaped, almost with impunity, until May when

---

2   The USA declared war on Germany on April 6, 1917.

3   Rear-Admiral William Sowden Sims, US Navy, Commander of US Naval Forces operating from Britain.

4   General John Joseph Pershing, Commander American Expeditionary Force.

two British destroyers, the HMS *Broke* and the HMS *Swift*, encountered half a dozen of them and in a most gallant attack sunk two and dispersed the remainder.

The British public had no more commenced to grumble at the blindness of naval policy, which had allowed this marine hornet's nest to develop within striking distance of their shores, when the series of aeroplane raids already referred to were launched from the same centre of enemy activity. Quite suddenly it seemed to be realized that self-preservation demanded that Britain's immediate interests become, for the time, paramount, even to clearing France of the common enemy. This was accentuated by the activities of the German submarines, which showed no sign of relaxing, and it was known that a large number of these boats had their bases on the Belgian coast. Thus it came about that, coincident with the victory of Messines, the plan of campaign in France apparently underwent a change. The Fifth Army was moved from the extreme-right near Peronne early in June so as to prolong our extreme-left towards the sea at Diksmuide. The Belgian troops were withdrawn from that portion of the front, and three French Corps assisted to prolong our line from just north of Ypres to where the Fifth Army took over.

In the meantime, General Allenby,[5] who commanded the Third Army to the south of Arras, was transferred to Egypt, and General Sir Julian Byng, the victor of Vimy, was placed in command of the Third Army, then consisting of eight corps, which extended to the south to take over the front vacated by the Fifth Army. Though the operations, commenced on April 9, became known as the Battle of Arras, the only real success was achieved by the Canadian Corps of the First Army in capturing the Vimy Ridge immediately north of Arras. As a matter of fact, the operations of the Third Army southward were not productive of success commensurate with the casualties involved. Hence the translation of General Allenby to Egypt, where the situation was by that time quite normal.

With General Byng's promotion, Lieutenant-General A.W. Currie became Commander of the Canadian Corps.

Throughout the latter part of June there was strong evidence of the preparation of a strenuous offensive aimed at clearing the Belgian coast and relieving the shores of Great Britain of the triple-menace of air raids, destroyer raids, and submarine boat activities in the southern area of the North Sea. During the same period the role of the First Army, whose front extended from Arras to near Armentières, was to keep

---

5   Later Field Marshal Edmund Henry Hynman Allenby, 1st Viscount Allenby, GCB, GCMG, GCVO.

the enemy employed and impress him with the idea that a new offensive was preparing on the southern portion of that front, having for its probable object the capture of Lens. Trench bombardments, wire cutting, and nighttime harassing fire were commenced about June 15 on the front of the 13th Canadian Division and 1 Corps, the latter being immediately west of Lens.

It was decided that on June 28 the 46th Division of 1 Corps should capture Reservoir Hill, which is only a mile from the centre of Lens and looks down into it, and that the 3rd and 4th Canadian Divisions should capture a line running through Éleu-dit-Leauwette to just outside of Avion. The 1st Division, on our right, was to put up a feint barrage, and the XXIII Corps, to the south, was to capture the German trench in front of Oppy.

As part of the preparation, and in order to keep the enemy guessing, the Canadian Corps put on a feint barrage on Sunday, June 18, along its whole front. It was the intention to follow this up with two practice barrages along the fronts of the XIII Canadian and 1 Corps before the final operation. This was forestalled by the enemy's evacuation of Reservoir Hill and of a portion of trenches in front of Éleu-dit-Leauwette on the afternoon of June 25. During the night, the 4th Division sent out fighting patrols and captured Coulotte, with little or no resistance. On June 26 the 3rd Division prolonged the advance to within a short distance of Avion Trench, and the 4th Division made another slight advance.

There was desultory patrol fighting until the night of June 27–28, when raids were launched by each division, and by the morning of June 28 we had captured Éleu-dit-Leauwette and the whole of Avion Trench from there to the Toronto Road, southwest of Avion, which was to have been our objective for the attack timed for 7:10 PM on June 28. In view of this, orders were issued for a new objective: to establish a line from the Toronto Road through the middle of Avion to a point on the Lens–Arras Road, a short distance northeast of Éleu-dit-Leauwette.

Chapter 19

HILL 70

The success of the limited operations of the Canadian Corps during the latter part of June suggested to the Corps Commander, Lieutenant-General Sir A.W. Currie, that the holding operation, pending the development of the great Northern Offensive, might as well become a real operation against Lens. The First Army authorities were not very keen about this, and were also desirous that if anything of the sort be done, the attack be made on the Méricourt front. Opposed to this, there was a strong and unanimous feeling in the Canadian Corps that the point of attack should be northeast so as to capture the celebrated Hill 70, just east of Loos, from which point Lens could be dominated. This led to considerable discussion.

On the north and south of Lens, and about equidistant from it, are two elevations known as Hill 70 and Sallaumines Hill, while the city lies in a basin between them. From the position of the Canadian Corps on the plain in front of Vimy Ridge, the obvious thing to do was to attack Méricourt and Sallaumines Hill, and so dominate Lens from the south. But it was pointed out that there was great difficulty in siting our artillery on the flat Douai Plain south of the Souchez River, whereas north of the Souchez River, as far as Loos, there was rolling ground and many fosses[1] and mining villages, affording both cover for batteries and observation of the enemy's position. Besides this, the capture of Hill 70 would give better observation of the

---

1   A type of coal mine shaft tower.

approaches to Lens from the east than Sallaumines Hill. Finally, the northern attack was sanctioned.

In this connection the question arose as to the sufficiency of artillery for the operation. The remarkable condition resulting from the failure to manufacture sufficient guns had arrived at the point that none of the 18-pounders or 60-pounders that went out of action for any reason could be replaced. In addition to this, the Lahore (Reserve) Divisional Artillery had been withdrawn from the line and relieved by the 4th Canadian Divisional Artillery, made up from the surplus of the other three divisions on the reduction to the new establishment. Also, a large number of Heavy batteries had been withdrawn and sent north to take part in the great offensive. This reduced the Canadian Corps Artillery to 164 heavy guns of various calibres and 282 eighteen-pounders, with a full compliment of 4.5-inch howitzers. This would give a barrage on the intended battlefront of 25 yards per gun, while on the remainder of the front, which we would hold, there would only be about one gun per 100 yards for feinting purposes.

I advised the Corps Commander that with the guns we had the operation could be carried out, provided the Army undertook to maintain 75 percent of our heavy guns in action (i.e., 120). This was an important proviso, because in denuding us of heavy guns for the Northern Offensive the best guns had been taken, while those left with the Canadian Corps included a large percentage of guns that had been nearly shot out or otherwise crippled, so that about 25 percent were normally in the workshops for repairs. It was a pretty close decision, and only made after I had a report on the remaining "life" of each individual gun. In addition to this, there were one 15-inch and four 12-inch howitzers on which we had the call when required. The First Army agreed to this arrangement.

On July 2, the 2nd Canadian Division relieved the 46th Division of the I Corps on our left, and took over the front from the Souchez River to the Double Crassier east of Maroc. About the same time we relinquished our southern area as far north as Méricourt to the XIII Corps on our right. The 1st Canadian Division moved north and took over an additional division front from the I Corps, which extended our left north of Loos, to a point opposite Fosse 14 bis.[2]

The battle plan was that the Canadian Corps should attack with the 1st and 2nd Divisions from the northern outskirts of Lens to Fosse 14 bis, on a front of 4,000 yards, and that the 4th Division, which now relieved the 3rd, on our right, should

---

2   An abbreviation from the French, Fosse 14 bis de mines de Lens.

make a feint in front of Lens and Avion. The depth of the objective at its widest point was about 1,500 yards. Hill 70 was to be captured by the 1st Division, which was to push on beyond the hill and down the farther slope close to Cité St. Auguste. The 2nd Division was to prolong the attack to the right, parallel with the northern edge of Lens, to a final objective that would swing round to the northeast and join up with the 1st Division in front of Cité St. Auguste, with the 4th Division farther to the right, holding Avion and the immediate western edge of Lens. This would contain the city on the southeast, west and north, while the capture of Hill 70 would dominate the place and put the artillery observation on all the exits from it to the test.

The artillery preparation was particularly difficult because Lens was surrounded by large mining towns and villages, the houses of which were built of brick and so close together that there were only small open spaces, like large commons, between these settlements. In addition to this there were numerous collieries, with fosses built of steel and iron, each surmounted by a high tower or shaft, all of which afforded good observation posts. Cité St. Auguste contained large manufacturing buildings, but on the 1st Division's front, Hill 70 was quite bare and heavily entrenched, as was the strip of enemy territory running north to Fosse 14 bis.

In addition to dealing with the trenches and wire, most of these mining towns had to be thoroughly smashed to make way for the attack, as the buildings and their cellars afforded cover for numerous machine guns. It was really one of the most difficult artillery preparations of the War. Just south of Lens, the high ground in our possession fell away steeply to the north, and the town of Loos itself was in the bottom of a deep hollow, which made it almost impossible to site guns between Hill 70 and the ridge running from Maroc to Hulluch.

Another difficulty was that the enemy, in addition to a superiority of artillery on our immediate front, had a large group of batteries in the vicinity of Wingles, and from the towers of the big metallurgical works at that place our left flank was commanded to enfilade. The artillery of the 1 Corps undertook to neutralize the Wingles batteries, and performed that duty fairly effectively.

Within a space of twenty-four hours our batteries on the Vimy Ridge were shifted northward and located in Maroc, Bully-Grenay, Calonne, Liévin, and the Souchez River Valley, leaving one weak group to support the 4th Division on our right. The Field Artillery for the support of the attack was moved into positions behind Riament Wood, Liévin, and the Double Crassier, and in the low ground between the Double Crassier and Loos. In the two latter areas it was necessary for the field batteries to remain dormant, as they were entirely overlooked from Wingles.

The artillery programme went into operation on July 13, before the transfer of the batteries to the north had been completed. The orders from the First Army were that the attack should be made about July 25, but this was almost immediately seen to be impossible, and the time was gradually extended to July 28, and then to July 31, by which time it was still more obvious that the period for preparation was entirely inadequate.

The First Army appeared to have the idea that the assault must be coincident with the commencement of the great offensive to the north, but the Commander-in-Chief[3] paid a visit to the Canadian Corps, and at a corps conference gave the assurance that operations were in no sense interdependent. He definitively informed the Corps Commander that there was no necessity of assaulting until both the Infantry and the Artillery were satisfied that the preparation was complete. He also said that the Army would furnish us with additional artillery, but when the Army was subsequently approached on the subject, the Canadian Corps was informed that there was no more artillery available. Later on, we were reinforced with thirty 13-pounder guns, brought in from a cavalry division that was resting in rear, pending anticipated employment when the Northern Offensive broke through.

As already stated, our bombardment had commenced on July 13, and gradually increased in volume as the batteries got into position. A large proportion of the strongest trenches and wire had be taken on with aeroplane observation, especially on the eastern slopes of Hill 70. This necessitated good visibility, but on July 31 a period of heavy rain and mist set in, which continued for a week, precluding all observation or the taking of photographs to discover what damage was being done. Luckily nearly all the targets had been registered by aeroplane before the bad weather set in, and the bombardment continued steadily. Also, the Field Artillery kept up harassing fire to prevent the enemy repairing his wire and trenches. It was a period of considerable anxiety. For about a week no aeroplane observation or photographs were available, and our allotment of ammunition for the operation was being steadily expended. If the subsequent observation, when good visibility returned, showed that the shooting had not been accurate, most of the work would be yet to do.

In addition to this, our heavy guns began to deteriorate rapidly, and the enemy developed a system of counter-battery work modelled on our own, which, while far less effective in proportion to the ammunition expended, was still seriously destructive to material, and necessitated our counter-batteries shooting very heavily and

---

3   Sir Douglas Haig.

further using up the comparatively short lives of most of the guns. Those lame ducks and casualties were going into the workshops and remaining there much longer than the amount of repair necessitated.

As an example of the enemy's activity, on July 22, he strafed ten of our Heavy Battery positions, putting in over 3,500 rounds of heavy shell in one day. Our actual casualties only amounted to two guns injured and a normal percentage of personnel: but our counter-batteries had to fire so heavily in order to neutralize this offensive that on the following day our available heavy guns were down to 42 percent, instead of the original 75 percent, of the number guaranteed us at the beginning of the operation.

The situation was that practically no reinforcement of heavy guns was being received, while the slowness of the army workshops did not keep pace with the deterioration of the guns in action. Urgent representations were made, and the Corps Commander visited all the army workshops to see if the repairs could not be expedited. The result was that we got no more heavy guns, but repaired guns came out of the workshops within the next few days in such numbers that we soon again had 137 out of 164 in action. Our heavy gun power did not again fall below 75 percent, until after the operation.

The Counter-Battery Officer, Lt. Colonel McNaughton, estimated at the beginning that we had 102 enemy batteries in front of us, but so accurate and effective was our system of locating batteries by aeroplane, sound ranging, and ground observation, that by the day of attack only 63 batteries remained active. When the weather was favourable, our counter-batteries took on for destruction as many as fifteen to twenty batteries a day, and the subsequent photographs usually showed from one to four gun emplacements per battery done in. At the same time, it was estimated that a silenced battery became active again within five to seven days. Besides this, when visibility was impossible, days elapsed when no counter-battery work could be done.

Eventually the assault was fixed for 4:25 AM on August 15. After the period of bad weather already referred to, the aeroplane observation and photographs showed that our blind shooting had been remarkably successful, and only a few areas required to be dealt with in order to complete the destruction of trenches and buildings. On "Y" day[4] the Counter-Battery Officer was confident that he had the situation in hand and could neutralize the enemy's barrage. The Infantry were more confident than before any previous battle, and expressed complete satisfaction with the Artillery's preparation.

---

4   The day before "Z Day," i.e., the day before the attack.

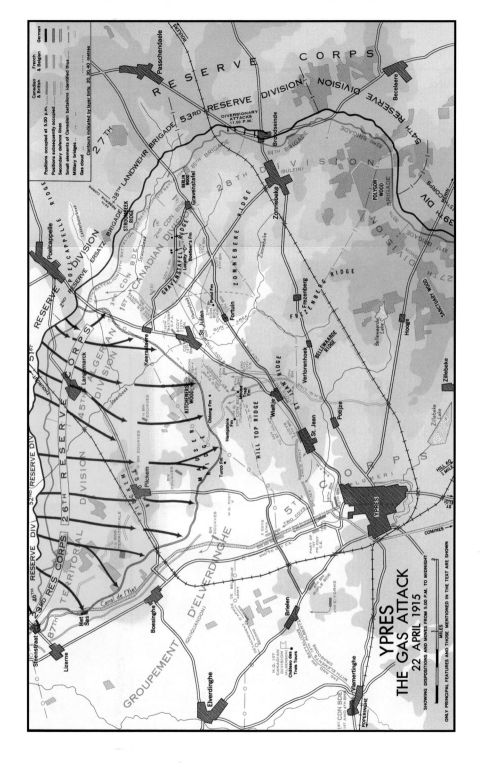

Ypres Gas Attack Map. DEPARTMENT OF NATIONAL DEFENCE (DND)

June Ypres Battle Map. DND

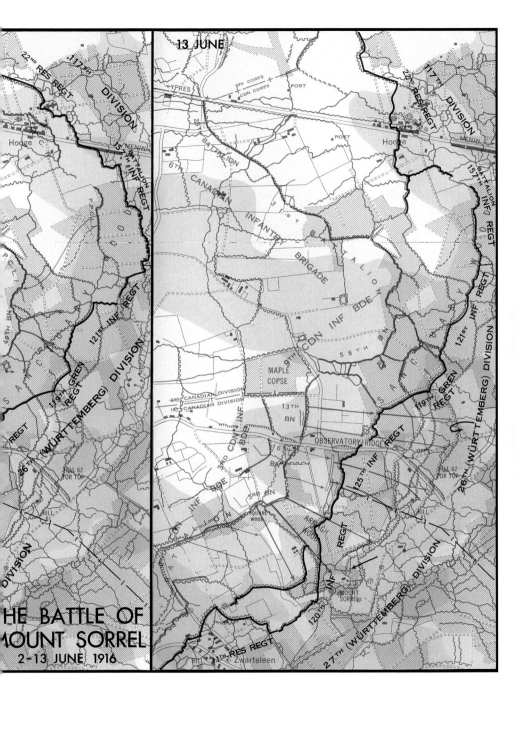

THE BATTLE OF
MOUNT SORREL
2-13 JUNE 1916

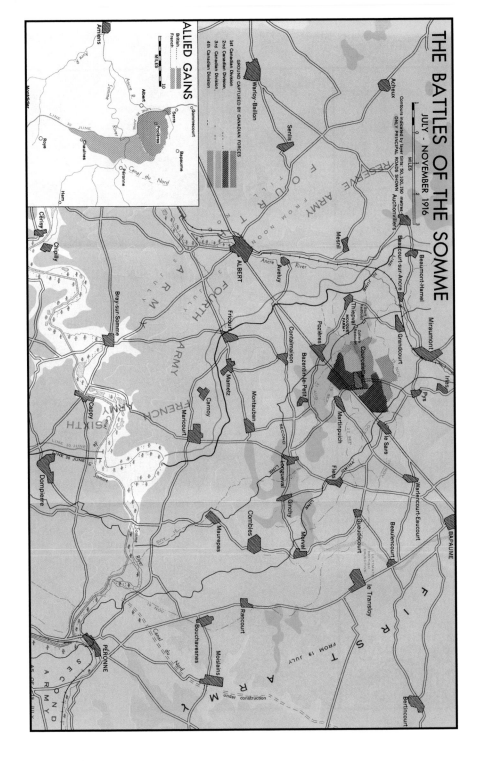

Somme Battle Map. DND

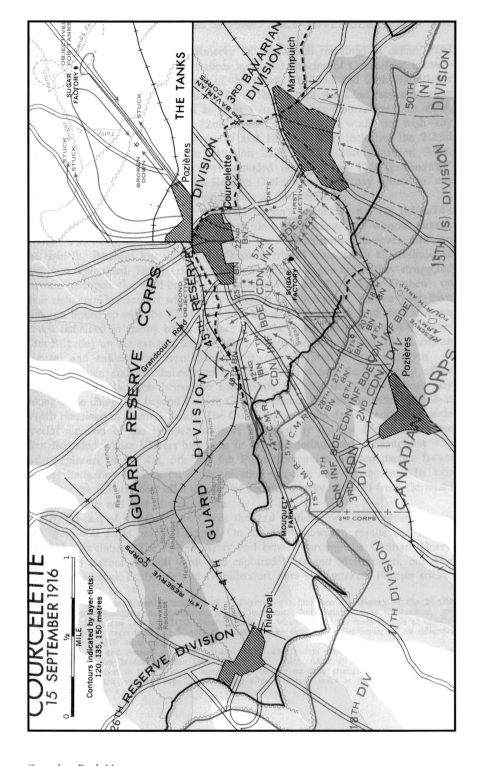

Courcelette Battle Map. DND

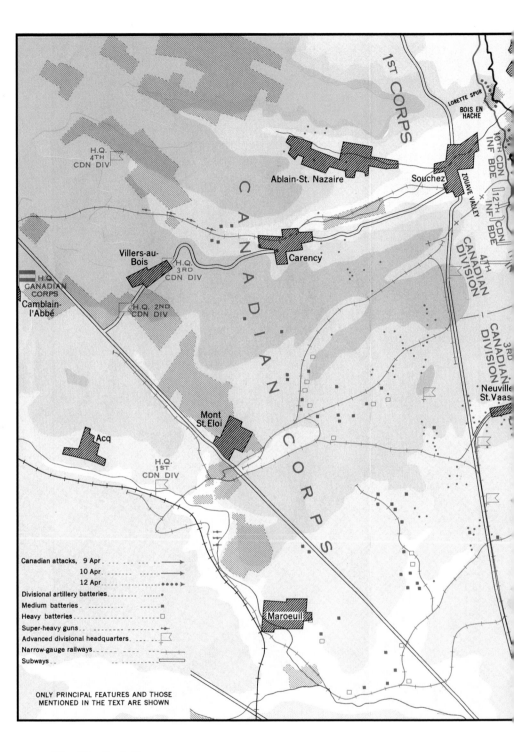

Vimy Ridge Battle Map. DND

VIMY RIDGE
9-12 APRIL 1917

MILES

Contours indicated by layer tints: 80, 100, 120, 140, METRES

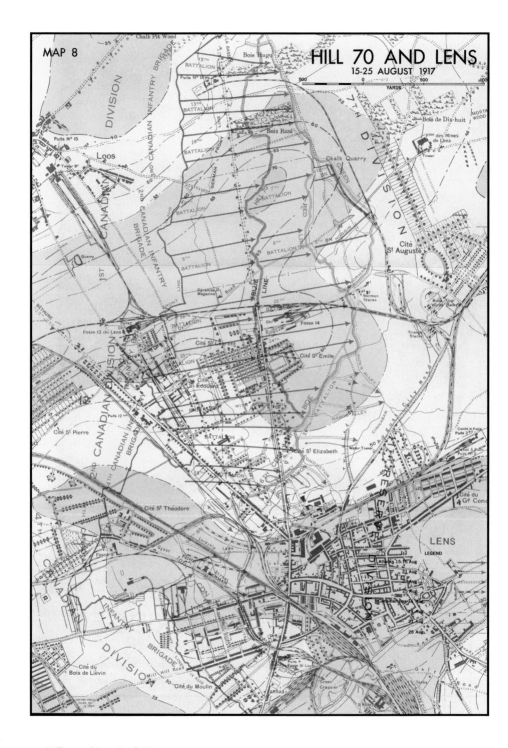

Hill 70 and Lens Battle Map. DND

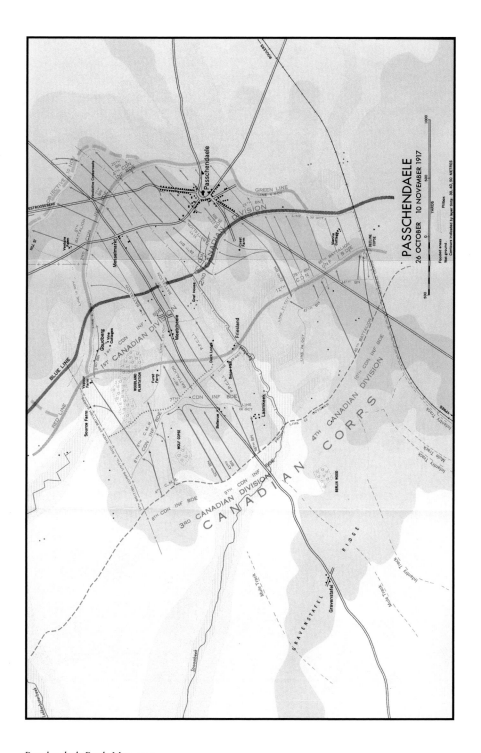

Passchendaele Battle Map. DND

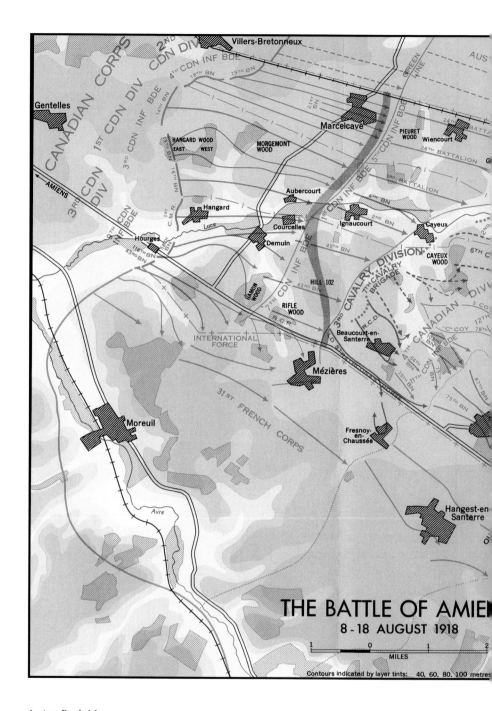

Amiens Battle Map. DND

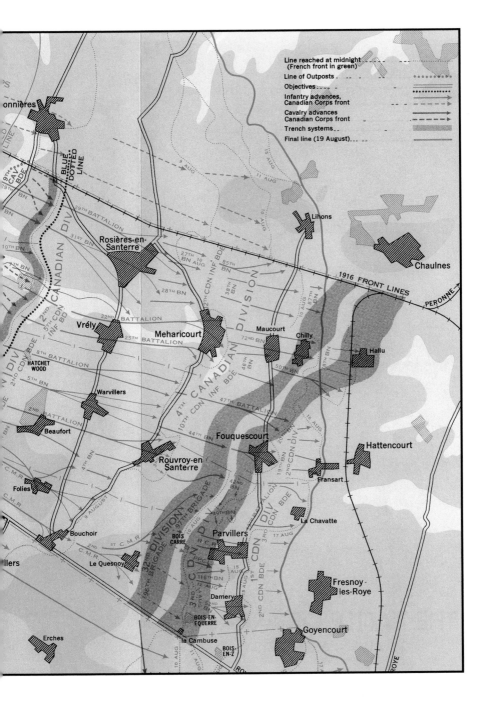

onnières

BLUE DOTTED LINE

9TH CAV. BDE.
29TH BN

31ST BN

29TH BATTALION

10TH BN

7TH BN

CANADIAN DIV.

Rosières-en-Santerre

27TH BN 10 AUG

85TH BN

22ND CDN INF BDE

9 AUG

15 AUG

10 AUG

11 AUG

Lihons

Chaulnes

1916 FRONT LINES

PERONNE

28TH BN

38TH BN

87TH BN

Vrély

2ND 5TH CDN INF BDE.

22ND BATTALION

25TH BATTALION

Meharicourt

72ND BN

Maucourt

Chilly

Hallu

CANADIAN DIVISION

46TH BN

50TH BN

2ND CDN DIV

HATCHET WOOD

8TH BATTALION

5TH BATTALION

Warvillers

47TH BATTALION

4TH CDN INF BDE

2ND BATTALION

Beaufort

10TH CDN INF BDE

44TH BN

Fouquescourt

Hattencourt

4TH BN

Folies

C.M.R.

Rouvroy-en-Santerre

19TH BN

22ND CDN DIV CDN BDE

Fransart

C.M.R.

La Chavatte

Bouchoir

9 AUGUST

2ND

9TH BRIGADE

1ST C.M.R.

3RD CDN DIV.

1ST CDN DIV

BOIS CARRE

R.C.R.

Parvillers

17 AUG

llers

Le Quesnoy

C.M.R.

8TH BRIGADE

116TH BN

15 AUG

3RD CDN P.P.C.L.I.

52ND BN

Damery

2ND CDN BDE

Fresnoy-les-Roye

Erches

196TH BN

BOIS-EN-EQUERRE

la Cambuse

BOIS-EN-Z

Goyencourt

10 AUG

11 AUG

ROYE

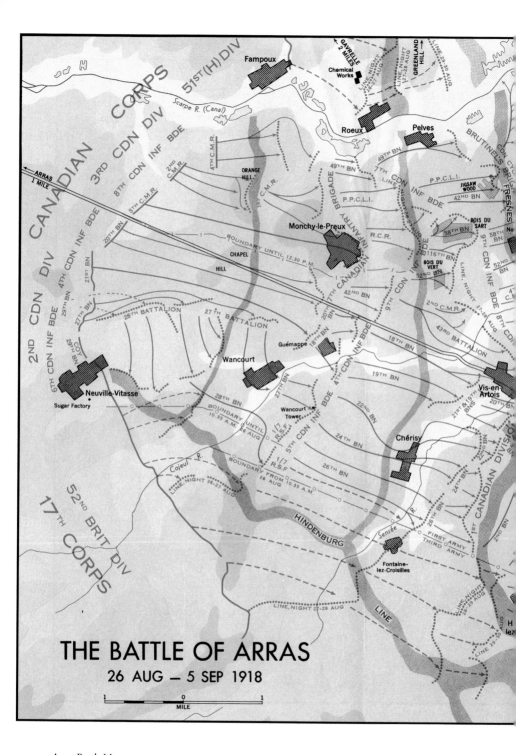

THE BATTLE OF ARRAS
26 AUG – 5 SEP 1918

Arras Battle Map. DND

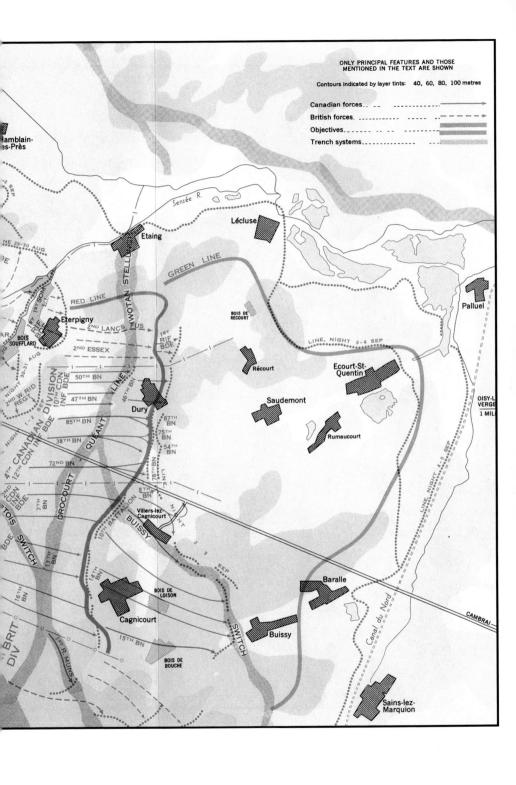

ONLY PRINCIPAL FEATURES AND THOSE
MENTIONED IN THE TEXT ARE SHOWN

Contours indicated by layer tints: 40, 60, 80, 100 metres

Canadian forces
British forces.
Objectives.
Trench systems

Hamblain-
es-Près

Sensée R.

Lécluse

Etaing

GREEN LINE

RED LINE

Palluel

Eterpigny

2ND LANCS FUS

BOIS DE
RECOURT

1ST
RIF
BDE

LINE, NIGHT 3-4 SEP

Récourt

Ecourt-St-
Quentin

2ND ESSEX

BOIS
SOUFFLARD

50TH BN

47TH BN

46TH BN

Saudemont

OISY-L
VERGE

1 MIL

85TH BN

Dury

87TH
BN

75TH
BN

Rumaucourt

38TH BN

54TH
BN

72ND BN

78TH BN

8TH
BN

Villers-lez-
Cagnicourt

107 BATTALION

BUISSY

Baralle

BOIS DE
LOISON

Cagnicourt

Buissy

BRIT
DIV

15TH BN

SWITCH

CAMBRAI

Canal du Nord

BOIS DE
BOUCHE

Sains-lez-
Marquion

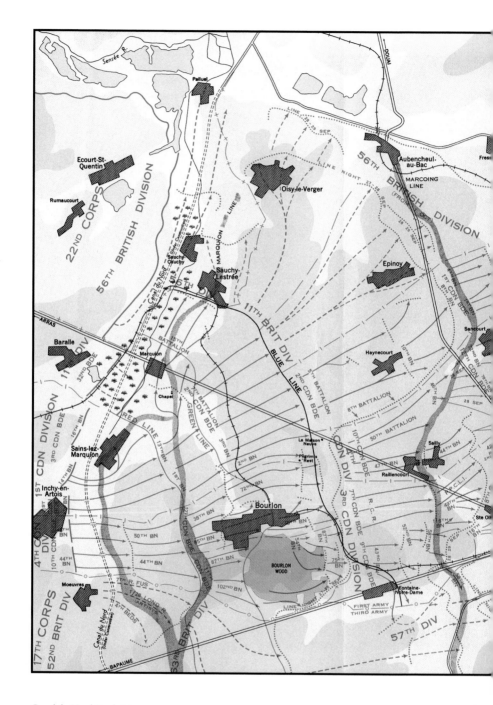

Canal du Nord Battle Map. DND

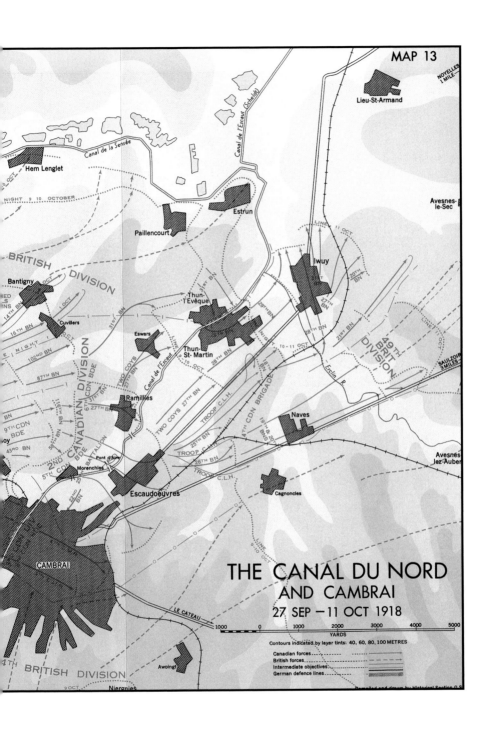

MAP 13

NOYELLES
1 MILE

Lieu-St-Armand

Canal de l'Escaut (Schelde)

Canal de la Sensée

Hem Lenglet

NIGHT 9 10. OCTOBER

Estrun

Paillencourt

Avesnes-
le-Sec

BRITISH

DIVISION

Iwuy

Bantigny

Thun-
l'Evêque

Cuvillers

Eswars

49TH
BRIT.
DIVISION

Thun-
St-Martin

SAULZOIR
3 MILES

Ramillies

Naves

9TH CDN
BDE

CANADIAN DIVISION

6TH CDN BDE

4TH CDN BRIGADE

43RD BN

2ND CDN BDE

5TH CDN

Pont d'Aire

Morenchies

Avesnes
lez-Auber

Escaudœuvres

Cagnoncles

CAMBRAI

LE CATEAU

THE CANAL DU NORD
AND CAMBRAI
27 SEP –11 OCT 1918

Awoingt

1000   0   1000   2000   3000   4000   5000
YARDS

Contours indicated by layer tints: 40, 60, 80, 100 METRES

Canadian forces
British forces
Intermediate objectives
German defence lines

4TH BRITISH DIVISION

Niergnies

Compiled and drawn by Historical Section G.S.

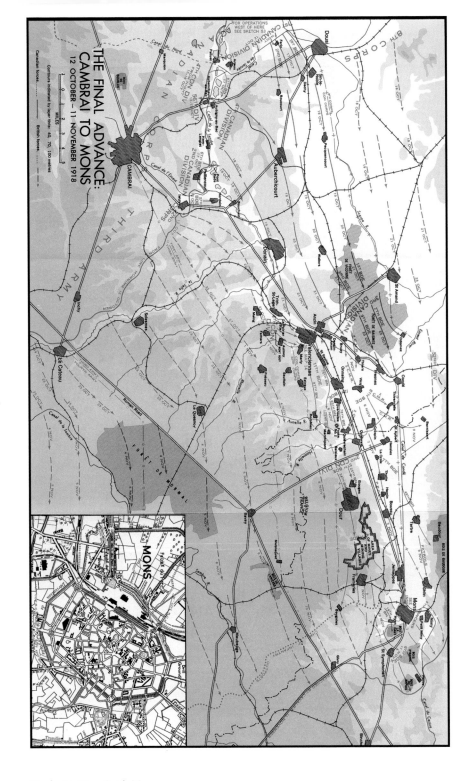

Cambrai to Mons Battle Map. DND

Meantime, feint barrages and continual raids had been put on along the front of the holding division to the west of Lens, and in front of Avion, with the purpose of deceiving the enemy as to the extent of the battlefront. To the last, the Germans, now evidently thoroughly alarmed, neglected their counter-battery work to put frequent barrages on prospective points of attack, as well as the front- and support-line trenches. These barrages indicated that he was entirely at sea regarding our intentions. Notwithstanding the extensive bombardment to the north of Lens, the enemy remained obsessed with the idea that this was the feint, and that the real attack was to be on the 4th Division front: a direct frontal attack on Lens.

On the night of August 14–15, as afterwards discovered, the enemy was thoroughly aware than an attack was to be made at dawn. Still, in pursuance of his rooted idea regarding our intentions, instead of shooting up our infantry, who were massed in the trenches on the front of the 1st and 2nd Canadian Divisions ready for the assault, he heavily bombarded our batteries with gas and other shell, and put down occasional heavy barrages in front of the 4th Canadian Division. As the latter only intended putting on a feint attack with two companies against Lens, their front trenches were sparsely held, and practically no damage resulted.

At 4:25 AM on August 15, the weather was fine, but it was still comparatively dark. The barrage went on with beautiful accuracy. A rolling barrage of the 18-pounders (102 to each attacking division) immediately preceded the Infantry, while ahead of it at a distance of 400 yards was a jumping barrage of 4.5- and 6-inch howitzers, and beyond that again a moving barrage of heavy howitzers, which dealt in succession with enemy strongpoints. On the right and left, smoke barrages blinded the observation of the enemy's artillery groups behind Méricourt and Wingles respectively.

The assault proceeded without a hitch, and on scheduled time both assaulting divisions reached their ultimate objectives with comparatively slight losses. Three minutes after zero the enemy put down a scattering barrage on the battlefront, but our counter-batteries, with good aeroplane observation, went back at him with such energy and accuracy that the barrage soon dwindled away. For a short time the enemy artillery was almost completely neutralized.

At this psychological moment the 4th Division developed its feint attack with two companies on the western portion of Lens, and to our great satisfaction the enemy put down a tremendous barrage in front of Lens and Avion, and even farther south. Obviously the Germans were still convinced that the attack on our left was a feint, and that the real assault would push directly into Lens, on the front of our right division. He was entirely outmanoeuvred. The barrage on the right continued for over an hour, and by the time the enemy discovered his mistake the attacking troops were in their final objective.

When the German Command realized the situation, and that they had lost Hill 70, immediate counterattacks were organized in frantic haste to recover the Hill. In preparation for the attack, of which he had in some way received previous intimation, large bodies of infantry had been brought up in the rear of Lens, including a regiment of the Prussian Guard. These were now diverted towards Hill 70, the remainder of the 4th Guard Division was hurried up in support, and infantry streamed across the open from the direction of Wingles towards our left flank.

At a distance of 600 or 700 yards from the left flank there were three woods, the Bois Hugo, Bois de Dix-Huit, and Bois Quatorze. It had been foreseen that the enemy, arriving across the open, would assemble in these woods for counterattacks against our new flank, and in the buildings in Cité St. Auguste for counterattacks on Hill 70. Accordingly, concentrations of heavy artillery had been arranged for these points at stated hours subsequent to our infantry reaching their final objective. Now the Bosche played right into our hands. As their infantry approached in scattered groups from Wingles, they were first taken on by the artillery of the corps on our right, and as they approached our flank were heavily shot up in the open by our own guns, with the obvious result that they rushed into the woods for cover and to assemble for the attack. Then we put our heavy, five-minute concentrations on these assembly places. The same thing happened to the troops coming up from the east to Cité St. Auguste: our 60-pounders took them on in the open before their arrival, and the heavy howitzers pounded Cité St. Auguste where they were assembling. This delayed their counterattacks until nearly noon, and inflicted terrible casualties on them.

The enemy was madly intent on recovering Hill 70 at all costs. Between noon and 9:00 PM, he launched five heavy counterattacks from the woods on the left, and was met by annihilating barrages, so that not a man reached our front line trenches. In the same way, launching counterattacks from the northeastern suburbs of Lens and the Cité St. Auguste, he furiously assaulted the 2nd Division again and again, but on every occasion the counterattack was smashed before it reached our front line. Counting the smaller local counterattacks earlier in the day, and the massed attacks that took place later in the evening as the enemy's reserves came up, eighteen attacks were repulsed with what must have been terrible slaughter, and by midnight, when the fighting died down, not a German soldier had reached our line alive.

The early part of August 16 was fairly quiet. On the previous day, the 1st Division had been holding a railway cutting northwest of Cité St. Auguste. This cutting was directly enfiladed by German machine guns from houses in the city, so the Infantry deliberately withdrew a few hundred yards west and established their line until the machine guns referred to could be dealt with. On August 16 these houses were battered down, and a rolling barrage was put on opposite the railway cutting to enable the Infantry to resume possession of the cutting.

From subsequent information it would appear that the enemy had been preparing a heavy counterattack on that portion of the line, which was to come off at about 6:00 PM. Our advance anticipated them, and the barrage killed a large number of Germans in the railway cutting. When our infantry advanced behind the barrage they found the cutting littered with dead, and had no difficulty in establishing their line some 100 yards behind the railway cutting. In addition, dugouts in the railway cutting were bombed and 210 prisoners captured. Some surprise was expressed that the line at that point should be so heavily held, but about 7:00 PM, the enemy counterattack, which had been massing in the support lines, developed. The troops belonged to the 4th Prussian Guard Division, and seeing them advance in semi-massed formation, our line of posts beyond the railway cutting sent up an S.O.S. and retired before the onslaught. The result was that the artillery barrage that came down between the retiring line of posts and the Prussian Guard's counterattack repulsed the latter with very heavy losses. Our infantry waited until the barrage had done its work, and then advanced and re-established the posts, and the line was consolidated.

The next few days passed in consolidation, repulsing occasional counterattacks, and harassing the enemy in Lens and on the roads leading to it from the east. On August 21, the 2nd Division in the centre and the 4th Division in front of Lens attacked again, at 4:35 AM, to close in upon the city from the west and north. The objective of the 2nd Division was Cinnabar Trench, 600 yards nearer Lens on the north and northwest, while the 4th Division pressed into the city for about 200 yards from the west.

Again our attack coincided with a counterattack by the enemy. By this time the 1st German Guards Division had been brought in, and they held Cinnabar Trench in force. At zero hour it was not yet light. Apparently both forces advanced at almost the same instant and met between their respective objectives. Desperate bayonet fighting ensued, which lasted for a quarter of an hour. At the first, the Prussian Guard greatly outnumbered our first line, but as the latter was reinforced by the successive lines of the attack, the terms became equal, and the Germans were driven back to their starting point at Cinnabar Trench, which was captured by our infantry. What was left of the Guard made a hasty retreat. The Bosche never had any stomach for cold steel.

On our right the 4th Division got into all their objectives in the western environs of Lens, except at the point on the left they joined up with the 2nd Division. There the 50th Battalion was apparently caught in the barrage that preceded the attack of the Prussian Guard, and was held up, sustaining heavy casualties. The 4th Division had heavy hand-to-hand fighting in the houses throughout the whole day, but retained its objectives from the Green Crassier (exclusive) to Amalgam Trench, at the northwest corner of Lens.

With the 2nd Division it was a day of ding-dong fighting against persistent counterattacks issuing from the northern side of Lens with the aim to retake Cinnabar Trench. Lens was evenly crowded with German reinforcements: eight fresh regiments in addition to the 1st Prussian Guard Division being identified on the two divisional fronts in the course of the day. Counterattack followed counterattack from 7:00 AM till 4:00 PM that afternoon, and every one was beaten off by artillery, machine gun, and rifle fire.

In the meantime our heavy artillery and Super-Hows[5] shelled Lens, and inflicted heavy casualties on the Bosche infantry who were crowded in the cellars and ruined buildings of the city. It was one of the busiest days the Canadian Corps Artillery ever had, and the enemy casualties must have nearly equalled those of August 15. About 5:00 PM our infantry, holding the 100 yards of Cinnabar Trench, were exhausted but unconquered, and as it was very difficult to reinforce them across the open, they were deliberately withdrawn to the position they'd held in the morning and the line adjusted. Their retirement from that part of the line was not interfered with, and the other objectives gained were all held.

On August 22, both sides rested, and early in the morning of August 23 the 4th Division carried out a small operation to capture what was known as the Green Crassier, in the suburbs of Lens, near the Souchez River. The Crassier was an immense slag heap, about 200 yards long and 75 feet high, with the spurs running eastward. A short distance behind it was a railway cutting filled with dugouts and lined with machine guns. It was a very strong position, with brick buildings all around it, and a large colliery known as Fosse 4 a few hundred yards to the north. The whole objective constituted a sort of fortress within the city of Lens.

---

5   Super-heavy howitzers.

After the preliminary bombardment, the 4th Division captured the Green Crassier and Fosse 4, together with some scores of prisoners and half a dozen machine guns. Throughout the morning, the enemy concentrated heavy artillery fire on the position, and repeatedly counterattacked. There was much hand-to-hand fighting, but the Crassier became untenable and by 1:30 PM our infantry were driven off the top and finally withdrew to the place from which they had started. The same thing happened in connection with Fosse 4.

The prisoners taken reported that the cellars in Lens were crowded with German infantry, who were being continually reinforced, as the enemy was determined to hold Lens at any cost. Accordingly, at 3 PM and throughout the afternoon, we bombarded the portions of Lens where the cellars were situated with 12-inch howitzers and in the evening searched the streets with shrapnel and the roads leading out of Lens towards the east with heavy shell. At 2:30 AM, on August 24, the place received two thousand rounds of lethal gas shell, so that the garrison must have had an unhappy twenty-four hours. The days that followed were passed in a general exchange of artillery reprisals, when gas, shrapnel, and high explosives were used on both sides, with effect more terrible than words can tell.

On September 25, 1915, the British had fought the first Battle of Loos. The indomitable persistence of the attack, particularly on the part of the Scottish regiments and Guards Brigade, coupled with the comparatively inefficient artillery support of which the latter arm was capable at that stage of the War, had resulted in a semi-success by the British, though at a terrible loss in infantry casualties. But the general result had been disastrous. The subsequent successes of the Canadians in capturing Vimy Ridge led to the latter being given the task of finally taking Loos in August 1917. The action was carried out under the name of Hill 70—perhaps because it was not desirable for the public to know that what a magnificent force of British troops had failed to accomplish in several days' fighting in September 1915 should be accomplished by noon on an August day by the Canadians.

The Canadians, with their customary determination to make good their motto, "What we have we hold," hurled back literally scores of counterattacks with bullet, bayonet, and barrage, so that a series of German Guards division attacks, made to retrieve what was evidently regarded as a fatal loss, practically resulted in not a German soldier reaching the Canadians' first line trenches. The Canadian Infantry secured Hill 70 by noon on August 15, 1917, the date of the attack. So exasperated was the enemy that large bodies of reinforcements were hurried up and sent continually to counterattack throughout a long summer afternoon, but were as continually beaten off by the Canadian Artillery, though, by sundown, the Gunners were nearly exhausted.

It was an afternoon of the most furious and successful artillery engagements the Canadians sustained during the War. About the end of the day a staff officer arrived at my headquarters from the Commander of the 1st British Army, when I was rather irritated and worn out by the pressure of the day's work, and exclaimed breathlessly, with an air of conveying a reprimand: "General Morrison, do you know that the Army Commander is appalled at the amount of ammunition you have used today?"

"So are the Germans," I retorted, and he stared at me and departed.

Chapter 20

SEPTEMBER OF 1917

The centre of interest during September of 1917 lay in the north where the Second, Fourth, and Fifth Armies were trying to push the enemy out of Zeebrugge and capture his submarine and air bases along the coast. But the operations had been held up, and progress had been very unsatisfactory, in spite of the fact that the southern portion of the Western Front had been ruthlessly denuded of both infantry and artillery to tend to the Northern Offensive.

General Byng, now commanding the Third Army, humourously described himself as holding his extensive front by Christian Science. He mobilized a considerable portion of the few heavy guns left in his command into what he termed a "Travelling Circus." His tactics consisted in moving this circus from one point of the line to another under cover of darkness, putting on a three- or four-day bombardment followed by an energetic trench raid, and then slipping the heavy guns away to another point where the operation could be repeated. Thus he impressed the Germans with the idea that there were very many more heavy guns in front of them than was actually the case.

Early in September the Canadian Corps was similarly weakened. All the army brigades that had assisted at the Hill 70 fight, and a large proportion of the Canadian Heavies, were moved north. The daily allotment of ammunition for the remaining guns was reduced to such a minimum as to remind the Gunners of the dark days of 1915. In other words, the Canadian Corps, which from its very entrance into the European conflict had been striking deadly blows at the enemy, found itself with its claws clipped. It was reduced to a peace footing almost overnight—a purely defensive unit for the first time since its arrival in France.

But, until that happened, the Canadians still had the hope of capturing Lens. They held Hill 70 to the north of the city; they held the suburbs on the west; and they held Avion on the south. Lens was thus nearly two-thirds surrounded. It was a reasonable expectation that, if the offensive were continued, the Artillery would gradually render the city untenable, and the Infantry would gradually fight their way into the place until it was captured. Lens had no strategic importance, but the possession of the city stood for the possession of France's greatest coal mining district, and its capture would have a tremendous moral effect on both France and Germany.

The dream of conquest was rudely shattered when the Canadian Corps was ordered to hand over its positions, all the way from Souchez to Hill 70, to the I Corps, and to resume its old sector from north of Acheville to Souchez. To the south of Lens there was a hill called Sallaumines Hill, which stood in the same relation to Lens on the south as Hill 70 did on the north. Once Sallaumines Hill was captured, Lens automatically would become untenable, and any tired troops that happened to be handy could walk into it from the western suburbs. There was a good deal of disappointment among the Canadians that they should not have the satisfaction of actually taking the city after they had done the hard work of rendering it takeable.

However, the weather was fine, and the *esprit* of the Corps had never been higher, and all branches manfully realized that, after all, their business was to win the War, and the minor matter as to who should actually enter Lens was not worthy of soldierly consideration. The sooner the job was done the better. So everybody went to work. Like at Vimy, the Corps itself was to do all the planning, dig the gun pits, get up 1,200 rounds of ammunition per gun, reinforce trenches, and do all the other dirty work necessary to the success of the offensive, though other troops would share the benefit when the day to advance arrived. In spite of the fact that most of this work had to be done out on the flat Douai Plain, when guns were so few and ammunition so scarce that the enemy's artillery could not be neutralized, the work of constructing gun pits, laying tramway lines, digging jumping-off and communication trenches, laying buried cables, and training over the tapes proceeded with commendable zeal throughout September. The weather was fine, and in the case of the Artillery, nearly four hundred gun pits were finished by October 1, and the storing of them with ammunition was well underway.

Meanwhile, the fine weather, which continued throughout September, had stimulated the offensive in the northern Ypres sector, and a series of heavy operations had been undertaken which had gradually driven the enemy back beyond Zonnebeke and St. Julien, so that all the main ridges in that part of the country, with the exception of the Passchendaele Ridge, were now in our hands, and the German armies in that region were being forced down into low ground. These ridges had long dominated the famous Ypres Salient, and now the tables had been turned.

Notwithstanding these successes, there was a feeling throughout the army that the Northern Offensive had not accomplished what was expected from such an immense concentration of infantry and artillery; that there was a lack of organization and efficient staff work; and that some of the commanders had suffered from an embarrassment of riches and had failed to use the enormous resources at their disposal to the best effect. Also, that while the Guards Division, and the Australians, New Zealanders, and Scotch troops, had fought with great verve and local successes, they had not been adequately supported by what had commenced to be known as the Conscript Divisions.

More conservative critics in the army were disposed to await the final outcome of the Northern Offensive without prejudging it, but towards the end of September, rumours commenced to fly about to the effect that the Commander-in-Chief might be relieved. It was reported that the Australian Corps had asked to be transferred from the Fifth Army to the Second, and that General Gough might be replaced. There was no way of ascertaining whether there was anything behind all this talk, but the fact that it did exist was characteristic of the state of things at this time.

In England the civilian population had evinced an unencouraging indifference when the progress of the Northern Offensive had slowed down, and declined to take much interest in the really splendid fighting of the troops, which only resulted in gains of so many thousand yards of front and so many thousand yards of depth, and did not appear to get any nearer the Rhine.

South of the front held by the British armies, the French were engaged in desultory operations without undertaking anything in the nature of a "Big Push"; the single American Division, which as yet was all that represented the power of the United States in the War, had not yet entered the line; and the Russian Division, which had been brought over by Japanese warships a year before amid great acclaim, had mutinied and been removed from the line, where it was rounded up in a concentration camp, and there refused to do anything except eat the rations furnished by the French Government. The Italian armies had met with greater successes than any of the others, and had captured some hundreds of thousands of prisoners on the Austrian front, but operations there towards the end of the month were in a state of stagnation.

As for Russia, the Germans had captured Riga, the troops were abandoning their front on large sectors, and the clash between Premier Kerensky[1] and General Kornilov[2] had nearly precipitated a civil war.

Germany, aided by the Pope,[3] was busily proffering peace—but it was a German peace, and bore no relation to the peace that the Allies had set out to dictate in Berlin. Naval affairs were at an absolute standstill, but the success of Germany's submarine warfare had diminished by about 50 percent. Such was the state of affairs at the end of September 1917.

---

1   Alexander Fyodorovich Kerensky, 2nd Minister-Chairman of the Russian Provisional Government and Minister of War, then Prime Minister of Russia from July 2, 1917.

2   General Lavr Georgiyevich Kornilov was Commander-in-Chief of the Provisional Government military forces. He attempted a coup against the Kerensky government.

3   Pope Benedict xv.

Chapter 21

BACK TO YPRES AGAIN

The month of October had barely opened when rumours commenced to float about in the Canadian Corps that a move north was impending. First of all, an order was received to detach six more Heavy batteries to be sent north. A few days later an order came out stopping all preparation for the Sallaumines operation. By this time some four hundred gun emplacements had been built beside light railways, forward dressing stations, and observation posts. Communication, assembly, and jumping-off trenches had also been dug, and all the staff plans for the attack and consolidation of the position had been completed. There was a good deal of disappointment that, after all the hardest work had been done, the Corps should not have the satisfaction of carrying through the operation and completing the capture of Lens.

It was not a matter of surprise when, on October 9, orders were received that the Corps should move north and join the Second Army under General Sir Herbert Plumer.[1] It was a surprise, however, that when orders had actually been received, all ranks appeared highly pleased at the prospect of returning to their old fighting ground at Ypres. The season was late, and there had been a good deal of wet weather—enough to turn the fields of Flanders into seas of mud.

---

1   See chapter 13, footnote 14.

The Corps began its march northward on October 12. The 3rd and 4th Divisions had been withdrawn from the line early in the month, and the 1st and 2nd were now brought back into the rear areas, being relieved by the V Corps, which had come south after three weeks of hard fighting in front of Ypres. The Infantry of the 3rd and 4th Divisions went north by rail, and their divisional artilleries marched by way of Lillers, Morbecque, Eecke, and Poperinge.

The Corps Staff took over from the II ANZAC Corps on October 18, and for a few days the interesting Imperial spectacle was presented of a corps composed of the New Zealand Division and the 3rd Australian Division commanded by Lieutenant-General Sir Arthur Currie and the staff of the Canadian Corps. On October 20 and 21, the 3rd and 4th Canadian Divisions of Infantry relieved the II ANZAC troops. The 3rd and 4th Canadian Divisional Artilleries took over a portion of the front, reinforcing a body of field artillery then in support, including the New Zealand, 3rd Australian, 49th and 66th Divisional Artilleries, and five army brigades.

The front taken over thus extended from Zonnebeke on the right 3,000 yards to the vicinity of St. Julien, and covered almost the exact ground that the 1st Canadian Division had held when the Second Battle of Ypres was inaugurated by the original German gas attack. A great change had taken place in the appearance of the country during the two and a half years that had supervened. The villages of St. Jean, Wieltje, and Fortuin had practically disappeared. The destruction of woods, farmhouses, and other landmarks had reduced the countryside to a waste of ridge and hollow, and nothing remained but a mere trace of the Wieltje–Passchendaele Road and the Ypres–Zonnebeke Road by which the returned Canadians who had fought there in 1915 could orient themselves.

The road from Zonnebeke to St. Julien was now represented by a line of badly battered trees sticking up drunkenly from a sea of mud. The Valley of the Hanebeek was a circuitous line of bog, developing in spots into swampy ponds. Beyond it, Gravenstafel Ridge was a bare hill of mud over which could be seen the ruins of Passchendaele.

The rotting debris of three years of war covered the ground: tumbled-in trenches, roofless dugouts, torn and trailing remnants of camouflage screens, rusty shells, broken rifles, rotting scraps of clothing and accoutrements, the occasional remains of dead men and horses, and a plentiful crop of brightly white or sadly weatherbeaten crosses completed the picture.

There was, however, one feature that was distinctly new. It consisted of dozens of the so-called German "pillboxes": dissolute-looking erections of concrete dotted here and there over the muddy fields, especially along the tops of ridges, some of them tipped over bodily in the mud by the overwhelming impact of shellfire, which could not smash what it was powerful enough to overset.

On reporting to the Major-General, R.A. of the Second Army,[2] I was informed that my command would consist of about 250 heavy guns (comprised in twelve groups ranging in calibre from 60-pounders to 15-inch howitzers and 6-inch and 9.2-inch guns) and fifteen field artillery brigades. Our front was about 3,000 yards, extending from the Ypres–Roulers Railway on the south to Wallemolen on the north. For this extent of front the gun power seemed ample, but when I made a personal reconnaissance of the front on October 16, prior to taking over, I had a rude awakening. Instead of twelve groups of Heavies I could only find ten, and of the 227 remaining heavy guns, 89 were out of action.

To make matters worse, none of the guns out of action had been sent back to the ordnance shops because the Assistant Provost Marshall[3] of the II ANZAC Corps had given orders that no guns were to use the roads lest they should block traffic. As the four I.O.M.[4] shops were west of Poperinge and the Heavy Batteries were on a line running north and south through Wieltje, the chance of getting the guns back and repaired in time for October 26 was anything but bright; in fact, it was an impossibility.

The condition of the field brigades was even worse. The 18-pounders, on paper, were 306, but in action they were not half that number. One brigade I visited, southeast of St. Julien, had only seven out of eighteen 18-pounders in action, and these were dotted about in the mud wherever they had happened to get bogged. Only a minority of batteries were properly organized and in action. Generally speaking, the Field Artillery was in a state of disorganization. The Heavies were in much the same state. Of forty-eight 60-pounders, only seventeen were in action, and of twenty-six 9.2's, only six were in action.

---

2   Major-General Royal Artillery C.R. Buckle.

3   Lieutenant-Colonel F.S. Tatham, South African Defence Forces. Provost Marshall personnel were military police.

4   These workshops were equipped to repair guns. Light shops repaired field guns and medium shops repaired heavy guns. An Inspector of Ordnance Machinery (I.O.M.) was in command of each workshop, or "I.O.M. shop."

The whole layout of the artillery was about as bad as it could be. The heavy guns were mainly sited in two clusters, one from Potijze to Frezenburg on both sides of the Ypres–Zonnebeke Road, and the other near Wieltje on both sides of the Ypres–Passchendale Road, providing irresistible targets to the enemy. In the same way, the Field Artillery was bunched roughly in two groups, west of Kansas Crossroads and west of the Kink on the Ypres–Zonnebeke Road.

The Zonnebeke Road was the only traffic avenue forward for the Right Division, and the Ypres–Pascchendaele Road the one for the Left Division, the latter being fit only for pack mules east of Wieltje and the former almost destroyed by shellfire east of the Kink. The ground between these roads was almost impassible for man or beast, and the roads themselves were lined with dead horses and abandoned guns and ammunition wagons that could not be taken forward. In one case a howitzer battery was in action, with its guns in a parallel line to the front, just pulled into the mud off the road, and as the distance between them was only about fifteen yards, the guns could not be fired without blowing away the gun crews in front of them. The problem of getting forward ammunition presented almost insuperable difficulties.

No information as to the above condition of affairs was vouchsafed me by anybody, and it was only by personal reconnaissance that I discovered the conditions. The explanation then was that the offensive in the direction of Passchendaele had been hurried forward regardless of obstacles, under the impression that Passchendaele could be captured by a *coup-de-main*.[5] The result was that the II ANZAC Corps had attacked on October 12, with such artillery support as could be expected under the conditions above described, and had met with a serious repulse. The Right Division got on comparatively well, but the Left Division was held up almost at the outset by strong uncut wire and numerous pillboxes, manned with machine guns, at the western extremity of the Bellevue Ridge. By the morning of October 13, the two divisions were back in their original trenches, with a loss of six thousand men. Not the least paralyzing feature of the operation was the fact that, owing to the lack of preparation, the wounded had to be carried several miles back across almost impassible mud, so that it took six men between six and seven hours to transport one wounded man on a stretcher.

In view of existing conditions, and of what had to be accomplished before our first operation in the way of reorganizing and readjusting the artillery situation, I

---

5   A sudden surprise attack.

asked to be put at once in charge of the Artillery, and this was done at 10:00 AM on October 17. For similar reasons, General Currie and the Corps Staff took over command on the following day, though our troops were not due to relieve until October 22. At a conference held at Corps Headquarters on October 16, General Sir Herbert Plumer, Commanding the Second Army, and a number of his staff were present. They appreciated the situation and were very helpful in making preliminary arrangements regarding the repair of the roads and so forth to enable us to get ready for the capture of Passchendaele. I proposed that as soon as the roads could be made available I would push forward three brigades of field artillery, roughly east of the line from Zonnebeke to St. Julien; get forward six batteries of 6-inch howitzers and two batteries of 60-pounders to the place vacated by the field brigades (in order to be able to counter-battery the more distant German guns which were at present out of range); get forward heavy guns, including the super-howitzers, which were useless back near Ypres; and get up the derelict field guns that were still strewn along the roads east of Wieltje and Frezenburg. I also got permission to use the roads for getting disabled guns back to the ordnance shops.

As long stretches of roads had to be rebuilt—or entirely built—before most of this readjustment could take place, and the first operation was timed for October 26, it looked like a hopeless proposition. It had been decided that Passchendaele should be taken in three operations: one on October 26 that would include the Bellevue strongpoint; the second on October 30, which would include Crest Farm, Meetcheele, and Goudberg; the third would see the 3rd and 4th Divisions relieved by the 1st and 2nd, and Passchendaele taken on November 6. The long wait was necessitated by the delay that would be necessary for the Corps of the Fifth Army, on our left, to fight their way forward in line with us and finally get their guns up in time for the third operation.

For the preliminary move of guns and the establishment of general communication forward, the southern road had to be rebuilt from the Kink to Zonnebeke, and a spur from there to the station crossing and north 400 yards into our area. A double-plank road also had to be constructed from just east of Wieltje to and beyond Kansas Crossroads to parallel that portion of the northern road which was beyond repair and almost impassible for pack animals. Forward dumps had also to be established and filled up. Altogether, it was a fairly Herculean programme, especially as our own troops would not be available for four or five days, and the troops of the II ANZAC Corps were fairly exhausted and waiting only to be relieved.

Not the least obstacle was the camouflage of misinformation, or lack of information, consequent on the adoption of the post: that everything was all right when in reality everything was all wrong. For instance, we were assured that our flying corps had control of the air. This confidence was rudely shattered two or three days afterwards when I was taking General Mitchell[6] over the left division to show him the layout of the battery positions on that front before he took over: enemy aeroplanes were fighting our own as far back as Wieltje, and others were swooping down over the forward area and shooting up our infantry with machine guns from a height of three to five hundred feet.

As we were returning in the afternoon, sixteen Gothas[7] crossed our line, manoeuvring beautifully in double columns, and then deliberately deploying on a front of about a mile. The only opposition they encountered was a brief and frantic barrage from a few A.A.[8] guns, which, as the big fleet approached closer, became silent. The batteries stopped shooting, and everybody who could find cover took it as the long line of Gothas proceeded to drop barrages of bombs at intervals of 300–400 yards until they disappeared westward to the vicinity of Vlamertinghe. Having unloaded about 150 of these huge projectiles, the fleet swung in column of route to the north and withdrew, apparently unmolested.

The seriousness of this drawback consisted in the fact that the counter-battery office we took over had its records in such a state of unreliability that Lieutenant-Colonel McNaughton had practically to start the counter-battery work afresh, and for this purpose he must have aeroplane observation, which was very difficult to obtain, owing to enemy aeroplane interference. We also needed photographs of the enemy's positions. The latter we got, but they were taken at such an altitude as to be practically useless. It was the same difficulty that we had had to contend with in the early days before Vimy—the army squadrons[9] were chiefly employed in bombing raids over the enemy hinterland instead of defending our own front and preventing the artillery observation planes from being driven in and interfered with by the enemy. This condition of affairs we succeeded in getting partially remedied before the first zero hour.

---

6   Brigadier-General James Henry Mitchell, DSO. GOC 3rd Canadian Divisional Artillery, June 20, 1916–December 29, 1917.

7   The Gotha was a German heavy bomber.

8   Anti-aircraft.

9   I.e., Royal Flying Corps aircraft squadrons assigned to support Second Army.

On the night of October 21–22, the 4th Canadian Division took over the right front and the 3rd Canadian Division the left front. The guns brought in by these divisions proved a welcome reinforcement, but on the morning of October 26 we had only ninety 18-pounders on the right division front and 120 on the left division front, instead of the total 306 that were supposed to be handed over to me.

From day to day the artillery situation improved, though it was uphill work, as with the exception of our own two divisions all the troops were tired out with the previous fighting and the awful state of the mud in which they had to work. The weather proved our best ally, as it unexpectedly turned fine on October 15 and remained so until the night of October 25–26, when the rain resumed in torrents. But by that time our preparations for the first assault were completed, if not to my satisfaction, at least to the point of assuring success.

A new barrage had been in use on the front, consisting of five lines about 200 yards apart: (1) a creeping barrage; (2) a barrage of 18-pounders and 4.5-inch howitzers; (3) a machine gun barrage; (4) a barrage of 6-inch howitzers and 60-pounders; (5) another of 8-inch and 9.2-inch howitzers. This we varied considerably in the light of our previous experience. Every morning and afternoon previous to Z Day, this barrage was put down so as to keep the enemy guessing when the assault would actually take place. During the interim the enemy heavily bombarded the two roads of communication, as well as our batteries, a number of which near Zonnebeke were in plain view from Passchendaele Ridge and suffered considerably. One battery lost ninety-three, killed or wounded, in a period of three days.

On the morning of October 26, the barrage was put on at 5:40 AM, and the Infantry attacked. The right division reached its objective with comparative ease and penetrated a considerable distance beyond, along the southern ridge, where they established posts.

The left division found the strong wire around Bellevue entirely out, and the first two waves pressed on past the pillboxes that crowned the slopes without stopping to mop up. The result was that when the third wave came up the ridge onto the plateau, the Germans had come out of some of the pillboxes with machine guns, and were firing into the backs of the troops that had passed on and into the faces of the third wave as they emerged on the ridge. The Infantry behaved with splendid steadiness. The two front waves immediately took cover in shell holes and sat pat. The third wave retired below the crest of the ridge and held on.

Their reappearance coming over the crest gave rise to a report that the attack had been driven back, and there was at one time a question of drawing back the barrage onto the pillboxes, which might have been disastrous. However, this was not done, but strong reinforcements were sent forward, and in the afternoon these advanced with the greatest spirit, capturing the pillboxes and Bellevue (out of which they had got forty prisoners), Dad Trench, and a line of pillboxes farther east of the ridge, capturing eighteen machine guns and a total of about 350 prisoners.

This gave us the strong point of Bellevue, which had held up the attack of the II ANZAC Corps. It had been the intention to advance our flank farther forward on the left of the 3rd Division, but the word came that the 63rd (Naval) Division, on our left, had failed to get forward to make a flank for us, so our troops held on where they were, having captured their main objective.

Through some misunderstanding on the right, the I ANZAC troops relinquished Decline Farm before our people took it over, and it was promptly occupied by the Bosche, but on the following night[10] our 4th Division recaptured it after a stiff fight. By the evening of October 26, both of our divisions were counterattacked several times, but beat off the enemy with comparative ease, and the first operation against Passchendaele was finished.

Our losses were light, being about 1,500 for the Corps.[11] The counter-batteries handled the enemy's artillery fire well, and there were comparatively few casualties from that source. During the day of the battle it rained heavily nearly all day, but on October 27 the weather became fine again, which greatly ameliorated the conditions for the troops, who, apart from the captured pillboxes, had no shelter from the weather in the forward line, which consisted only of connected shell holes. On October 28, the Commander-in-Chief visited the Canadian Corps Headquarters, and warmly congratulated General Sir Arthur Currie and his officers and men on their achievement.

No sooner was the first operation involving the capture of Bellevue completed than preparations were commenced for the next operation, which included the capture of Crest Farm on the right and Meetcheele on the left. There were two positions farther along the twin ridges leading towards Passchendaele, the 4th Division continuing on the right and the 3rd Division on the left. The opportunity was taken of the time intervening before this attack to push forward as many Heavy and Field batteries as possible, not only to somewhat distribute the grouping already described but to secure better ranges for dealing with the enemy's counter-batteries, and to prepare for the barrage that would ultimately have to include the assault on Passchendaele.

---

10   Night of October 27–28, 1917.

11   This refers only to October 26. By October 28, total casualties were 2,481.

The engineers and labour battalions had succeeded in pushing the repairs to the Zonnebeke Road down the railway crossing from whence ran a track, negotiable for artillery, parallel to the railway and branching off towards Windmill Cabaret Hill. On the north the double-plank road had been extended to Kansas Cross, beyond which the Gravenstafel Road was fairly passable. The weather continued mild and sunny, with occasional light rain, so that the condition of the ground was no worse, though it did not improve a great deal.

The enemy shelled these two roads of communication very heavily day and night, and about a thousand men were lost during their construction. It was my good fortune to pass unscathed one Sunday morning through the sort of experience which was an every day occurrence to the pioneers who built those roads, to the brave men who brought forward guns and ammunition and supplies, and to the heroes of the stretcher-bearer sections who carried their heavy burdens of wounded to the dressing station along that deadly corduroy. I had set out early with Major Cosgrave and an orderly to inspect some battery areas. We had not gone far beyond Wipers[12] when we came on a block of ammunition lorries, ambulances, pack mules, and miscellaneous transport double-banked for 3,000 yards. I knew what that meant, so I left my nice new car in a place of safety (there was a pile of dead mules and empty tin hats in front of it when we returned) and proceeded on foot. Dodging in and out among the transport, we eventually reached the head of the column, and in front stretched the Zonnebeke Road, along which several thousand pioneers were going through the motions of road building.

This terrible thoroughfare was thickly garnished with dead horses and mules and—other things. The sea of mud through which the road ran was continually erupting in numerous places, the way the sea does in pictures of naval engagements. The memory of it often causes me to think what base motives force people to do their duty under such circumstances. For my part I saw a vision of myself turning back to solemnly report at the corps conference in the evening that I had been "prevented by shellfire," etc., etc., from making the necessary reconnaissance for the batteries to move forward, and I was more scared to do that than to go down the road. So we gave the orderly the field dressings, and posted him, like Gunga Din, fifty paces right flank rear, and we moved off in column of route. I may add, incidentally, that the orderly, a young Canadian who had never been under shellfire before, scrupulously maintained his distance and dressing throughout all the varied happenings of the morning.

---

12   Slang term for Ypres.

We went on down to the new battery area, and returned without incident. I had never had a higher respect for the pioneers than I did for those troops working on the road. They had absolutely no cover, not a shelter, trench, or dugout to go to, no matter how heavy the shelling became, but they worked steadily on with their officers sauntering up and down the road among them, and there was not even the possibility of getting an ambulance to them to pick up the wounded.

The Bosche was using their new 106 fuze,[13] which was very effective. Every time one of these landed, the fragments would go squattering across the mud in every direction for 200 or 300 yards, for all the world as if a flock of wild ducks had been stricken with a sudden panic. One particular 106 landed 50 yards from us, but as luck would have it there was a hummock of mud on the side next to us and close to the burst, which took all the splinters on that portion of the arc of dispersion.

To shorten the story, we got to our objective and back to the head of the stalled transport with nothing worse than a splattering of mud, and just then the Bosche put down a barrage on the devoted road builders, not 500 yards behind us, and through the smoke we saw them scattering across country out of the danger zone, to wait until the barrage had let up.

Then the Bosche commenced to shell the transport, and we were making our way along through the pack mules and ammunition lorries. I was just opposite the wheel of an ammunition lorry when a shell alighted in the middle of it and the lorry blew up. About fifty cubic feet of flame flashed out in front of me, so close that it almost singed my eyebrows, and for a fraction of a second I could see and feel splinters and debris flying past my head, so near that I wondered how my face could squeeze in between them. Then large chunks of stuff commenced to descend all round me. I judged that it was time to act with decision and commendable initiative, so I flattened myself closely against the unsmashed rear of the lorry and remained perfectly safe. Six men who were immediately beside me were killed or wounded. When the main portion of the debris had lit I slid round the tailboard of the lorry, just in time to meet Major Cosgrave, who had been a lorry-length behind and had arrived to pick up the pieces. He broke into his usual cheerful grin.

The remains of the exploded lorry were burning fiercely, and around it, as closely as could be packed on the road, were double-banked lorries loaded with 9.2-inch shells. Everybody who had any sense was clearing off across country and diving into

13   Morrison is using a British super-quick point-detonating fuze to describe the latest German version, which looked similar to the British 106 fuze.

shell holes. I ordered my companions and orderly to conform to my movements, and proceeded to take ground to the flank at what we used to call in the dear old days "the normal pace of manoeuvre." You know how it feels to be in a nightmare, where you draw your revolver on a large "Bosche" who is intent on capturing you, and the thing snaps and snaps and won't go off? Or when you are trying frantically to run away from something impending and can't get any speed on? Well, trying to get away from that impending explosion, in more or less heavy marching order, through that mud and inundated shell holes, was something like that.

When I had gone about 75 yards I looked round and Major Cosgrave was nowhere to be seen. The orderly, still faithfully preserving his distance right flank rear, had not seen him, so we stopped. I shouted for him several times, but a shout carried about as far as a whisper in a boiler factory. So we had to go back, and there he was, pulling people out of shell holes to get stretchers for the wounded, and ordering the motor drivers to try and back away their ammunition lorries so that they would not take fire. He succeeded to some extent, and the drivers played up bravely, but the jamb on the road was so hopeless that it would have been necessary to move half a mile of double-banked lorries on either side of the burning one, and long before that the explosion was bound to come.

After we had obtained stretchers for the wounded, and they were started off, I ordered him out and we proceeded across country. We had gotten about 350 yards when six motor loads of 9.2-inch ammunition blew up together. We lay down on our faces in the mud, and for the next minute it felt like we were being bombarded with cobblestones. Once or twice we got up thinking it was all over but a rushing sound in the air overhead, followed by a dull, sickening thud of a large piece of debris, would announce that everything that had gone up had not yet come down. A good many of the thuds were accompanied by the arrival of pave blocks from the road, many of which were blown nearly half a mile. One advantage of the big explosion was that it blew the fire out; otherwise the explosions might have been going on yet.

As there did not seem to be anything else we could do, I relieved my pent-up feelings by giving the major a good scolding and threatening to transfer him to an ambulance unit, and we went on, preceded and followed by a perfectly good barrage, which distributed the dead mules round our car, as already mentioned.[14] Near

14   It should be noted that, in addition to scolding Major Cosgrave, Morrison also nominated him for a second DSO for this action, which was awarded in early 1918.

the Asylum we divided the attention of a high-velocity gun between ourselves and some more mules, and then a Gotha tried to lay some eggs on us, after which we passed through a barrage of Archie empties.[15] Otherwise, the return journey was quite uneventful. The weather was like an April day, and after we had scraped the mud off ourselves, we unanimously concluded that the day ranked among the most enjoyable Sunday outings we had spent.

The batteries suffered heavily in guns. By almost superhuman effort, six guns were placed on the mounds of mud, between shell holes on the position the 2nd Howitzer Battery was to take over as their guns just north of the Zonnebeke Road were out of range. A guard was placed on these guns, but before morning one of them was rendered utterly useless by a shell, and about 10 AM the next morning another one was tipped into a shell hole ten feet deep by a bomb from an aeroplane. It was uprighted and cleaned off, but just before it was fired an observant gunner noticed a dint in the nose of the piece. That afternoon, under shellfire, those guns were taken back across the mud and sent down to the shops. The 18-pounders supporting the right division got down as low as sixty-two, owing to the number smashed or going out of action, and practically none could be obtained to fill in dents. A similar state of affairs existed among the Heavies. Out of 227, only 151 were in action. In the face of this, the Army ordered out of the line the 66th Divisional Artillery and the 108th Army Brigade; but by strong representations the guns of the 66th D.A. were left to form a pool from which to replace the 18-pounders.

The situation at that time was that, though the Canadians were debited with a total of 306 eighteen-pounders, only 162 were in action, the remainder being made up of unfilled indents: guns that had been left stuck in the mud by the British previously in occupation, and were known as "derelicts" at the I.O.M., and four guns that were actually reported as "lost." The loss of the latter forms an illustration of the state of disorganization that prevailed among the British Army brigades. One Brigade Commander had abandoned three guns on the road, nominally bogged, and had left no guard on them. When the Canadian Corps took over, he was ordered to salvage these guns, but when he went to look for them he reported that somebody had taken them away! In some cases the Canadian Artillery had to take up ammunition, and even the guns, for some of the British Army brigades. The condition of these units

---

15   Anti-aircraft was commonly referred to as "Archie." The spent shrapnel shells fell back to earth after being fired.

absolutely justified the criticism that had been unanimously passed against this system of artillery organization in the early part of the year.[16]

The second attack was fixed for the morning of October 30, zero hour being 5:50 AM. The morning was bright, and visibility remained good until about 10:00 AM, during which time the aeroplanes did good work, sending down over seventy calls to the counter-batteries. The barrage was 100 yards for eight minutes, and extended along the fronts of the x Corps and the II ANZAC Corps on the right and the XVIII Corps on the left.

Our 4th Division on the right got Crest Farm and its other objectives at the first rush. The 3rd Division was held up by a block of pillboxes at Meetcheele. After desperate fighting, one large pillbox was captured, which commanded the other pillboxes, and not only blanketed their fire against the left division front, but prevented machine gun interference with the attack on the right. This was a brilliant piece of work, but the Princess Pats suffered heavily, having over twenty officers killed and wounded and the battalion's attacking strength reduced to about 150.[17] On the extreme left, Vapour and Source Farms were captured. Again the enemy barrage was quick in coming down after the attack commenced, but fortunately did not interfere with the assembly of our troops for the attack. The counter-battery work on our side was excellent.

The x Corps took advantage of the occasions to attack Gheluvelt and Polderhoek Chateau. The latter was captured, but Gheluvelt was not reached, and later in the day the troops in the chateau, considering themselves isolated, withdrew without being counterattacked. The enemy counterattacked the left Canadian division five times, from the north of Passchendaele, but those attacks never got through the artillery barrage. About four hundred prisoners were captured.

---

16   Brigades that reported directly to Army Artillery HQ with no equivalent of a Divisional Artillery HQ over them. This system was much criticized as it left the units largely unsupervised by a consistent higher commander.

17   Approximately six hundred men of the PPCLI began this attack; 354 were casualties. Stragglers could easily have reduced effective fighting strength to 150 at the culmination of the assault.

Chapter 22

THE CAPTURE OF PASSCHENDAELE

After the attack of October 30, efforts were made during the following nights to capture the rest of the pillboxes at Meetcheele, and also to take Vanity Farm (but without much success), the intention being to straighten out the line and afford a better jumping-off place for the 2nd and 1st Canadian Divisions, who relieved on the right and left respectively for the attack on Passchendaele. The 1st and 2nd Divisional Artilleries came in with their divisions, and brought the field gun conditions up to a more satisfactory basis, so that the barrage was increased to 110 guns on the right and 120 on the left. Notwithstanding the utmost efforts, the condition of the heavy artillery gradually depreciated until on the day of the attack there were only 131 guns in action.

However, in spite of the mud and the precarious state of the roads, a considerable number of guns were moved forward, including four 12-inch howitzers, six batteries of 6-inch howitzers, and four batteries of 60-pounders. This enabled us to engage the enemy's counter-batteries for a distance of 7,000 yards past Passchendaele. Six more brigades of field guns were advanced beyond the Zonnebeke–St. Julien Road, so as to enable the Corps to barrage the Infantry into and past Passchendaele. The work of getting up all these guns, together with the supply of ammunition, was little less than Herculean, and was accomplished under constant shellfire, from which the Artillery suffered considerably.

It may be mentioned here that when the Canadian Corps took over they inherited a system of counter-battery work that was quite opposed to our methods in the past and seemed to have been in force throughout all the operations of the Second Army up to that time. It had been our system to obtain the fullest possible information regarding the positions of the enemy's batteries through flash spotting, sound ranging, and aeroplane observation, and only deal for destructive purposes with the batteries we actually located, depending upon neutralizing fire to keep the others quiet. The Second Army system appeared much less scientific and of a more "rule of thumb" character. The sound ranging system had not kept pace with the advance and was practically out of action; the flash spotting arrangements were not satisfactory; and the aeroplane observation, though bravely attempted by the Corps Squadron[1] when the visibility was good, was rendered almost equally impossible by the lack of protection afforded the non-fighting planes by the Army fighting wing. The aeroplane photographs had to be taken at such a height, on account of the same interference, that they were almost valueless and afforded no information to the counter-batteries. The condition of affairs had given rise to a system of employing huge concentrations on spots where it was suspected the enemy's batteries were. It was like a blind man throwing stones and hoping that, if he threw enough of them, he would hit something.

Major-General Buckle[2] strenuously objected to our counter-battery system, as if its adoption reflected to a large extent on the previous method in vogue in the Army. Notwithstanding that we had already carried through two successful operations at a minimum cost to the attacking Infantry, while two previous corps had failed in the same attacks owing to the lack of Artillery support, he insisted that the concentration system should be adopted, and made it almost a personal matter. At my request the Corps Commander strongly recommended to the Army Commander that the Canadian Corps Artillery should be allowed to adopt its own methods, which had proved so successful at Vimy, Lens, and Hill 70, and he finally secured immunity for us from interference. This is worth noting in view of the slow progress made on the northern front, in the months just preceding, notwithstanding the immense force of artillery, which should have been sufficient to blast away all opposition to the Infantry attacks.

---

1   Each corps was normally allocated one RFC observation squadron to work with.
2   MGRA Second Army.

In addition to this, curious customs had crept in which I had to reform. For instance, if there were three Divisions of Artillery supporting one Division of Infantry, all but one C.R.A.[3] went out of the line with their staffs, leaving a colonel in command of their divisions, which were nominally termed groups. Then the other colonel of each division considered himself free to go out of the line or go on leave, leaving the "group" in charge of his colleague. Then two majors took charge of the brigades, which formed the groups, leaving their batteries in the charge of captains, and other majors went on leave and did the same thing. The ultimate result was that there were but a few junior officers in the fighting line and most of the senior officers were out resting; consequently, discipline deteriorated and gradually disorganization ensued. It was relatively the same with the Heavy Group commanders, all of whom were living in Ypres or farther away from their batteries, which were in action several miles off.[4]

The attack on Passchendaele took place on November 6 at 6:00 AM. The enemy had information of the pending attack, and brought down his barrage one minute after it was launched, but strangely enough he did not interfere with the assembly of the troops before zero, which might have been fatal to the whole operation. The attack included Passchendaele on the right, and Mosselmarkt and Goudberg on the left, being on a front of about a mile. It was carried out exactly as planned, and in a little over an hour and thirty minutes all objectives had been gained with comparatively little loss, and about five hundred prisoners taken, making a total of over a thousand since the beginning of the operations.

The Bosche's morale had been seriously impaired by the two former operations, and by the heavy harassing fire which we had maintained night and day against the approaches to the east of the town and over the whole sector. As the artillery barrage opened, the enemy could be seen leaving their trenches and running away ahead of it. When the objectives had all been reached, there was a counterattack from the northeast, but it was lacking in spirit and was easily shattered by our artillery. By night the Infantry were thoroughly dug in and the S.O.S. lines established.

Field-Marshal Hindenburg[5] had publicly announced that Passchendaele was to be held at all cost, and if lost was to be counterattacked until retaken. In the face of

---

3 Commander Royal Artillery. This is the same position as GOC Divisional Artillery. CRA was adopted in 1917 to emphasize that these generals commanded the division's guns.

4 This refers to British units.

5 Field Marshal Paul Ludwig Hans Anton von Beneckendorff und von Hindenburg, Chief of the German General Staff 1916–1919 and subsequently President of Germany 1925–1934.

such an easy victory the whole Second Army metaphorically held its breath, expecting that the Canadian Corps would be driven from its position by an irresistible counterattack, but the day passed and nothing happened. That night the enemy was quiet, and there were numerous prophecies that the irresistible counterattack would come at dawn on the following day, but again nothing happened, and I was satisfied that the barrage, prepared for such a contingency, could annihilate anything that approached it. The possibility of counterattacking on the German side was reduced to a minimum by the fact that there were large stretches of wet ground on the reverse slopes of the ridge, as there were on our side, thus limiting the assembly of a counterattack to three comparatively dry areas. During the next day we kept these areas under occasional bursts of fire, which were quite sufficient to discourage the enemy from even assembling for a counterattack.

I had not been able to understand why, during the previous operations on the Western Front, the Germans could successfully counterattack, if the immense amount of artillery at the disposal of the British armies was properly handled. We had held Hill 70 against thirty-five counterattacks, none of which ever had a hope of succeeding because our properly organized barrage broke them up at their points of assembly and almost annihilated the attackers when they attempted to advance. After my experience regarding the condition of affairs after the Canadian Corps had taken over on this front, the slowness with which precautions were taken to deal with counterattacks, and the general inefficiency of supervision in seeing that orders were carried out, I understood the reason why. These three operations had confirmed my opinion that with a properly organized barrage that brought to bear the full force of gun power, successful counterattacks were almost an impossibility.

It was amusing to read, in the newspaper reports of the capture of Passchendaele by the Canadians, that almost every description was tempered with a restraint, such descriptions being frequently sprinkled with "ifs": "If they can hold the ground that they have taken," in view of Marshall Hindenberg's threat. The subsequent accounts in the papers were in a much more jubilant key, when it was discovered that this fear was unfounded.

The capture of Passchendaele left the Canadian Corps holding a very pronounced salient, because none of the corps on either side of us had taken advantage of the enormous expenditure of ammunition in putting on "Chinese barrages"[6] in order to advance abreast of us and improve their positions. Having taken all of our

---

6   Army slang for diversionary bombardments. "Chinese attacks" were feint attacks.

objectives, it was not without some slight surprise that the Corps received an order to attack northwest along the Passchendaele Ridge on November 10, practically across the front of the 2nd Division, which in the meantime had relieved the 18th on our left. In conjunction with this attack the 1st Imperial Division was to push forward, also going north parallel to the front it had been holding.

It was a peculiar operation and had peculiar results. Again the Germans failed to interfere with our assembly for the assault, which was launched at 6:05 AM. On November 10 the Canadians were successful at every point, and even overran their objectives on a front of about 1,600 yards' depth, carrying them well beyond Vindictive Crossroads.

By this late date the Germans had moved back their artillery a considerable distance, with the result that the corps on either side of us had their batteries sited so far back that they could not effectively deal with the enemy's, though they loyally attempted to do so. Consequently, no sooner had this last attack succeeded then the counter-batteries of five German Corps were turned on the Canadian Corps front, and submitted it to a frightful bombardment which lasted all day. At nightfall our infantry still grimly held all their objectives, notwithstanding heavy losses. But the troops of the 1st Imperial Division had been driven back to their original positions. It was one of the heaviest artillery engagements of the War, and everybody was thankful when the German fire died down at dusk. But it left the Canadian Corps what had almost *ceased* to be a salient and was nearly a letter "L" extending out on the Passchendaele Ridge. The situation was precarious, but neither on November 11 nor 12 did the enemy counterattack, evidently having a wholesome respect for the Canadian barrage.

It is due to the 1st Imperial Division to say that the troops fought well, and that the failure was due to staff work which allowed a division to come fresh into the line and immediately launch a difficult attack over ground which neither the staff, the officers, nor the men were acquainted with.

During the past week news had arrived of the overwhelming defeat of the Italian Army, with the capture of a quarter of a million men and 2,300 guns by the Austro-German Army. Also that Kerensky had been deposed in Russia and a new pro-German government formed. General Cavan[7] had been dispatched to Italy with what was reported to be ten British divisions. On November 10, General Sir Herbert

---

7   Later Field Marshal F.L.R. Cavan, 10th Earl of Cavan, KP, GCB, GCMG, GCVO, GBE, DL.

Plumer received orders to proceed to Italy with a portion of his staff, in what was stated to be an advisory capacity. The command of the Second Army was taken over by General Rawlinson.[8]

A few days longer to hold their gains, and the Canadians were done with Ypres forever. But—*oh!* What a tale for the generations to come! Never in civilian life are men called upon to labour as those men laboured—with all the might of their bodies, to lift, and carry, and pull, for the sake of their comrades and their cause.

The Infantry went forward to the firing line in single file, winding along the muddy ridges between the water holes, slipping, floundering, helping one another along through the dark, in conditions where no one could get through alone. "Up front" they lay in the mud, and found it good at times to lie still in the one place for a long while, till the wet slime about them had become warm with their bodies' heat. When the hour to advance came, they got out of their watery beds, and by an effort of heroism almost unequalled in the history of war, bombed the enemy's cement emplacements and drove him from his strongholds.

And if they were wounded? Could one whose leg had been shattered by a dum-dum[9] crawl on his hands through that bog—a mile, a mile and a half, two miles—to a dressing station? If he had a bullet in his lungs or through his stomach, where the least exertion meant that the deadly bleeding would begin, could he survive the effort of dragging himself through miles of mud? Let no secrets be kept. The Canadians took Passchendaele but Canada's sons paid for every inch of ground gained, a price more terrible than the human tongue can tell.

The stretcher-bearers who ventured into that hell came struggling out with their burdens only to be blown to bits, perhaps, when they reached the plank road just half a mile from their destination. Through water to their waists, in mud to their knees, they crept foot by foot along, till their burden was in safety or themselves had died en route. Nor ever once was heard a complaint or whine. Wounded men, seeing the danger their bearers were in, pleaded to be left to die; begged their comrades to seek safety to the side. Yet they plugged steadily ahead, through the enemy barrage, along the duck walks, down that plank road, to the pillboxes where the ambulances took

---

8   General Sir H.S. Rawlinson, 1st Baron Rawlinson, GCB, GCSI, GCVO, KCMG.

9   Hollow-point bullets designed to create more severe wounds, initially designed at Dum Dum Arsenal for the British Army in India. Dum-dum bullets were prohibited in warfare at the Hague Convention in 1899. All sides accused their enemies of continued use of dum-dum bullets during the First World War, "proof" that their opponents were "barbaric."

the wounded away. Then back the bearers went, up front again. Even then, there were hundreds who never got the help they needed, and died because they could not be taken out.

There were gunners who were in action twenty days out of the twenty-one their unit was in the line. In all that time they never had dry feet. They drank tea made with the gas-poisoned water in the shell holes. They laboured day and night without supplies, when rations and water were destroyed by shellfire on the way up. They ate dry raisins and mouldy biscuits—sometimes they ate nothing at all. The morning of the second advance, one battery had only tea in a space of twenty-eight hours. Under a deadly fire that destroyed two entire gun crews, the battle went on. And after six hours and twenty minutes of firing, when the count of ammunition was made, the gun that had been directly in the enemy's line of fire was found to have fired only three shells less than orders called for.

In the years to come, when the last of the veterans are telling tales of the things that happened in the Great World War, the three Battles of Wipers will be most vivid in their memory.

There the Canadians faced three mighty tests—the gas attack of April 1915 was met by the old 1st Division; the German onslaught of June 1916 was borne by the courageous 3rd Division just after they came into the line; and the last victorious affray was an offensive in which the whole corps cooperated in the capture of Passchendaele Ridge in October and November of 1917. Every one of these battles was a supreme test of the military genius of the Canadians, of their will to win, and of their courage to hold on against heavy odds. And in every test they covered themselves with glory.

Chapter 23

ELECTION ISSUES

On November 18 the Canadian Corps "handed over" to the VIII (Imperial) Corps in front of Passchendaele, and moved back to its old quarters in front of Lens and Hill 70. The troops who marched out of Flanders during the next month—for it was all of a month before the different elements were once more united under General Currie's command (the heavy batteries and the Eighth Army Brigade[1] arrived just before Christmas)—were tired troops. Their equipment was in a sorry state; their horses had suffered from the mud and wet; and the men themselves were more done up than they had been since they left the Somme. Yet before they were two days' march from Ypres they had thoroughly cleaned their equipment and were ready for whatever lay ahead. They returned to their old familiar haunts, glad that their turn in Flanders was over, and willing enough, for a time at least, to go back to the routine business of "holding the line."

During December the Federal Election in Canada created a great deal of both excitement and anxiety. It was fought out on the question of conscription, but really turned on the point of whether Canada was to continue to take part in the War. Voluntary enlistment had decreased to the point that it did not nearly make good the losses in battle, so that unless conscription was adopted the Corps would eventually

---

1 Eighth Army Brigade, Canadian Field Artillery.

dwindle to nothing for lack of recruits. Quebec, which had furnished only one battalion in the field up to that time, seemed unitedly opposed to conscription, and Laurier had adopted the sinister slogan: "A cross on the ballot for the Union Government means another cross in Flanders."

As election day approached, the eyes of the world were on Canada. A short time before, Australia had pronounced against conscription, and as a result her two ambitious, weak corps had dwindled to one. There had been no election in Great Britain since before the War, and there was considerable unrest and dissatisfaction among certain portions of the populace over the food restrictions, together with a certain amount of war weariness. The United States had come in during the previous April with a great flourish of trumpets, but as yet the Americans had not a single man on the firing line. France had only been kept in the War recently by Britain continually relieving her of the defence of more and more of her front, and furnishing her with enormous stores of food and material. To Germany, the Canadian election was fraught with hope and fear: hope that the defection of Canada would be the first indication of the defection of the overseas dominions; fear that a firm lead on the part of Canada would have a heartening influence on all the Allies, and indicate to the German people that, notwithstanding the heavy sacrifices in blood and money the Dominion had already made, she was in the War to the finish.

Among Canadians both at home and abroad, the possible result of the election was viewed with the greatest anxiety and uncertainty. It remained to be seen to what extent the initial resolve of the English-speaking population of the Dominion had been shaken by the severe losses of two years of almost constant battle. The wives, sisters, and mothers of all soldiers had the vote, and there was for them the great temptation to do something to stop the War, so that their fathers, sons, and brothers might come back to them. Then the heads of families, who had sons eligible for conscription, might vote to prevent them being sent to the War.

There was much proud rejoicing throughout the Canadian Corps when it was learned the day after the election that the Union Government had been returned by one of the largest majorities ever accorded a government since Confederation. This had been done by the people of Canada without the soldiers' votes.

Voting of course had been held in the field, often under fire, during the week preceding December 17, when the election took place in Canada. It was subsequently found, though the ballots of the soldiers were not counted for nearly two months after the election, that they stood about 95 percent for the Union Government and conscription. This brought the Union Government majority up to seventy-one.[2]

Had the soldiers' vote been necessary to sustain the government, the result would not have been viewed with such utter satisfaction. Not only did it have an inspiring influence on the soldiers in the field in evidencing how splendidly they were supported by the feeling in Canada, the decision of Canada in this election was a great disappointment to the enemy, and had a heartening effect on all the Allied people.

In view of the adoption of conscription, the question arose as to whether the Canadian force should be reorganized on the basis of two corps of three divisions each. The British divisions were reducing the number of their battalions from twelve to nine, and as the Canadians had a complete division, the 5th, in England, the necessary change to two corps could have been made without waiting for the conscript recruits. But after a prolonged consideration of the question it was finally decided to have one strong corps of four divisions, of twelve battalions each, twelve hundred men to a battalion, supported by five and a half divisions of field artillery and three brigades of Canadian garrison artillery. The advantage of this was that it kept down the numbers of corps and divisional staffs, while it very largely increased the number of rifles and artillery available for operations under one command. Consequently the 5th Division[3] in England was broken up, and its field artillery, engineers, and machine gun companies were embodied in the original corps, thus making the Canadian Expeditionary Force something between a corps and an army, and one of the most formidable fighting machines on the whole British front.

2   The Union Government under Sir Robert Borden obtained a seventy-one-seat majority.
3   I.e., 5th Canadian Division.

Chapter 24

TRYING OUT THE TANKS

After the close of the great British offensive in the north, guns of all calibres were very scarce. In the summer of 1915, when artillery ammunition had been nearly exhausted, every class of manufacturing establishment was organized for the manufacture of shells. To such an extent were the shops engaged in making ammunition that the manufacture of guns was neglected, with the result that by autumn of 1917 a large proportion of guns of all calibres were worn out, and no adequate arrangements had been made to replace them. When the Canadian Artillery returned to Lens, it was only half armed, and no guns existed to be drawn for the indents that had been filled at Ordnance. The situation caused some anxiety before it was finally remedied early in the new year.

The shortage of guns only intensified another anxiety that had been weighing on all ranks. A new instrument of war had appeared: the armoured tank, and it was not yet known to what extent these new monsters were dangerous, or how they might be dealt with in the field.

The Canadians' first experience of the tanks was at the Somme in September of 1916. Three or four of them had advanced to an attack there with the 38th (Ottawa) Regiment, without any great success, as the ground was full of deep shell holes and obstructed by trenches. The enemy had put nearly all of them out of action; but it was evident that with more skill in the handling they would be of inestimable value in attacks against trenches, barbed wire, and machine gun nests.[1]

---

1   This refers to the attack by the 2nd Division on Courcelette on September 15, 1916. In fact, six tanks participated in the action. The 38th Battalion was not involved in this attack. Morrison may be confusing it with the 28th Battalion, which was.

Tank corps were formed in the British armies, and practiced assiduously with various forms of the new machine. In the northern battles of 1917, they had an extensive test, but the heavy rains of the late autumn left many of them lying like a great herd of hogs in the mud of the Ypres Salient.

When General Sir Julian Byng with the Third Army made his gallant assault on Cambrai, the tanks were given an important role in the battle. The ground was dry and rolling, eminently suitable for tank operations. But the chance of war along with an error in tactics proved their undoing. The tanks advanced against the enemy in what is known as "Indian file," and it was this play of "follow your leader" that caused the failure. For it happened that, at a critical point, the leading tank made its way through a gate in a stone enclosure on a hillside and a German battery was in action at the foot of the slope. The appearance of the tanks struck into the men manning the guns of the battery. They fled, with the exception of their major, who himself took charge of a gun and, one by one, put nearly a dozen tanks out of action as they came through the gate in the enclosure. It was easier for that one brave gunner to hit the tanks than it was for the tanks to "get" him; the result was that the major blocked the avenue of advance before he himself was killed.[2]

This incident caused a considerable sensation among all ranks. The dangerous usefulness of the new arm was obvious. It was not so obvious what tactics would need to be employed to prevent enemy tanks from damaging us in any future encounter, for it was plain that tanks moving freely in the open were not at all in the same position as tanks passing "Indian file" through a hole in a wall at point-blank range of field guns. Much as our infantry believed in the Artillery, they knew too little about the guns to be absolutely convinced that in an emergency they could successfully put tanks out of action. When all was said and done, the Canadian Gunners had never been in action against tanks, and until they had been, a grim doubt existed that it was imperative should be removed.

I had absolute confidence in my Gunners and their ability to deal with tanks. And, thinking the matter over, I decided that I would put them to the test and dissolve the doubt; for, in the words of Shakespeare: "He either fears his fate too much, or his deserts are small, who dare not put it to the touch, and win or lose it all."[3]

In December of 1917, the snow lay quite heavily on the ground, especially in the vicinity of Arras and in the valleys and gulches around Vimy Ridge. When I had

---

2   Well after the War this man was identified as (probably) Unteroffizier (Sergeant) Theodor Krüger, Feld Artillerie Regiment 108. This identification was made after Morrison's death.

3   The quote is misattributed to Shakespeare. It is actually by James Graham, 1st Marquis of Montrose.

finally decided to test the Gunners in the new warfare of tank-stopping, a suitable scene of action was selected: the Zouave Valley at the northern end of Vimy Ridge. A dozen imitation tanks were constructed, to move on steel cables a quarter of a mile long, drawn by eight gun horses. The tanks were concealed in the mouth of the Souchez Valley, and it was arranged that at a signal they would begin to move, crossing the end of the Zouave Valley and disappearing northward if they survived the test.

It was agreed that the gun for the test should be placed on the low ridge known as the Music Hall Line; that picked gun crews should be stationed at the foot of this ridge; and that when the alarm was given, they should double to the gun and do such damage as they could before the tanks disappeared.

The interest that was taken in the event showed how sportily it was regarded. Though it was quite cold, and the ridges were almost knee-deep with drifted snow, nearly five hundred generals were present, representing almost every branch of the British arms in that area. In addition to that, many hundreds of Tank Corps troops, infantrymen, and artillerymen crowded Lorette Ridge and the spurs of the Vimy as spectators. I was particularly surprised and pleased at the large attendance of Tank Corps officers who invited themselves that Sunday to our mess. With true British confidence in the efficiency—if not the invincibility—of their own branch of the service, and the consequent lack of appreciation of other arms, many of them prophesied the failure of the test. Indeed, some of them endeavoured to persuade me to call off the event, insisting that the Gunners would not be able to stop the tanks, and that the result would not be beneficial to the morale of the troops, especially the Infantry. My reply, somewhat emphatically given, was that if the Canadian Gunners could not protect their infantry from tanks, the sooner we knew it the better for everybody.

After lunch the test was made. A single gun stood on the crest of the ridge ready for action; crack gun crews, representing every brigade of the Canadian Corps Artillery, were drawn up under their sergeants at the foot of the hill. A trumpet blew. The first attack began to move, and the first gun crew doubled to their gun. Eyes and field glasses were directed on the Souchez Valley. A minute or so, and the first dummy tank came lurching along the railway, out of the mouth of the valley. The gun layer reported "Ready" and the order to fire was given. As the smoke drifted leeward, "the boldest held his breath for a time." Certainly I held mine, and my heart jumped with elation as the dummy tank reared in the air and fell in a splintered heap.

At a second signal, another crew doubled to the gun. A second tank wobbled out on the tramway for 50 yards or so, then collapsed, its running gear demolished. One after the other, each of the twelve tanks attempted the hazardous journey; and one after the other, each collapsed, stricken, before it reached the end of its cable. Not a tank escaped.

At first each hit was saluted with applause, but as tank after tank was destroyed, the successive hits were received in silence. If the Infantry had ever seriously doubted the Artillery, they did so no longer; if they had ever feared German tanks, they knew now that, once the Artillery had come into open action against them, they would quickly be rendered harmless.[4]

All ranks had need of that newborne confidence in the ability of the Gunners to stop the tanks, for early in 1918 it was rumoured that the Germans intended to make a great push in March, and that tanks were to be a leading feature of this final effort to push the British Army into the sea. The German Army in the west had been heavily reinforced from Russia, and was openly bragging of what it intended to do to the Canadian Corps. The enemy even went so far as to announce the date of the big push as March 21.

The Canadians were by no means terrified by the German boast; on the contrary, they welcomed the prospect of an effort on the part of the Kaiser's troops to take back "The Bastion of France." During the winter, preparations were made for the expected attack. That was only prudent. Scores of miles of trenches were dug, and wire entanglements laid; reserve gun pits were built and supplied with ammunition; stores of army materials were cached many miles back of the line; and everything possible was done to ensure effective resistance in the face of overwhelming odds.

Meanwhile, changes were being made in high places that were to affect seriously the course of events. After the Battle of Cambrai, which was such a brilliant success when first launched on November 20, and which later—under the onslaught of sixteen German divisions—left things pretty much "as you were," there was a great deal of talk in England regarding the reorganization of the leaders of the Army. Until the facts were known, some two months later, General Sir Julian Byng was severely blamed for the failure of the Third Army to hold the ground so boldly taken. Admiral Sir John Jellicoe,[5] First Sea Lord, was suddenly retired in favour of Admiral Wemyss,[6] whose chief qualification to be head of the British Navy seemed to be that he had

---

4   This demonstration occurred on March 10, 1918.

5   Admiral of the Fleet Sir John Rushworth Jellicoe, 1st Earl Jellicoe, GCB, OM, GCVO, SGM, DL, First Sea Lord November 30, 1916–January 10, 1918.

6   Vice Admiral (later Admiral of the Fleet) Sir Rosslyn Wemyss, 1st Baron Wester Wemyss, GCB, CMG, MVO, First Sea Lord January 10, 1918–November 1, 1919.

been a very successful commander of the Royal Yacht. And—what was equally serious—a section of the British press instituted a campaign against Sir Douglas Haig, Commander-in-Chief of the British Army.

Finally, in February, the Allies decided to establish what was known as the Versailles Council, to be composed of military representatives of the British, French, Italian, and American armies. A good deal of mystery surrounded the question of the exact powers of this tribunal, but the general idea was that it should really command all the Allied armies. If that principle were accepted, then the British representative on the Allied Council would practically be superior to the Chief of the General Staff and to the Commander-in-Chief. General Sir Henry Wilson was given the post at Versailles. Neither the post nor the applicant was regarded with much favour by the best military authorities in England.

Soon friction ensued, with the result that General Sir William Robertson, the British Chief of Staff, resigned (as the government stated; he was retired as he said himself) and was given an inconspicuous command on the east coast of England. General Sir Henry Wilson was made Chief of the Imperial Staff, and General Rawlinson, a subordinate army commander, whose record consisted of an almost unbroken succession of failures since the beginning of the War, was sent to Versailles. These changes were not regarded in the Army as adding any strength to the British position, but there was a general feeling of relief that Haig remained in the post of Commander-in-Chief, though two of his juniors had been put over his head.

Winter on the Western Front passed rather pleasantly as compared with former years, on account of the good weather. An increasing proportion of the Canadians took their leave in Paris and southern France in preference to going to England. The Americans had been sending over troops for many months, but a good deal of mystery existed as to whether they were many or few in number. The guesses varied from three divisions to 300,000 men, but whatever was the number the French were frankly disappointed at the Americans' lack of keenness in taking over portions of the fighting front. When the much heralded German offensive opened on March 21 on a front of fifty miles, from the Scarpe to the Oise, the general impression was that if the decisive battle of the War had now commenced, the War would be lost or won before the Americans had enough trained troops in France to be any factor in the decision.

Chapter 25

THE LAST ATTEMPT ON PARIS: FIRST STAGE

E arly on March 21, it was known that the German offensive had been launched—not against the Canadians in the Lens–Arras sector, but against the Fifth Army in the south. For the next three or four days the almost hourly bulletins told the story of how the Fifth Army was practically being driven out of the theatre of war in the south, while the Third Army was making a magnificent fight but was having to fall back constantly on its right to keep in touch with the Fifth. By March 27 the Third Army was practically on the same line that had been held by the British before the Battle of the Somme, while the Fifth Army had lost most of its field and heavy guns and was demoralized to such an extent that most of its personnel was withdrawn beyond Amiens. The Third Army was left with its right flank exposed, and was forced to reach out as far as possible to link up with the oncoming French to the south of Albert.

The linking up process brought into action men of all ranks whom only needed proper leadership to carry out desperate and effective fighting. As the disorganized Fifth Army disappeared out of the line it left a space of about one division front between the right of the Third Army and the French, who were rapidly coming up to our assistance. This gap was hastily filled up by a miscellaneous body of troops that achieved a gallant reputation under the name of Carey's Force when they rallied under an artillery officer, Brigadier-General Sandeman Carey.[1]

At first this force was only about three thousand strong. It was augmented by a Canadian machine gun brigade, under Lieutenant-Colonel Walker,[2] which was dispatched from the Canadian Corps to assist in blocking the way to Amiens. The Canadian Cavalry Brigade also did very gallant work, fighting both mounted and on foot. On one occasion they made a mounted charge on a wood filled with Germans and completely cleared it out, subsequently handing it over to the Infantry. For the first time on the Western Front armoured motorcars did magnificent service. Under the charge of Canadian officers and men, these cars darted about on various roads, shooting up the advancing German Infantry, and materially assisting in blocking the road to Amiens.

This situation continued for nearly a week during the latter days of March, and as the presence of the French from the south gradually became heavier, the German advance on Amiens, southwest of Albert, was retarded and eventually stopped, though they had reached to within ten miles of the railway running south to Paris. Amiens was evacuated by over 100,000 of the civil population, and the Germans shelled and bombed it night after night until it became almost uninhabitable.

Meanwhile things were happening in high places. The French had not been kept in sufficiently close liaison with the British armies, and would appear not to realize the extent of the disaster which, in one short weekend, led to the Fifth Army's retirement from in front of St. Quentin almost to the gates of Amiens, and, worst of all, to the loss of nearly all its guns and other equipment. Whether reluctance or ignorance on the part of the British representative in Versailles was the cause of the failure to impress the French with this portentous fact is as yet only a matter of surmise. But the fact was that about March 26, General Haig arranged a meeting with the President of France and the French military chiefs at Doullens, with a view to thoroughly arousing them to the situation, in order that they might more speedily cooperate, and in greater strength, to save the situation.

A few days after, General Rawlinson, who had been the British representative at the Versailles Council, suddenly arrived on the battlefront with a hastily arranged staff and was reported to have taken command of the Fifth Army from General

---

1   Later Major-General George Glas Sandeman Carey, CB. "Carey's Force" was mainly British Royal Engineers with five hundred American Railway troops, four hundred men from 2nd Battalion Canadian Railway troops, and a Canadian machine gun battery.

2   Lieutenant-Colonel William Keating Walker, DSO, MC. Commanding Officer 1st Canadian Motor Machine Gun Brigade.

Gough, who was relieved and sent home, as was supposed. A few days later it was announced that General Rawlinson was to command the Fourth Army, while Gough was to remain in command of the Fifth, the name of which was to be changed to the Reserve Army. The grim humour of this situation was that the Fifth Army had practically ceased to exist as an organization, and the Fourth Army was only coming into being after a lengthy period of organismal eclipse, presumably being made up of the reinforcements that were now commencing to come from England or from other parts of the line. The actual fact was that during this period of disorganization of one army and the reorganization of another, the vital few miles in front of Amiens were being held by Carey's Force and by various heterogeneous units, all fighting on their own to prevent the Hun from seizing Amiens.

In the latter days of March the situation so far as the Canadian Corps was concerned was most important. The left of the Third Army was practically pivoted on the right of the Canadian Corps on Vimy Ridge, and extended southwestward to a point immediately west of Albert. In other words, the gallant Third Army had held on with its left practically to the original line, but had been forced to swing back on its right to keep touch with the disappearing Fifth Army until Carey's Force and the miscellaneous units above described had stopped the Germans in front of Amiens.

On March 26 the XVII Corps, without being attacked, evacuated Monchy-le-Preux, a hill to the east of Arras which was regarded as the key to the city, and to some extent dominated the south end of Vimy Ridge. Matters became serious on this sector, and the 1st and 2nd Canadian Divisions were transferred to the XVII and VI Corps respectively to strengthen the line from Arras southward. The I Corps relieved the Canadian Corps as far south as Souchez, and the latter prepared to relieve the XIII Corps to the Scarpe River, holding this very wide front with only two divisions. On March 28, before the relief was completed, the XIII Corps was heavily attacked north of the Scarpe by at least three divisions, but drove off the enemy with considerable slaughter. Previously, in pursuance of the system that appeared to have become very common in the British armies just before the big offensive commenced, the XIII Corps had been holding its front line trenches with outposts. These front line trenches were now abandoned, and the line on the right of the XIII Corps at the Scarpe was drawn back in a sort of defensive flank.

About this time the VI Corps is credited with having warned the XVII Corps that it might have to retire; and the XVII Corps warned the XIII Corps that it was about to evacuate Arras, with the result that the XIII Corps immediately commenced to draw back its Heavy batteries and field artillery, and the VII Corps withdrew practically all its Heavy batteries west of Arras. The evacuation of Arras would have turned the Vimy Ridge—and so on the rumour of these intentions reaching General Currie, he entered such a vigorous protest to the Army that immediate steps were taken to prevent it. But matters had already gone too far to prevent serious consequences.

As an actual fact the staff and other offices in Arras had been abandoned in such haste that maps, telephones and personal equipment were not removed. The city was being shelled and the panic among the troops communicated itself to the inhabitants of the city. There began from Arras much the same sort of flight as began from Ypres in May of 1915. Stores were left unlocked, the cash drawers emptied. Dinners were left half eaten; house doors wide open. The great mass of civilians fled without a moment's preparation, and poured down the roads in every conceivable sort of conveyance, hurrying out of a city that they believed would in a very few minutes be overrun with Germans.

The 1st Canadian Division, which had been in reserve, was ordered into the line to cover the southeast of Arras. For some days the uncertainty as to what had happened had caused more or less confusion everywhere. There had been some rushing about of troops when it was not known for certain just where they would be needed first or most. But as soon as Arras was threatened it was known that it would be the duty of the Canadians to hold the city against any odds. The confusion ceased.

The 1st Division went into the line, and on the way in there happened one of those things of which Canada can be proud. The 1st CFA Brigade was taking up positions at Agny. Moving in from behind the city, they met, some miles back, a large band of refugees. At once, excitement was noticeable among the French civilians. Questions were asked and answered; hurried consultations were held among little groups of refugees; then a cry went up: "C'est les Canadiens! Ce n'est pas nécessaire de partir!" (In other words, "It is not necessary to flee.") Three cheers were given, and right there on the road that long column of refugees turned left about and followed the Canadians back into Arras.

It was some time before order was restored in the city, and in the meantime considerable looting was done for which the Canadians were blamed.

The XVII Corps was now transferred from the Third to the First Army, and a readjustment was made by which the 1st Canadian Division came back to the Canadian Corps, bringing the 1st, 3rd and 4th Canadian Divisions together again, while the 2nd Division remained with the VI Corps, and was fighting to defend Amiens. That was roughly the situation in the latter days of March and the beginning of April 1918.

Chapter 26

THE LAST ATTEMPT
ON PARIS: SECOND STAGE

In the first week of April the great German offensive in the south was held up, the enemy having made so much headway that he had to complete his communications. During this time, by the consent of all the Allies, General Ferdinand Foch of the French Army was given command of all troops on the Western Front. There was desultory fighting at various points, and strong rumours were abroad that the next phase of the offensive would be in the vicinity of Ypres. As in the case of the first German drive, this turned out to be accurate. On the anniversary of Vimy Ridge, in the early morning of April 9, in a dense fog, the enemy attacked furiously from Givenchy to Armentières. This included the front held by the Portuguese divisions, who promptly broke and fled, letting the Germans through behind the British lines in the vicinity of Neuve-Chapelle. The Portuguese were to have been replaced the next day, and if other troops had been in the line there might have been no German advance in the north. But such is the fortune of war.

On the northern portion of the sector attacked, the enemy advanced so rapidly that he had penetrated by evening from Bois-Grenier to Bac-Saint-Maur and the Lys River. The 55th British Division was driven out of Givenchy, but recaptured it, together with 650 prisoners, and held the line as far north as Festubert, but north of that the enemy advanced nearly to Estaires.

To the north of Armentières, on April 10, the Germans made another thrust, capturing Messines Ridge. This was recaptured by the British but subsequently lost, and it became necessary on the following day to evacuate Armentières, the line withdrawing to Nieppe. The Second Army fought well but, owing to the loss of Messines, had to abandon Passchendaele and all the ground gained in the campaign of 1917, which brought the line back just to the east of Ypres. Fighting steadily, but meeting with increasing resistance, the enemy, by April 15, had captured Merville, Estaires, Neuve-Église and Nieppe. Apparently their original objective had been Béthune, but being firmly held on the line, Givenchy–Festubert–Robecq, and finding the going better towards the northwest, the head of the offensive swept past, south of Bailleul, and by the night of April 14 had penetrated as far as Méteren and Merris. The resistance of the left of the First Army and the right of the Second Army had been much more steadfast and effective than that of the Fifth Army during the southern offensive, and the German progress had been relatively slower. But the situation was critical in the extreme.

To release reinforcements for the north, the Canadian Corps had its three divisions stretched from Arras to a point northeast of Loos, a front of 27,000 yards, and had some of its artillery taken away. The barrage gun power was less than one gun per 100 yards. An undesirable feature of the heavy artillery reinforcements sent to the Canadian Corps was that an undue proportion consisted of heavy siege batteries. This came about from the fact that Heavy brigades of other corps and formations, desirous of increasing their mobility, gladly divorced themselves from their 8-inch and 9.2-inch batteries, which were a great hindrance to manoeuvre, with the result that the Canadian Corps had thrust upon it eleven batteries of heavy siege guns, which was more than it needed, while it was short of medium howitzers, 60-pounders and field artillery for the defence of the abnormal front it was holding, a front more akin to that of an army.

On April 14 the position of the Corps was not exactly fortuitous. To the south, the Third Army front sloped away to the rear in the direction of Albert. On the north the First Army was holding from Loos to Festubert, but from there the defensive line slipped sharply back to a point within 4,000 yards of Bethune. Together with one division of the XVII Corps to the south, and two divisions of the I and XI Corps stretched out very thinly to the north, the Canadians were holding the peak of the salient created by the two German offensive operations already described. In its keeping were the city of Arras, Vimy Ridge, and the great coalfields which lie between Vimy Ridge and La Bassée Canal, stretching back to Béthune.

The Canadians were perfectly confident that they could hold their own front against all comers, but it only required the incursion by the Germans in Béthune on their left rear, or at a corresponding point on their right rear, to threaten their flanks and possible line of retirement, thus placing the Corps in jeopardy, with the disagreeable possibility of having to abandon their extremely strong frontal defences and fight their way out to the rear. For a frontal fight, even on our very extended front, we were well prepared, but if the Corps had to manoeuvre to protect its flanks, we were more or less anchored by a mass of heavy artillery, most of it of a very immobile character. This heavy artillery alone would stretch out forty miles when on the move.

On April 14 I suggested that six heavy siege batteries should be withdrawn and echeloned in positions on our left rear, to protect that flank and incidentally to afford us that much more freedom of manoeuvre. Under normal conditions each of these Heavy batteries would require at least three days to be drawn out of the line, taken back a few miles, and put into action again on the line designated. I figured that without these batteries we would still have barely sufficient artillery to repel any frontal attack, but it would essentially strengthen our position by providing for flank eventualities. This plan was submitted to the Army and approved, but it appeared to create the impression that we had more artillery than we actually needed, because the approval carried with it an order that we were to hand over four batteries of medium heavies, which we were by no means in a position to spare.

This was the situation on the morning of April 14.

During the next fortnight a series of engagements ensued along this northern front, ending in the taking of Kemmel Hill after one day's fighting. For a few days it looked as if the enemy was going through to Calais and Boulogne, as Kemmel Hill commanded Ypres and the only remaining range of hills, which included Mont Noir, Mont Rouge and Mont des Cats. From there to Calais is practically a level plain. After a few days' rest, an attack was launched, from Voormezele on the north to Loos on the south, by ten divisions, with the intention of capturing Ypres and the hills already mentioned, including Scherpenberg to the north of Kemmel.

A furious battle ensued, but the British had been reinforced by a considerable number of French troops from General Foch's reserve armies. The successive attacks on this ten-mile front were beaten off with a loss to the Germans of over thirty thousand men, a notable success at a time when matters were commencing to look serious.

On the morning of April 26, the Germans made another attempt to reach Amiens, and had some success at first, but after forty-eight hours' stiff fighting they were driven out of Hangard and Villers-Bretonneux. I had occasion on this day to pass through Amiens, from which the German advance was then only eight miles distant. The city, which had contained a month before nearly 125,000, had been almost entirely deserted by its civilian inhabitants, who had locked up their houses and fled with whatever they could carry in their hands. The city had been bombed and shelled a good deal, but the damage as yet was comparatively slight. The panicked departure by the inhabitants was no doubt largely due to a terror of Bosche frightfulness.

During the last few days of April, orders arrived for the Canadian Corps, less the 2nd Division (which still remained with the VI Corps), to prepare to be relieved in order to proceed to a new field of action. This news was received with general satisfaction. The Canadian troops were not enamoured of the situation that had left them practically isolated on a salient between the deep indentations in our line caused by the German southern and northern offensives.

Chapter 27

THE LAST ATTEMPT
ON PARIS: FINAL STAGE

On May 7 the Canadian Corps, less the 1st CDA, moved from the Vimy front to training areas in the hinterland of the First Army. At this time the 2nd Canadian Division, with its Artillery, still remained attached to the VI Army Corps, and was in action south of Arras. The Corps Headquarters were established in Pernes, and the three divisional headquarters on a line extending roughly from Savy to Auchel.

It was stated that the three divisions and the whole Corps Artillery, less the 2nd CDA, was within ten days to launch an attack in a north-easterly direction on the Béthune–Saint-Venant line. This was held by the XIII and one division of the XI Corps, the proposition being that the Canadians should advance through these troops and launch an attack, the first phase of which would carry us to the outskirts of Estaires and Merville. The initial advance would be supported by the whole artillery on that front, up to a distance of 3,500 yards, after which the Canadian Artillery would advance in close support of its Infantry to carry the attack to its final objective. A hundred tanks were to take part in the operation, the chief purpose of which was to clear the Germans away from the vicinity of the coalfields.

About ten days was to be spent in reconnaissance and preparation, including the training of all troops in open warfare. However, within forty-eight hours from the time the Corps moved out, presumably authentic information was received that the enemy was to make a heavy attack from Arras to the La Bassée Canal. That attack had been expected from the time the thrust was made in the north, for it was plain even to a non-military eye that so sharp a salient as the Lens–Arras sector had become was a deadly menace to the enemy's flanks, and must ultimately be wiped out before he dared advance any farther on either side. The result of this information, regarding the impending attack, was that all plans were changed. Three brigades of field artillery and three brigades of heavy artillery, which had not yet been relieved at Vimy, were retained in the line, and the 1st, 3rd and 4th Infantry Divisions were told to form reserves for the XVII and XVIII Corps, which had relieved them on the Vimy front, and the XIII Corps on the Béthune–Robecq front. Reconnaissance for the operation, which the Canadian Corps had been taken out of battle to carry out, was stopped.

The expected attack failed to materialize, but nothing further was said about our proposed offensive operation. The situation then resolved itself into a practical disintegration of the Canadian Corps, whose three remaining divisions, with their supporting artillery, were widely distributed and held in army reserve, either to act as divisional units in support of the troops in front of them or as potential reserves in case of another big German offensive on any of the fronts.

As the enemy continued to be very quiet, and the whole of the Canadian Corps had been very much averse to being even temporarily broken up and assigned piecemeal to other corps, it became a moot question as to whether the proposed Northern Offensive had not been merely a means to an end. However this might be, the weather became fine and active training in the hinterland continued, though nothing further was heard of our Northern Offensive, which appeared to have been tacitly abandoned. This was the condition of affairs as late as May 18.

Meantime, affairs in England had not been going smoothly. Brigadier-General P. de B. Radcliffe, BG, GS[1] of the Canadian Corps, was transferred to the War Office to take the place of Major-General Maurice[2] as Director of Operations under General

---

1   Brigadier-General (later General) Sir Percy Pollexfen de Blaquiere Radcliffe, KCB, KCMG, DSO. He was known as "Pee de Bee" by his friends. He was Brigadier-General, General Staff (BG, GS) Canadian Corps (Senior Staff Officer) from June 5, 1916, to April 7, 1918.

2   Major-General Sir Frederick Barton Maurice, 1st Baronet, GCB, GCMG, GCVO, DSO. He was Director of Military Operations for the Imperial General Staff from 1915 until forced to resign for publicly criticizing Prime Minister Lloyd George in 1918.

Sir Henry Wilson,[3] who had succeeded Sir William Robertson[4] as Chief of the General Staff, and was gradually gathering a new staff about him at the War Office and elsewhere. Brigadier-General N.W. Webber,[5] formerly GSO 1 of the 2nd Canadian Division, became BG, GS of the Canadian Corps.

After the big German offensives on March 21 and April 9, Mr. Lloyd George had stated in the House of Commons that the British Army was as strong numerically in January 1918 as in January 1917; also that there was only one white division in Egypt and three in Palestine. As an excuse for the debacle of Gough's Army, it had been alleged that the taking over of the French line as far south as Saint-Quentin during the winter of 1917–18 had unduly weakened the British front in that sector, and that this taking over had been contrary to the advice of the British military authorities. In the speech referred to, Mr. Lloyd George absolutely denied this, and stated that the proposed extension of the line had been concurred with by Sir Douglas Haig and everybody concerned.

On May 7, nearly a month after the speech had been delivered and immediately after General Maurice had been relieved of his appointment at the War Office, the latter published a letter stating that he was impelled by his duty as a citizen to inform the British public that these statements were incorrect.

The underlying tendency of the action was to excuse the failure of General Gough, but the immediate result of the Maurice letter was a political hubbub in the House of Commons, and the giving of notice by Mr. Asquith,[6] before he had even heard the premier's reply of what was practically a resolution of lack of confidence in the British Government.

During the few days that elapsed until this motion came before the House for discussion, the leading London papers debated the situation in lengthy editorials. The *Post* and a few others lauded General Maurice as a patriot of the first order, while the *Times* and most of the other influential journals denounced Maurice's action as insubordinate, and intimated that even if his version was correct, it was no time, with

---

3   Field Marshal Sir Henry Hughes Wilson, 1st Baronet, GCB, DSO. Chief of the Imperial General Staff February 19, 1918–February 19, 1922.

4   Field Marshal Sir William Robert Robertson, 1st Baronet, GCB, GCMG, GCVO, DSO. Chief of the Imperial General Staff December 23, 1915–February 19, 1918. Robertson rose from Private to Field Marshal.

5   Brigadier-General Norman William Webber, CMG, DSO, RE. He was a British Army officer who served as BG, GS Canadian Corps until October 27, 1918.

6   Herbert Henry Asquith, 1st Earl of Oxford and Asquith, KG, PC, KC, FRS. He was leader of the opposition December 6, 1916–December 14, 1918.

a great German offensive impending, to sow the seeds of dissension as between Britain and France. The gossips went so far as to allege that Maurice was playing into the hands of the Asquith party to overthrow the government, a tool in the hands of a military clique.

As the day arrived for Mr. Lloyd George[7] to reply, interest was at a fever heat. Cool headed, disinterested people of all classes viewed the situation with alarm: for on the brink of what was believed to be the enemy's greatest attempt to smash the Allies on the Western Front, here was the Imperial Parliament in the throes of an internal strife which might result in the downfall of the British Government. For the first time since the coalition government had been formed, Asquith's party sent out whips and made great preparations to carry the vote of want of confidence. When the House met, Mr. Asquith moved the resolution, but, possibly having got wind of an impending counter-stroke, he weakly argued that he did not mean the resolution as a want of confidence. This was greeted with ironical laughter, and he was goaded into the further indiscretion of vehemently declaring that he did not want to supplant the premier.

Then Mr. Lloyd George took the floor, and gave an unqualified denial to each of General Maurice's statements. He went farther and showed that the figures regarding the strength of the army in France and the number of white divisions in Egypt and Palestine had been furnished from General Maurice's own department; that ten days later the Hansard copy of his speech had been submitted as a matter of routine to General Maurice's department and had been initialled as correct by his own deputy. He also showed that General Maurice's statement, that he had been at Versailles when the extension of the line was debated, was only a half-truth (while Maurice had been at Versailles he had not been in the council chambers), and that his assertion as to the opposition at the council meeting was untrue. The premier followed this up by pointing out that though four weeks had elapsed between the speech and the publication of the Maurice letter, General Maurice had never drawn his attention to the alleged incorrect statements, and that it was only after he had been relieved of his appointment at the War Office that he had rushed into print.

In the face of this reply by the premier, the House of Commons voted down the resolution by 293 to 106. There had been a previous proposition for a committee of inquiry, either by members of the House or a few judges, but after the revelation

---

7   David Lloyd-George, 1st Earl Lloyd-George of Dwyfar, OM, PC. Prime Minister of the United Kingdom December 6, 1916–October 12, 1922.

above referred to, the whole case went by the board. The net result of the incident was to greatly strengthen the government. A few days later, General Maurice was retired. The attitude of the Allies was signified by messages of congratulation to Mr. Lloyd George by the governments of France and Italy. And so the sensation died as suddenly as it was begun.

Up to the end of the third week in May, a state of tension existed in the hourly expectation of another great German offensive. Meantime, German troops had captured the Crimea, with the great fortress of Sebastopol, including a large fleet of Russian merchant vessels in the Black Sea, and were demanding that that Black Sea fleet be handed over. Their captures included the Dowager Empress of Russia, and three or four grand dukes, whom Germany held responsible for the original declaration of war by Russia in 1914.

On May 27[8] the long expected German attack was launched on a fifty-mile front extending from Soissons to about twenty miles east of Reims. From its inception, this attempt to reach Paris was only moderately successful. The line at Reims and to the east held fairly well, but the advance on the western half was rapid. The Aisne was crossed, Soissons captured, and the impetus of the attack had not spent itself until the enemy had captured Château Thierry and had crossed the Marne in many places. For a time, the capture of Paris seemed imminent, and deliberate preparations were made to evacuate the city, whose chief military value consisted in that it was the main source of aeroplane production in France. The sound of the battle could be heard in Paris, but the people were remarkably calm and determined. For the first time, American troops took an important part in the fighting. Eventually the enemy was held and General Foch[9] began to throw in his long anticipated reserves.

---

8   May 27, 1918.

9   Allied Commander-in-Chief.

Chapter 28

PREPARATIONS FOR AUGUST 8

At the end of May the Canadian headquarters moved to Château Bryas, two miles northeast of Saint-Pol. During the weeks that followed, the intensive training in open warfare (which proved of inestimable value in later operations) was carried out by infantry and artillery. All ranks entered upon the work with zest, but latterly it began to pall. The troops felt that they had mastered their job, and subsequent events showed that they had. Through no fault of their own, they had not been engaged in a battle since the beginning of the year, and they were "spoiling for a fight." This was amusingly illustrated by an incident that occurred when the Corps Commander had occasion to reprimand a distinguished battalion for its lack of ginger in its training operations. He concluded his remarks by telling the unit that if he noticed any further waning of interest in the training operations, he would put them in the back of the line. It was intended as a threat, but the battalion took it as a promise and unanimously burst into loud cheers.

During the month many distinguished Canadians visited the Corps, including the premiers of Manitoba,[1] Saskatchewan,[2] and Alberta,[3] as well as Major-General Logie[4] who commanded at Toronto throughout the War, the Prime Minister Sir

---

1   Tobias Crawford Norris.

2   William Melville Martin.

3   Charles Stewart.

4   Major-General William Alexander Logie, CB, General Officer Commanding Military District No. 2 and the 2nd Divisional Area, CEF, 1915–1918.

Robert Borden,[5] Honourable Mr. Calder,[6] Honourable Mr. Rowell,[7] Honourable Mr. Meighen,[8] and others. The prime minister and his colleagues had come over to attend the War Council in London. During the latter half of June there was a lull on the British Western Front and a large number of officers and men were able to go on leave; a very unusual circumstance at that season.

Steps were taken at this time to reorganize the Canadian Heavy Artillery into four mixed brigades of twenty batteries, consisting of two 60-pounders, two 6-inch howitzers, and one 8-inch howitzer battery each. The existing organization was considered lacking in mobility and long-range guns, whereas the proposed organization would give a uniformly heavy armament for each of the four Canadian divisions.[9]

Dominion Day was celebrated in France by the holding of sports and competitions at which over forty thousand troops, representing nearly all the British armies, were present. It was one of the largest events of its kind that was ever held. The following week a highland meet was held, where the programme included a pipe band of 480 pipers and drummers, the largest unit of that sort that ever played together. The premier, Mr. Borden, and a number of cabinet ministers were present. The arrangements for carrying out the sports and competitions were admirable, and the event was the talk of all the armies.

On the evening of July 2, the prime minister had a conference with the Corps Staff and dealt with various matters, including the reorganization of the Artillery, besides endorsing the policy that the Canadian Corps should at all times fight as a unit and not be dispersed except in the case of the greatest emergency. He returned to England on the morning of July 3. Honourable Mr. Calder remained and inspected the 4th Brigade CFA, besides visiting Arras and seeing batteries of the 5th DA in action northwest of that city.

On July 15 the Corps moved to Duisans and took over the line from Neuville-Vitasse to Thales. Earlier in the month the 3rd Division had relieved the 2nd Division on the left of the Third Army so that the Corps was practically reconstituted in the line. Preparations were at once begun for the capture of Orange Hill and

---

5 Sir Robert Laird Borden, GCMG, PC, KC. Prime Minister of Canada October 10, 1911–July 10, 1920.

6 James Alexander Calder, Minister of Immigration and Colonization.

7 Newton Wesley Rowell, President of the Privy Council and Vice-Chairman of the War Committee.

8 Arthur Meighen, Minister of the Interior and Superintendent of Indian Affairs. Meighen was prime minister from July 10, 1920 to December 29, 1921, and from June 29 to Sep 25, 1926.

9 This reorganization was approved but had not happened by the time of the Armistice. The Canadian Corps Heavy Artillery retained three mixed brigades with a total of fourteen heavy and siege batteries.

Monchy-le-Preux, the latter point overlooking Arras and most of Vimy Ridge, since it had been surrendered by the XVII Corps in April.

Preparations for this attack were well underway, when, during the last week of July, General Currie, General Webber and I were apprised of the fact that the Canadian Corps was to be secretly withdrawn and transferred to the front of Amiens, where a surprise attack was to be made from that city and the railway line to Paris. No one else in the Corps shared the secret.

On July 27, under the guise of attending a tank demonstration in the Fourth Army (but with a view to acquiring knowledge for use in the Orange Hill operation), a lot of officers went down to the Fourth Army area. General Webber, Chief of Staff, and myself, together with Colonel McNaughton, CBSO, slipped away from the party and visited the Australian headquarters, where we got a guide to show us over the Villers–Bretonneux battlefield. During the afternoon, Colonel McNaughton and I reconnoitred the French front from Villers–Bretonneux to Cachy for Field and Heavy positions. We stayed that night with the Australians and next morning reconnoitred the southern half of the area from Domart-en-Ponthieu to Gentelles by 11:00 AM. We succeeded in locating all of the forward Field and Heavy areas that could be made available for placing guns for a surprise attack. After lunch at the Australian headquarters, we motored to the Fourth Army's headquarters at Flexicourt. This was a very difficult trip, as in addition to the special work we had to do we had to keep the object of our visit secret from both the Australians and the French. To the Australians we posed as Canadian joyriders, and while in the French area we took off our Canada badges and posed as Australians.

On the afternoon of July 28 I had a long talk with Major-General Budworth,[10] MGRA of the Fourth Army. He demanded to know if the Canadian Corps Artillery would put down a barrage for a surprise attack without previous registration.[11] I promptly replied that they could, because I had taken care during the early weeks of summer to have every gun accurately calibrated.

The Canadian Artillery had had little rest since the fighting around Vimy, and the rifling of the guns had become very much worn. This interfered seriously with both the range and the accuracy of the guns. But the extent of that interference, the exact amount of error, either in range or lateral movement of the projectile in flight,

---

10   Major-General Charles Edward Dutton Budworth, CB, CMG, CVO. MGRA Fourth Army 1916–1918.

11   I.e., Without firing on the targets beforehand in order to ensure accuracy.

could be estimated accurately by a small electrical apparatus, and corrected by a resetting of the sights on the gun.

The guns of the 3rd Division, under Brigadier-General Stewart,[12] were first selected for examination. It was evident at once that all guns in the Corps would need to be examined and calibrated. With that intent, a calibration range (which early got the name of Petawawa) was constructed at Ablain-Saint-Nazaire, and as rapidly as possible the guns were sent to this range and there calibrated. The correction for each gun was noted on the gun itself so that any later adjustment in the sights would allow for the "error" of the gun.

Not only were the guns calibrated but the calibration was tested in the field by the 3rd Canadian Division. I was deeply impressed with the accuracy of the corrections, and it was at once evident to me that calibration could easily be substituted for the noisy "registration on targets," which had hitherto been the only means of securing accuracy, and which invariably betrayed the presence—and often enough the position—of the gun. Consequently I told General Budworth that, notwithstanding the fact that the Germans could overlook the area our guns would have to occupy, we could put on a surprise attack without previous "registration."

He informed me that I would have seventeen brigades of field artillery, including our own, and nine brigades of heavy artillery, with which to carry out a surprise attack on the front from Domart to Villers-Bretonneux, and that the attack was to take place on August 8 with the French on the right and the Australians and the III Corps prolonging the line to the left.[13] The utmost secrecy was to be observed. In the meantime, one brigade of Australians, with two heavy brigades of artillery and three brigades of field artillery, were to take over the front line from the French and act as camouflage while we brought in the artillery already mentioned, installed them in camouflaged positions well up to the front, and put forward dumps of six hundred rounds per gun field ammunition and four hundred rounds per gun heavy ammunition. This artillery was to be got in at night and remain dormant until zero hour. It promised to be one of the most difficult artillery operations undertaken by a corps, as the attack was to be inaugurated by a barrage

---

12   Brigadier-General John Smith Stewart, CMG, DSO. GOC 3rd Divisional Artillery December 29, 1917– January 5, 1919.

13   Morrison was ultimately assigned seventeen brigades of field artillery, nine brigades of heavy artillery, and four siege batteries (three with 6-inch and one with 12-inch guns).

larger than the one with which the battle of Vimy opened. There was to be no preliminary bombardment.

On our returning to the Corps, a secret camouflage report was spread that it was the intention to withdraw the Canadian Corps and send them north to take part in an operation near Kemmel. Divisional commanders were informed that they were to continue with active preparations for the Orange Hill attack in order to camouflage for the alleged *real* intention of taking the Corps north. To mystify still further, secret orders were issued on July 30 for a battalion each of the 2nd and 3rd Divisions to proceed northward, together with the 1st and 4th Canadian Casualty Clearing Stations and some other auxiliary units.

On July 31, the CRAS of the 1st, 3rd and 5th Divisions[14] arrived at Corps Headquarters at Molliens Vidame. The new front had been divided into five sections. I took the three CRAS over the ground and pointed out the brigade positions already selected, and they were directed to reconnoitre the battery positions. The CRAS of the 2nd and 4th arrived on August 1 and were similarly directed, together with the GOC CCHA.[15] In every case the necessary positions were found by evening and topographers were detailed to resect each battery position.[16] Most of the Canadian guns had been calibrated before leaving the Vimy front. Those that were not, together with the guns of the army brigades allotted to the Corps, were calibrated during the next two days at Vaux. On August 3 and 4 advance parties of brigade and artillery commanders located their positions, and arranged for O Pips and communications. The Corps Staff allocated forward dumps and commenced sending up the ammunition required for the attack.

The situation was complicated for the Artillery by the fact that a fleet of tanks and a division of cavalry were to be used in the offensive. It was by this time fairly easy to arrange either a creeping or a jumping barrage behind which the Infantry might steadily advance to an objective; it was a much more difficult matter to arrange a barrage which would allow for the free movement of tanks and cavalry. To prevent the Infantry barrage from blowing up our own tanks, it was decided to use only shrapnel, with a small proportion of smoke shells. And in order that the Heavy Artillery should not interfere with the Cavalry's movements, a "coarse" barrage was laid

---

14   Brigadier-General H.C. Thacker, GOC 1st Divisional Artillery; Brigadier-General J.S. Stewart, GOC 3rd Divisional Artillery; and Brigadier-General W.O.H. Dodds, GOC 5th Divisional Artillery.

15   Brigadier-General H.A. Panet, GOC 2nd Divisional Artillery; Brigadier-General W.B.M. King, GOC 4th Divisional Artillery; and Brigadier-General R.H. Massie, GOC Canadian Corps Heavy Artillery.

16   This means that survey data was provided to each battery in order to ensure that their locations and aiming points would allow accurate firing, without registration, prior to the attack.

down by the Heavies, with the "jumps" measured by miles instead of yards, and the time spaces in hours instead of minutes. The Cavalry was required to conform to this barrage.

The Canadian divisions in the line were quietly withdrawn. Of course this gave occasion for a tremendous amount of speculation on the part of both the adjacent troops. As was expected, the alleged secret regarding our northward destination spread insidiously and with such success that the French mission attached to the Corps actually started off ahead for Cassel to secure for themselves comfortable billets after the manner of their kind. It may be added that several days elapsed before they discovered that the Canadian Corps had not gone to Cassel.

When the move commenced, all columns marched west: under sealed orders to be handed to them by Road Control when they reached St. Pol, which was on the trunk road leading north and south. On their arrival there, to their astonishment, they were turned south instead of north. From then on, they moved in a maze of mystification that took many of them as far as Abbeville.

On the night of August 4–5, the guns were got into position and camouflaged. During the next few days, the gun pits were filled with ammunition, the tanks nosed like great beasts of prey into the corners prepared for them, the engineers—that brave band of fellows whose story is one long tale of heroic adventure—moved up their pontoons, and everything humanly possible was done to prepare for the great day.

Meantime, back in the forest around Boves were massed troops of every sort. The weather was hot with occasional showers of rain; the nights were moonless. Visibility was very poor for the great part of the time: light fog or haze all day long. That alone made possible the movement of troops on such a large scale.

So much moving about had been necessary that it was feared that the enemy had become suspicious of what was pending. But as far as possible every emergency was planned for. It was even arranged that if, during the night of August 7, the enemy got suspicious and laid down a heavy barrage on our infantry—massed in the front line trenches and ready to go "over the top"—the battle should begin at once. If the enemy anticipated our barrage, the church bells would begin to ring and this would be taken as the zero hour signal. Then our barrage would be laid down, the tanks would uncover and get on the move, and the Infantry would go "over the top."

That the enemy was nervous was evident to all who used the roads that night. But no serious happening suggested that he was aware of what was "to be served for breakfast."

Chapter 29

THE TURN OF THE TIDE

Whindrive a wedge between the British and the French armies. But in modern warfare, where mighty howitzers can hurl their shells a distance of twelve miles and drop four out of five of them practically into the same hole, the driving of wedges is a very dangerous business.

The Germans halted their advance towards Amiens in order to consolidate their position and make it secure. Then the French struck. In the southern corner of the salient, where the bend came in the enemy's new line, stood Reims. From Reims the French pushed out in the direction of Soissons, and forced the enemy to defend in strength this exposed southern flank. The German Staff did not know what was to happen next. Would the Allies apply the pinchers—attack from the north as well as from the south, in an effort to squeeze him out of the salient? The 2nd Canadian Division, under VI Corps, south of Albert, had been making raid after raid, and the Third Army was a constant menace to the success of the German push. The obvious thing to expect was a thrust through, by Albert. That would imperil communications and force the enemy to retire to his old line.

But the German Intelligence was completely deceived. They were taken utterly by surprise when, instead of attacking from the side, an irresistible assault was made on the very nose of his salient. The manoeuvre was daringly conceived and brilliantly carried out. It turned the tide of battle. When the Allied barrage came down at

4:20 AM on August 8, the last phase of the War was ushered in. Thenceforward, the enemy faced certain defeat. He never again assumed the offensive, but dropped back on every front till his troops were pushed beyond the Rhine.

The Canadian Corps was in the centre of the attack; on their right, the First French Army, which for the time being was under Field Marshal Sir Douglas Haig's command; on their left, the Australian Corps; and beyond the Australians the III British Corps was to attack in the direction of Morlancourt. The entire front of the attack was approximately 20,000 yards, a little over eleven miles, and the Canadian Corps, in the centre, was responsible for 8,500 yards of that line. The French, being forced to advance over a flat plain that was under full observation from the high ground in front of them, refused to advance—wisely enough—without a preliminary barrage to neutralize the enemy's defence. They were willing, however, that the barrage should not begin until the zero hour came, and it was planned that they should go over the top forty-five minutes after the barrage had opened. The advance of all troops was to be synchronized with the advance of the Canadians.

In addition to the regular corps force, General Currie had command of the 3rd Cavalry Division, which included the Canadian Mounted Units, a tank brigade, and a squadron of the Royal Air Force. To assist the Cavalry and maintain communications, a cosmopolitan group of Cyclists,[1] motor machine guns and trench mortars set on motor lorries, was organized under Brigadier-General Brutinel[2] into one mobile unit known as the "Independent Force."

The plan of battle was the simple one of laying down an intense barrage and, under cover of that barrage, overrunning the enemy's forward area. The 3rd Canadian Division was on the right and in touch with the French; the 1st Division was in the centre and the 2nd on the left, both in liaison with the Australians. The attacking divisions would follow the barrage to the first objective some 3,600 yards in, then the reserve troops would pass through and carry on to the second objective supported by tanks, the Cavalry, and the Independent Force. Meantime, certain units of Artillery would be in close support, and immediately any battery that was out of range would move forward and be in readiness to barrage our infantry into their final objective.

The battle plan worked perfectly. In the mad hurley-burley that followed the opening guns at 4:20 AM, there was on our side confusion of noise only. But the

---

1   Canadian Cyclist Battalion.

2   Brigadier-General Raymond Brutinel, CB, CMG, DSO. General Officer Commanding Canadian Machine Gun Corps 1916–1919.

enemy was taken completely by surprise; his intelligence was deceived, his outposts were caught napping, his batteries were neutralized before they could fire a return shot. Simultaneously, the tanks and infantry moved to the attack. A brigade of field batteries, with huge trestles roped to their gun wagons to enable them to bridge trenches, followed in close support, using their guns to destroy nests of machine guns, clearing out clumps of forest at point-blank range, and doing all in their power to hurry the retreat of the foe. At the conclusion of the barrage, three other brigades limbered up and joined the infantry divisions, followed shortly by three mobile Heavy brigades. By night, ten brigades of field artillery and four brigades of heavies were deployed in close support. The engineers were ahead of them, throwing trestles over trenches and making roads ready.

Less than an hour after the attack was launched, prisoners began to pour down the road: pale, broken men, amazed at the suddenness of what had happened, fully aware that the end had come. All of them believed that the Canadians were at Kemmel. There were heavy casualties of course, especially among the Cavalry. With brilliant dash our troops did their work, and paid the penalty in losses. Advances in broad daylight against a desperate foe armed with machine guns are costly. Many men died, but by night more than a dozen villages were in our hands and our troops rested eight miles within the enemy's defence line. Every objective for the day had been taken except for Le Quesnel, where the enemy put up unexpected resistance behind the railroad track. The prisoners captured more than equalled the total of our casualties, and so many enemy batteries were seized that it was possible to organize two complete artillery brigades of enemy guns and put them in action against their late possessors. There had been detailed to each division nine officers and fifty gunners who accompanied the Infantry to man the enemy's guns and turn them on the German retreat. Excellent work was done. A total of twenty-six hostile guns were put in action, and 1,500 rounds were fired.

The French and Australians, on our right and left, had done brilliantly, though the French had met unexpected resistance and the Australians had been slightly held back on their left by difficulties encountered by the III Corps.

By dawn the next morning Le Quesnel had been taken and the advance went on, but the enemy's resistance had stiffened. During the night fresh enemy divisions had been rushed up from the rear, and the Corps Commander refused to expose his troops to needless losses. The kick-off did not come as early as was planned, and heavy machine gun fire had to be faced from the start. But the 3rd Division took Le

Quesnel and all its other objectives for the day, and helped the French take Arvillers. The 1st Division, with machine gun and field batteries in close support, and with twelve tanks to assist it, cleared Beaufort Wood and fought its way through to Rouvroy and Warvillers. The 2nd Division and the Australians had a bad time of it. The whole ground in front of them was studded with machine guns, and the enemy had a ravine and a railway embankment to cover the concentration of troops and to strengthen his defence. But one by one the defence posts were captured, and with many prisoners to their credit, the 2nd Division reached Meharicourt.

From the church tower in Rosières, observation officers recorded a complete train of enemy reinforcements captured by our cavalry. All night long great bursts of flame could be seen in the enemy's territory, indicating that he was destroying the ammunition he did not expect to use and burning the war material he would have no time to move.

The next morning the attack was carried on by the 3rd and 4th Divisions, on the right and left respectively. The 1st and 2nd Divisions were withdrawn into reserve. When the 3rd Division had captured Le Quesnoy, the 32nd (Imperial) Division passed through, while the 4th Division on the left was having desperate fighting. With an utter abandon of recklessness, individual men among the Germans were making a savage defence with machine guns. Even artillery was being brought up, and during the night a strong counterattack had to be beaten off. The 32nd Division was confronted with an old Roman defensive position, which the Germans had fortified strongly in 1916. From the crest of Zed Wood, and from the high ground on both sides of it, machine guns and artillery could sweep the open plateau that would need to be crossed if any frontal attack were to succeed. The 32nd Division made a gallant try for the position, but was met by a withering fire and suffered heavy casualties without getting any appreciable distance ahead.

The 3rd Canadian Division relieved them on the night of August 11–12. Meantime, our heavy howitzers, drawn by steam tractors, were getting into position. The medium heavy guns were made available for counter-battery work, and the 8-inch and 9.2-inch howitzers were ready for whatever would be required of them. Major-General Lipsett[3] decided that the best way to win his objectives was to work round from the left by Parvillers. Step by step his troops worked their way through intense enemy fire to the edge of Parvillers, beating off five counterattacks in the process, until by Wednesday 14 the time was ripe for an open attack.

---

3   GOC 3rd Canadian Division.

A heavy barrage was laid down at 6:15 PM, and the 7th Canadian Infantry Brigade stormed the village. With only five casualties Parvillers was taken, but at once there began a series of counterattacks in which the Princess Pats, on one occasion, found themselves beset from both front and rear, and, like a famous British regiment that wears its insignia both front and back, they formed fronts both ways and beat off the foe. Many prisoners were taken and large numbers of the enemy were killed.

At Damery, three quarters of a mile to the south, equally thrilling things were happening. The 9th Infantry Brigade, after proper reconnaissance, put on a sharp and sudden attack, and took Damery almost without resistance. Lieutenant-Colonel Foster, the Commander of the 52nd Battalion, which made the capture, suspected a trap and withdrew his troops to the flank. Almost immediately a fearfully heavy barrage fell on the village, and then dense columns of troops, wave on wave, followed to attack. Our artillery caught them in the very centre of their massed advance, and our infantry poured machine gun and rifle fire into them at point-blank range. Only a few reached the village, to die on our bayonet points. The dead numbered more than a thousand. About 250 were taken prisoner. Again, in the afternoon, a second attack was made, with further loss to the enemy.

That night, and the succeeding one, the 1st Division relieved the 3rd, and the 4th relieved the 2nd. A few minor operations resulted in a straightening of the line and the securing of more advantageous positions. But, apart from the capture of Fransart by the 2nd Division, assisted by the French, most of the Corps' work consisted in beating off enemy counterattacks and in consolidating the position until they were finally withdrawn.

The fourteen days' operations of the Canadian Corps had resulted in the capture of more than nine thousand prisoners, 190 guns of all calibres, and more than a thousand machine guns and trench mortars. Twenty-seven towns and villages had been liberated. The deepest penetration was about fourteen miles: sufficient to secure the Paris–Amiens railway from interference and to dissipate the danger of dividing the French and British armies.

Between August 8 and 22 a total of 409,838 shells had been fired, and 11,822 casualties had been sustained, nearly 600 of which were officers. The operations had been costly, but they had turned the tide of battle, and had given opportunities, such as had never occurred before, for the display of individual initiative and individual courage.

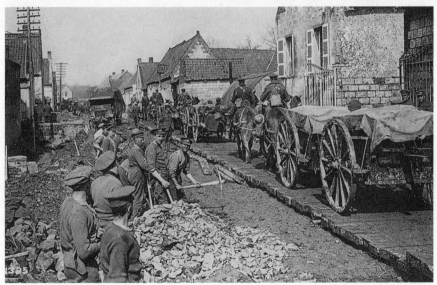

TOP Somme field kitchen. woD

BOTTOM Bringing up supplies for Vimy on plank road. woD

TOP Siege gun being loaded. wod

BOTTOM, LEFT Passchendaele, Belgium, general view. wod

BOTTOM, RIGHT The Menin Road. wod

TOP Morrison Artillery and Railway and Staffs, Passchendaele, November 1917. *Front row (L to R)*: Capt. Herbert Fripp, Maj. Andrew McNaughton, Brig.-Gen. Edward Morrison, Maj. Alan Brooke, Capt. Lawrence Cosgrave. LIBRARY AND ARCHIVES CANADA

BOTTOM, LEFT General Julian Byng. LAC, PA-001284

BOTTOM, RIGHT Mules transporting artillery shells. WOD

TOP Cathedral in Denain, France. *(L to R)* Gen. Arthur Currie, ʜʀʜ The Prince of Wales, Maj.-Gen. Edward Morrison, Maj.-Gen. David Watson. ᴡᴏᴅ

BOTTOM Armistice Day, November 11, 1918, in the square in Mons, Belgium. Lt.-Gen. Currie saluting; Maj.-Gen. Edward Morrison is the 4th right of Currie, Maj. Lawrence Cosgrave beside Morrison to left. ʟᴀᴄ, ᴘᴀ-003524

OPPOSITE, MIDDLE BOTTOM Canadian howitzer, Bonn, Germany, 1919. wod

OPPOSITE, BOTTOM Generals Currie and Morrison ride to the Rhine. lac, pa-003642

TOP, LEFT Canadian soldiers with German POWs. WOD

TOP, RIGHT Aerial view, Canals Sensée and du Nord. WOD

MIDDLE, LEFT Funeral of Lieutenant-Colonel John McCrae, attended by hundreds, Wimereux, France, January 29, 1918. Major-General Morrison and Lieutenant-General Arthur Currie stand beside McCrae's horse, Bonfire. GUELPH MUSEUMS

MIDDLE, RIGHT Cambrai burning as Canadian troops enter. LAC, PA-040229

BOTTOM, LEFT January 1919. *Front row (L to R):* Capt. Fripp, Lt.-Col. Crerar, Maj-.Gen. Morrison, unknown, Maj. Cosgrave. LAC, PA-003965

BOTTOM, RIGHT Bonn, Germany, 1919. *Front row (L to R):* Capt. Herbert Downing Fripp, Lt.-Col. Harry Crerar, Maj. Gen. Edward Morrison, Maj. Donald Alexander White, and (likely) Capt. Wilfred Josiah Finney. WOD

Chapter 30

THE CAPTURE OF
MONCHY-LE-PREUX

On August 21 the Canadian Corps handed over its positions in front of Amiens and moved rapidly north by way of Hautecloque, preceded by the 2nd and 3rd Divisions and followed by the 1st and 4th, with all Canadian Field Artillery. On August 23 it took over the front east of Arras, from the Scarpe River south to Neuville-Vitasse. Shortly it became known that the Corps was to attack and capture Orange Hill, an intermediate ridge about four miles east of Arras and west of the dominating height of Monchy-le-Preux. The XVII Corps was relieved and handed over nine brigades of field artillery and seven brigades of heavy artillery. It was another rush operation.

A corps conference was held on the night of August 22 at Hautecloque and the general opinion was expressed that the Corps might as well take Orange Hill and Monchy-le-Preux at the same time instead of making two operations of it as the Army seemed to propose. Artillery and ammunition were rapidly got into position and the attack planned much on the lines of the Amiens battle. The 2nd Division attacked on the right, from Neuville-Vitasse to the Arras–Cambrai Road, supported by seven brigades of field artillery. The 3rd Division attacked on the left, from the Cambrai Road to the Scarpe, also with seven field brigades. There were nine brigades of heavies. To the north of the Scarpe, the 51st Highland Division was to make a feint attack and prolong the barrage. As a matter of fact, though this fine division was very weak in numbers, it turned the feint into a real attack and captured Mount Pleasant, thereby considerably strengthening our left.

As in the Battle of Amiens, the plan of which had been adopted as a sort of "sealed pattern," the Infantry were to go forward under a barrage as far as possible, then four brigades of field artillery were to advance in close support of the Infantry, followed by two mobile brigades and a general advance to the Infantry reinforcements and reserve Artillery.

It was found that the "rolling" barrage would reach to the outskirts of Monchy, and it was decided that the first objective should be the eastern slope of Orange Hill where there would be a fifteen-minute rest to enable the troops to size up the situation before pressing on against the chief objective. Monchy was a hill of considerable prominence, on the top of which were the ruins of the town and a ragged fringe of bristling tree trunks that had once been thick wood. The Germans had held it from 1914 until April 1917, when it was captured by the British and retained for a year. During the German Spring Offensive it had in some unaccountable manner been given up by the XVII Corps without an attack, an action that nearly caused the fall of Arras at that time. The height not only dominated the city of Arras but the southern half of Vimy Ridge and the country behind it, affording very valuable observation to the enemy. It was extremely important that Monchy should be captured as a preliminary to any further operations on the Arras or Vimy fronts. In fact the subject of its capture had been mooted and some preparations had been made before the departure of the Corps for Amiens; therefore, though the notice was very short, our infantry and artillery knew the ground well and were quite prepared to take it on.

The attack was fixed for 3:00 AM as there was a waning moon, the weather was bright, and it was not considered that the enemy would be standing until dawn. For the attack no tanks were available, so that the Infantry depended entirely on the Artillery barrage. The two divisions of the Canadian Corps went through to their first objective on scheduled time and with comparatively slight loss. They paused there for fifteen minutes, and when the barrage resumed, they swarmed up the height into Monchy and before 8:00 AM had captured the height and were soon in the trenches beyond it, while the right division had taken Neuville-Vitasse, Wancourt and Guemappe.

This was a brilliant affair and the success was quite unexpected on the part of GHQ (General Headquarters) where it was expected that the redoubtable Monchy, which had proved such an obstacle in the spring of 1917, would require a second operation. All the enemy's guns in the area were captured along with about five thousand prisoners. Monchy was not only taken but held against all counterattacks, which were easily beaten off by our artillery with heavy loss to the enemy; the most important of these came from the northeast in the direction of Pelves. Before the night of August 26 our foremost troops were on the outskirts of the Bois du Sart.

The Commander-in-Chief[1] immediately decided to push the Canadian Corps on to smash the famous Drocourt–Quéant Line, which had so far resisted all efforts. It extended between the points named and consisted of a series of trenches, tunnels, and deep dugouts. These were heavily wired and defended in front by three extensive belts of wire about 40 yards in width and each 100 yards from the next belt. In order to prepare the Corps for this work, the Artillery was reinforced to a strength of twenty-two brigades of field and ten brigades of heavy guns—also, later on, by the 4th Imperial Division. Before the latter came into the line, the indomitable 51st Division, notwithstanding that most of its battalions were reduced in strength to under four hundred, gamely pushed forward and, by a series of minor operations, captured Greenland Hill: high ground north of the River Scarpe which overlooked our flank.

In order to secure a good jumping-off line the Canadian Corps had to advance 7,000 yards in a constantly widening front. On August 27 the VIII Corps on the north took over the line to the Scarpe. At midnight on August 28, the 1st Canadian Division relieved the 2nd on the right after the latter, by a hard day's fighting, had reached to Union Trench, south of Vis-en-Artois, capturing Chérisy on the way. The 3rd Division captured Remy Wood, Boiry-Notre-Dame, and Jigsaw Wood. This division was then relieved by the 4th Imperial Division on the left, the 4th Canadian Division being in close support. The position was then so favourable that the Heavy Artillery commenced cutting the wire on the Drocourt–Quéant Line, which it continued doing until the evening of September 1, when, with the later assistance of the Field Artillery, the lanes in the wire were reported sufficient for the attacking troops. All this had to be done with aerial observation and photographs, and was made more difficult by the fact that portions of the Heavy Artillery were repeatedly called off the work to support the numerous minor operations which preceded the capture of the jumping-off line.

On account of the constant widening of our front due to the advance on the Cambrai Road, our left flank was taken over, on August 30 at 6:00 AM, from the River Scarpe to Boiry, by the 11th Imperial Division. It was decided also that the 4th Canadian Division would push in astride of the Cambrai Road, for the 4th Imperial Division appeared to be exhausted and the Commanding Officer and his staff

---

1 Field Marshal Haig.

were not sanguine as to the success of their task. They remained in for the eventual attack, but the brunt of the operation fell upon the 1st and 4th Canadian Divisions. On August 31, the 1st Imperial Division was brought up in close support of the 4th Canadian Division.

From August 30 to September 1 there was heavy fighting all along the front. On August 31 the right division captured Ocean Work and extended its front line to an average depth of 1,000 yards, having already taken Upton Wood. On September 1 the Germans counterattacked our extreme right, but were driven back with heavy casualties and the loss of a hundred prisoners. Haucourt and St. Servins Farm gave a good deal of difficulty on the centre, while Eterpigny held the 4th Imperial Division up until shortly before the zero hour. The Crow's Nest, on a long ridge full of deep pits on the extreme right of the right division, was one of the last places secured before the day of the attack. All this preliminary fighting was very trying on the troops, but it was necessary to secure a line from which they could be barraged across the Drocourt–Quéant defences on the day of the battle.

In preparing the "rolling barrage" for the battle of September 2, the unusual experience was encountered of preparing a barrage map on August 31 for a jumping-off line that was not actually in our hands until the following evening. This was facilitated by the fact that the Infantry were not so anxious regarding the barrage as in any former battle, and even at the last moment asked to have it cut down in depth, to considerably less than the Artillery would put on. Our guns, both field and medium, had been constantly pushed forward since the beginning of the Monchy operation, so that even the medium howitzer batteries averaged 3,500 yards from the front line and the field batteries under 2,000 yards at the conclusion of the preliminary operations. The Infantry had formed such a high opinion of the tanks at the Battle of Amiens that they seemed to put their faith in them and a less than usual dependence on the barrage, forgetting that there was only one tank to 100 yards of front, and that they were not mechanically as fit as they were on the former occasion. This no doubt had its effect in the later battle. At midnight on September 1 all was ready for the attack on the redoubtable Drocourt–Quéant Line, the wire being reported to be well cut where required, the barrage ready to put on, and plenty of ammunition with the guns.

Chapter 31

SMASHING HINDENBURG

The order of battle on the morning of September 2 was as follows: the 1st Division on the right from Hendecourt-les-Cagnicourt half way to the Cambrai Road; the 4th Canadian Division extending the line 2,000 yards north of the Cambrai Road; and the 4th Imperial Division about 1,700 yards north of that. On the right the XVII Corps was to barrage and attack as a demonstration, with the exception that the 63rd Naval Division in reserve was to pass forward in rear of our right after the Drocourt Line had been pierced and turn south, taking the Drocourt Line in reverse and enabling the 57th and 52nd Divisions of the XVII Corps to break through. To the north of the Canadian Corps the 11th Imperial Division was to make a flank to the north once the Canadian Corps had pierced the line. The 1st and 4th Canadian Divisions were to spread out after the line was pierced and the 4th Imperial Division was to prolong the northern flank from where the 11th Division left off, leaving the Canadian troops free to make a dash for the Canal du Nord, which was the ultimate objective. On the Cambrai Road a force of armoured cars, preceded by one and a half regiments of cavalry, was to make a dash and endeavour to seize the bridge across the canal at Sans-lez-Marquion.

Zero hour was fixed for 5:00 AM. The weather was clear at the commencement but turned to rain by 7:00 AM, the rest of the day being bright and warm with occasional thunderstorms. The Artillery's arrangements were similar to those at Amiens and Monchy, except that on the close of the barrage, four field brigades and a mobile

Heavy brigade followed each division in close support, while the remainder of the Heavy Artillery put on a coarse barrage, in jumps of 1,000 yards, from the first objective to beyond the Canal du Nord. This "coarse" barrage was necessitated by the proposed rapid advance of the Cavalry and the Armoured Cars, and was intended to assist the Infantry advance after the Drocourt Line had been smashed. In addition to this, a lane 1,000 yards wide was left untouched along the Cambrai Road to further facilitate the proposed advance of the Armoured Cars and Cavalry. It is pertinent to mention at this point that the restrictive depth of the rolling barrage and the limiting of the heavy guns to the coarse barrage definitely affected the full results in gathering in the fruits of probably the greatest success the Corps had ever achieved.

The attack was launched at Zero and progressed under the barrage to the first objective with the wonderful success that so often carried the Canadian Corps to victory. At the narrowest part the barrage was barely 2,000 yards in depth and its widest under 3,000. The minimum depth of barrage heretofore had been 3,500.

Great was the jubilation when the contact aeroplanes brought back word, shortly after 7:00 AM, that the hitherto impregnable Drocourt Line had been smashed on a front of 8,000 yards, and that our infantry, with the exception of a small part of the 4th Imperial Division Front, were resting on the first objective beyond Dury. There the following barrage was to rest half an hour to allow the Infantry to dress their line, and then to lift entirely. From that forward the Infantry were to rely on tanks, motor machine guns, cavalry, and the "coarse" heavy barrage already referred to, for an advance of 7,000 yards across an undulating country, chiefly open, but with woods and villages sprinkled here and there. The early reports said that the losses had been light and that the prisoners were coming back in shoals, which subsequently proved to be true, as they finally amounted to over five thousand for that particular operation.

Further news was confidently awaited. The great task of the day had been completed with dash and brilliancy and it was confidently expected that the advance to the canal would be the finale of Canada's greatest victory in the War. At Headquarters the officers, who had been up since before dawn, went to breakfast in great spirits and returned expectantly to their telephones to receive the later good news. Already the task set had been splendidly performed and it only remained to gather the fruits of the victory. It was jubilantly recalled that in anticipation of this success, our long-range guns were steadily shelling the brigades along the whole front of the canal with shrapnel to intercept reinforcements and to prevent guns and fugitives from escaping beyond the canal.

But the news rather dragged. Hours passed without any definite information. About 10:00 AM, it became known that the Cavalry and the Motor Machine Gun Brigade had been held up 2,000 yards beyond the Drocourt Line, and that our troops were having heavy fighting on the Red Objective,[1] being opposed by innumerable machine guns. The Field Guns had gone forward with great dash and taken up positions in close support of the Infantry; the mobile Heavy brigades had also got well up. Earlier reports had stated that the enemy had put down his barrage one minute after Zero but without inflicting much damage. The counter-batteries failed to stop his barrage for a short time as it was found that many batteries had moved back during the night, but their positions were rapidly picked up by aeroplanes and within half an hour from Zero the enemy's Artillery was entirely under control.

Finally, movement was reported on our right: Cagnicourt and Villers-lez-Cagnicourt were captured; Hendecourt was taken; and the line extended forward to Bois de Bouche. Later in the afternoon the 63rd Naval Division was reported south of the railway, 2,000 yards southeast of Buissy. Still, the central division remained held up and the left (4th Imperial Division) was not yet on the Red Line. On our extreme left, Étaing was still in the enemy's possession. Towards evening the right division pushed on to the outskirts of Buissy and got in touch with other troops from the direction of Villers-lez-Cagnicourt, but failed to find the 63rd Naval Division on their right where they had been reported to be waiting to join up. The latter had not turned south along the Drocourt Line in front of the XVII Corps, whose 57th and 52nd Divisions reported the Drocourt Line held on their front, and got no farther that night. The 4th Division had fought hard all day without getting forward and reported heavy casualties, while the right division had made its advance possible by capturing nests of machine guns at the point of the bayonet. One of these nests contained no less than fifteen guns. When evening closed down, it was realized that, notwithstanding our success of achieving the main object of the attack, we had failed to cut off the enemy from crossing the Canal du Nord.

Later the news of what had happened was obtained. As soon as the rolling barrage had lifted, the 1st and 4th Canadian Divisions had pushed forward and were immediately met by heavy machine gun fire all along the front. The Independent Force of Cavalry and Motor Machine Guns had pushed down the Cambrai Road

---

1   The Red Objective, or Red Line, was the first objective of the battle, followed by the Green and Blue Lines, or Objectives.

gallantly, but at a large group of buildings collectively called the Factory they were brought to a stop by machine gun fire followed soon after by considerable artillery fire. The 10th Hussars retired precipitately without casualties, but the Machine Gunners attempted to push on and were met by German artillery fire at almost point-blank range. Five of our six armoured motors were smashed into scrap iron but the remainder of the force took cover in the Factory and along the Cambrai Road, and grimly hung on to the positions all day, suffering heavy casualties and inflicting losses on the enemy. On our centre division front our men had made gallant attempts to force their way forward against lines of machine guns, and only increased their losses by their determination to get forward. The 4th Imperial Division was barely holding its own, with its back to the Drocourt Line. On the right, matters had gone much better, and by skillfully avoiding the strong points, and manoeuvring the enemy out of his positions, the 1st Division had penetrated almost to the canal by nightfall.

Our heavy artillery and counter-batteries had been seriously handicapped by the optimism that had governed the settling of the coarse barrage already mentioned. By this barrage, the Heavy Artillery was debarred from using any unobserved fire west of each successive line, so that by midday they were shooting 1,000 yards beyond the canal and could not be ordered to draw in their fire until the situation was cleared up. Incidentally, this had stopped all counter-battery work west of the canal, and accounted for the batteries that had been silenced in the earlier part of the day being manned again and opening on the Infantry. On the other hand, the Heavy brigades with the Infantry, having no counter-battery information, and being intended solely for shooting up strong points and roads and otherwise helping the Infantry by close support, were unable to do any counter-battery work. In other words, the main force of the Heavy Artillery was neutralized until the situation in front of the Red Line could be cleared up, as a result of the arrangements made to allow the Cavalry and Motor Machine Guns to go forward. The situation when the Infantry was held up, as already described, was as if the heavy artillery barrage had "run away from them" and, like an ordinary creeping barrage, could not be brought back over the same ground until the situation was cleared up. This did occur later in the day, and counter-battery work was resumed, much to the relief of our troops.

That night the Corps Commander decided to bring all the Artillery under corps control in the morning, inaugurate a rolling barrage in front of the Infantry, and make a new attack on our final objective, namely, the Canal du Nord. A conference of commanding officers and their staffs was called for 9:00 AM and arrangements were made to put on the barrage, but the consensus of opinion seemed to be that the troops had suffered so heavily, and were so tired, that they were not in shape to make another attack immediately unless rested or relieved. Before the conference was over the news commenced to arrive that the enemy had been so alarmed at the break through the Drocourt Line that they had retired precipitately on the whole front, from the Scarpe to Péronne. This simplified the situation. Strong patrols were sent out on our front and by noon we held the whole area to the canal bank, from Palluel to Inchy-en-Artois.

On September 3 and 4 the 1st and 4th Canadian Divisions were relieved by the 2nd and 3rd respectively, and for the time being the Corps halted, holding the line of the canal. We had captured eighty-nine guns and about twelve thousand prisoners since August 26.

Two days later, Sir Noel Birch,[2] Chief of Artillery for Field Marshal Sir Douglas Haig, addressed the following letter to Major-General E.W. Alexander, VC,[3] Chief of Artillery for the First Army, of which the Canadian Corps at this time was a part. General Alexander forwarded a copy to me, knowing that I would be pleased with the high praise it contained for my own particular branch of the service.

Copy

General Headquarters
British Armies in France

October 6, 1918

My dear Alexander:

I don't want to trouble you about this until things slacken a bit, but I think for the sake of the Regiment we ought to have some record of the movements of the Artillery in the taking of the Hindenburg Line. I think you will agree with me when I say that it is one of the greatest performances that the Artillery have done in this war, if not the greatest. It is also extraordinarily interesting from a tactical point of view, as the taking of one part of the line made the next possible.

---

2   Major-General (later General) Sir James Frederick Noel Birch, GBE, KCB, KCMG, Major-General Royal Artillery General Headquarters (France) 1916–1918.

3   Major-General Ernest Wright Alexander, VC, CB, CMG, Major-General Royal Artillery First Army from April 9, 1918, to the Armistice. He was awarded the VC in 1914 for saving his guns and rescuing a wounded man under fire.

It would be very good of you when your staff has time to let one of them put on a map the sequence of the moves of your artillery, beginning on the 27th of September up to the 4th October inclusive. Of course the maps will bear no sort of detail. Just a ring round to say where Field or Heavy Artillery were on a certain day and where they moved to the next day, or where some of them moved to. I then propose having a map made out of the whole of the Artillery moves in the three Armies.

As you know, the Hindenburg Line was constructed to defeat the British Artillery and I think the way we defeated the Bosche over it will eventually be an interesting historical document.

(Sd) Thine,

Noel Birch

MAJOR-GENERAL E.W. ALEXANDER, VC, CMG

HEADQUARTERS R.A.

FIRST ARMY

Chapter 32

THE BATTLE OF BOURLON WOOD
AND THE CAPTURE OF CAMBRAI

On September 3, Corps Headquarters established itself on the recent battlefield southeast of Neuville-Vitasse. The holding line along the Canal du Nord was thinly occupied by the 2nd Canadian Division, from the Sensée River to Inchy exclusive. The enemy held the opposite side of the canal strongly with machine guns, and as the land on either side of the canal was wet and marshy, no serious effort was made to cross while our troops rested. Nearly fifty French inhabitants were rescued from the village of Escourt-St-Quentin, where they had hidden in the cellars during the enemy withdrawal. Some of them were wounded, and together with the sick had to be carried by our troops on stretchers for a long distance before they were out of range of the enemy.

As many artillery- and infantrymen as possible were withdrawn for a rest. Enemy aeroplanes dropped bombs by night and shot up the areas with long-range, high-velocity guns. Neither did much damage, except one shell which struck a trainload of troops in Arras Station, causing nearly a hundred casualties. About the same time, what was apparently a bomb from a British aeroplane dropped on a daylight parade of Canadian Machine Gun troops near Warlus, causing eighty-five casualties. A fuze picked up was of Vickers make, but how it came to drop was not discovered. The aeroplane must have been very high, as it was not seen.

About the third week in September orders were received that the Third Army would endeavour to capture Cambrai, and that the Canadian Corps was to operate on its left flank by taking a line running northwest from the famous Bourlon Wood. A few days later the objective was changed so as to include Bourlon Wood and Bourlon Village, thence northwest to Cisy-le-Verger. This was a very extensive but more satisfactory objective, because Bourlon Wood and Village dominated all the ground to the north, south, and west of it, and was really the key to Cambrai. Under the former scheme, had the Third Army failed to get Bourlon Wood, the Canadian line to the northwest would have become untenable. Under the new scheme the Canadian Corps was to take Bourlon Wood and the line already indicated, and then exploit its success in a north-easterly direction for about 17,000 yards, to the junction of the Sensée River and the Canal de l'Escaut.

This was not a very satisfactory proposition to the Canadians, as it meant that they were to capture the key to Cambrai and then sheer off and allow the other troops to secure the prize by entering the city. The XVII Corps was to play the same role as at the Battle of Drocourt by advancing under cover of our right wing until the main objective had been reached, then turning the Hindenburg Line, and passing a division down behind it, while two other divisions were to pass south of Bourlon Wood and, with the left of the Third Army, enter Cambrai. Correctly estimating the probable progress of the XVII Corps, General Currie had a tacit understanding that if the going was good and the Canadians were leading, they would take Cambrai before diverging to the northeast.

The Bourlon Wood position was an exceedingly strong one. At that point fierce fighting had taken place in November 1917 and it was by the failure to retain that commanding position that the ultimate objective was not reached in the gallant thrust made by General Byng on November 20–30. Especially for an attack from the west, the Bourlon Wood position was of formidable strength. Five thousand yards in front of the wood was the Canal du Nord, which we did not hold south of Marquion. On that front the canal was dry and its bottom was on the ground, level, so that the western bank was in the shape of a ramp sloping up to the western edge of the canal, while on the eastern side the top of the canal bank was level with the great hillside, which sloped starkly up to the edge of the wood that dominated the surrounding country for miles. In other words, Bourlon Wood and Village presented the appearance of a citadel with a huge glacis extending down to the west and north, with the canal a dry moat at the foot of it on the western side.

Additional difficulties were presented by the fact that the canal north of Marquion had water in it and the country on both sides of that was marshy and more or less heavily wooded. This necessitated the Canadian attack being launched on a narrow front of barely 2,500 yards between the Sains-lès-Marquion south. Consequently, the jumping-off line for the attack ranged from 300 to 750 yards from the canal, and the only means of judging what sort of obstacle the dry canal presented was with aeroplane photographs. The village of Moeuvres was nominally in the hands of the XVII Corps troops, but in reality only a part of it was held, and by posts who were being driven out and re-established from day to day. One day the Germans held it, and the next day the XVII Corps would claim to hold it. Neither side launched attacks of any consequence, so that the daily question as to who's Moeuvres it was became a recognized witticism over a period of ten days. The serious question was whether the enemy would be in possession of this village outflanking the Canadian jumping-off line when the zero hour arrived.

From an artillery standpoint the task before the Canadians presented very serious difficulties. In the first place, in order to put on a proper barrage it was necessary to concentrate twenty brigades of field artillery and ten brigades of heavy artillery on a front of 4,000 yards, and as close as possible to the jumping-off line in order that the barrage should "fan out" from an initial width of 3,500 yards to an ultimate width of nearly 9,000 yards at the final objective. In addition to this, the field guns could not reach the final objective of the division on the right, as it was out-ranged by about 2,000 yards. It was at first proposed that during the progress of the attack to the Red Line the engineers should construct crossing places in the dry canal, and that the Field Artillery should limber up and advance at a gallop through the canal to a position from which they could barrage the final objective east of Bourlon Wood. There were two almost insuperable objections to this: (1) that it would take at least three hours from Zero for the engineers to make the necessary crossings, which the enemy's fire might still further delay; and (2) it would be too long for the Infantry to wait on the Red Line, especially as the enemy had many batteries in folds of the glacis that could sweep the Red Line at close-range while the barrage halted. In addition to this, the batteries barraging the left division could barrage to the ultimate objective by using high-explosive shells in the final stages, and it was most desirable that the barrage should proceed without interruption throughout the whole front.

The attack was to be made by the 4th and 1st Canadian Divisions, and to be followed by the 3rd Canadian Division and 11th British Division. The Infantry plan was rendered very complicated by the nature of the ground. The 4th and 1st Divisions were to capture the ultimate objective from east of Bourlon Wood to a point 500 yards south of Sauchy-Lestrée on the left, about 1,000 yards east of the wet canal at that point. When this line had been reached, the 3rd Canadian Division was to pass through the 4th and take on the right flank, resting on the Bapaume–Cambrai Road while the 4th Division narrowed its front and became the right centre division. At the same time, the 11th Imperial Division was to cross the Sains-lès-Marquion, follow in the steps of the 1st Division on the left, and take over 3,000 yards of the line from the extreme left of that division at the ultimate objective, thus placing the 1st Division on the left centre.

If the ultimate objective of the Corps was reached on time, the 3rd Division was to push on towards Cambrai, the 4th Division to capture Raillencourt, the 1st Division to capture Haynecourt, and the 11th Imperial Division was to send one brigade northeast to capture Épincy and another brigade north to capture Oisy-le-Verger. For one day's work it was the most extensive task the Corps had ever been given, and the artillery arrangements rendered necessary were most complicated.

The problem on the right already described was solved in this manner: the portion of the barrage on the 4th Division front required six brigades as far as the Red Line, and from there eight brigades to the Green and Blue Lines. For this task, ten brigades were allotted. On Y/Z[1] night the brigades normally holding the line had to be relieved in order to occupy close battle positions, which had been prepared for them and stocked with ammunition. The defence of the line for that night was taken up by six brigades, which unlimbered 3,000 yards in rear of the front line. The rest of the battle positions on that front were from 1,500 to 2,000 yards from the line, in order to secure the maximum range for barrage purposes.

The following complicated solution was then worked out: from Zero to Zero plus 131,[2] six brigades would participate in the barrage to the Red Line. At Zero the other four brigades were to limber up and advance to the canal following the Infantry. From that point they could just put on the standing barrage at the final objective. These brigades at the canal, plus four of the other brigades, would then continue the barrage to the Green Line, which included Bourlon Village but just reached the western edge of Bourlon Wood. During the second phase, which would take sixty-seven minutes to reach the Green Line, two of the rearmost brigades were to limber up and

---

1   I.e., the night before the attack.

2   I.e., 131 minutes after Zero.

advance to the canal, making six brigades, all of which should fire from the Green Line to the final objective.

It had been decided that the Infantry should not pass through Bourlon Wood, as it had been heavily gassed for five nights previous, so that all that was necessary in front of the wood was a standing barrage by two brigades that would remain on while the other six completed the operation. Accordingly, two of the rear brigades were able to put on the standing barrage while the six brigades at the canal carried the barrage on both sides of the wood from the canal. This arrangement was so complicated that it had to be carried out perfectly without the slightest hitch.

In the afternoon, during the second phase of the battle, further to exploit the success by taking on the line of villages already mentioned, the twenty brigades of field artillery were divided up and placed under divisional control. The 3rd CDA and three additional brigades were allotted to the 3rd Division; the 4th CDA and the 2nd CDA to the 4th Division; the 1st and 5th CDAs to the 1st Division. Four army brigades were detailed to the 11th Imperial Division, which, with its own DA, made six brigades. By 12:20 PM the Corps' barrage was complete and all the Artillery, less three brigades, limbered up and advanced to close support of the divisions on the new line for the second phase. The 11th Imperial Division had to have two barrages: one in the direction of Épinoy and one in the direction of Oisy-le-Verger. In order to help out the latter attack, the 11 Corps put on an enfilade barrage from the northwest to the east of the canal, protecting the flank and front of the brigade attacking Oisy-le-Verger, whose left flank was nearly 2,000 yards east of the canal along an area that had not yet been mopped up.

This was a particularly good piece of Artillery coordination, as the enfilade barrage had to precede the advance of the 11th Division left brigade by 500 yards so as not to enfilade the advancing line with any long shooting, while the Infantry advanced immediately under its own parallel barrage, thus making a sort of "tartan" pattern of fire. This also worked out perfectly. By nightfall[3] the 11th Division had both its objectives: the 1st Division had Haynecourt, the 4th Division had made good progress towards Raillencourt, and the 3rd had captured Fontaine, southeast of Bourlon Wood (which was properly the objective of the Corps on our right, but which they had not reached), and was well started in the direction of Cambrai, two miles farther on.

---

3   On September 27, 1918.

The XVII Corps was held up at Graincourt-lés-Havrincourt and practically did not get any farther that day, so that the Canadians were well ahead of them in the race for Cambrai.

Another interesting phase of the artillery battle was the institution for the first time of what was practically a heavy artillery rolling barrage. It had been found in previous experience that when corps control[4] devolved on the divisions at the conclusion of the set barrage, the advance of the Infantry "into the blue" more or less blanketed the long-range fire of the Heavies. During the Drocourt operation, an attempt was made to get over this difficulty by drawing lines 1,000 yards apart across the front, marking the limits within which the Heavies could fire without danger to the Infantry as the line advanced "into the blue," which line was marked: "no fire west of this line after Zero plus—."

What happened in that operation was that, almost immediately after the Infantry emerged from the set piece barrage, it was held up all along the line by enemy machine guns. It was several hours before the position of the Infantry became clear, and in the meantime the fire of the Heavies had steadily moved farther away, leaving a large space in front of the Infantry that was not being dealt with by the counter-batteries. Within this space the enemy batteries that were not adequately dealt with by the divisional artilleries came to life again.

In the Bourlon operation I had a clear rolling barrage on a large scale drawn up by the Counter-Battery Officer in conjunction with the Infantry staff officers, the lines conforming to the expected pace of the advancing battalions, going slower where there was difficult ground and more rapidly where no obstacles were anticipated, the lifts being timed after the manner of a field gun barrage but on a larger scale. This gave the Heavy Artillery a much freer hand and also enabled the Infantry to know exactly where to anticipate the fire of our own Heavies. It also made it possible, in the event of a general hold-up much as had occurred in the Drocourt operation, to have the heavy-safety area exactly delimited to suit the positions reached by the Infantry. This innovation was also a great success.

On September 28 the advance continued on the right, but rather slowly on the left. The 4th Division completed the capture of Raillencourt. The Marcoing Line

4   "Corps control" meant that all guns (including divisional artilleries) were controlled directly by Corps Artillery HQ. Under division control, each Division Artillery HQ controlled all guns allocated to it without reference to Corps HQ. Corps control achieved better concentration of fire, but was less flexible when divisions were moving.

proved a fairly strong obstacle, and during September 29 and 30 there was considerable fighting, each division engaging the enemy more or less independently on its own front. By September 29 the 3rd Division had secured Saint-Olle, but was denied entrance to Cambrai by severe machine gun fire from the canal.[5] By the morning of September 30 the 3rd Division had secured Tilloy, and the 4th and 1st had reached the line of the Cambrai–Douai Railway, but had been driven back across it at Belcourt and other points until at noon the line of the three Canadian divisions extended roughly from the railway southeast of Tilloy, through Tilloy, Rancourt, and a point on the road immediately east of Epinoy. All the Artillery was then placed under corps control and it was decided to put on a coordinated corps barrage eastward from that line to a line running from Ramillies through Cuvillers, Bantigny, and north of Abancourt. The 11th Division was to put on its own barrage in a northerly direction to gain the high ground in the direction of Fressies.

This coordinated corps attack was put on at 5:00 AM,[6] with one of the heaviest barrages that we had ever used. There were a total of 780 guns of all calibres. On the front of the 3rd Canadian Division there was a field gun to every 25 yards, with a hundred 4.5-inch howitzers superimposed on strong points. This was preceded at 500 yards' distance by a rolling barrage of over a hundred heavy howitzers. The counterbattery groups, composed chiefly of 60-pounders, took on the approaches from the rear to deal with reinforcements coming up, while twenty heavy howitzers walked up and down the canal, which runs northeast from Cambrai parallel to our flank. It was the intention to secure the final objective and then have the 2nd Division, which had hitherto in these operations been kept in reserve, follow on in rear and swing to the southeast to force the canal crossings in the rear of Cambrai.

This attack practically reached its final objective but failed to mop up Belcourt Village in the centre, where a nest of the enemy subsequently held on throughout the day. But no sooner had the barrage lifted than the enemy counterattacked in great force, and there ensued one of the heaviest days of fighting the Corps had ever experienced. Enemy reinforcements poured steadily down from the junction of the Sensée River and the Canal de l'Escaut until the elements of at least ten divisions were identified on our front during the course of the day. It subsequently appeared that the Germans had decided to smash our line at 5:30 that morning with an overwhelming force, so that the attacks collided and, luckily for us, the initial assembly of the

---

5   The Canal de l'Escaut on the west side of Cambrai.
6   October 1, 1918.

enemy came under our rolling barrage. The day was fine, and our aeroplane observers had good visibility, so that they were able to turn the Heavies on to over 150 targets in the course of the fighting, while the Field Guns and 60-pounder Batteries got at their reinforcements continuously over the open sights.

Counterattack followed counterattack until late in the afternoon. The line swayed back and forth throughout the day, and while our losses were considerable, those of the Germans must have been extremely heavy. By three in the afternoon our guns were beginning to run short of ammunition, notwithstanding the most energetic efforts to keep it up. Most of the field brigades late in the afternoon had no ammunition left except that carried in their limbers, and the Heavies were rather in a bad way. The situation became so acute that the First Army dispatched a hundred lorry loads of heavy and field ammunition, direct from the army dumps, to supplement the regular flow of ammunition to the batteries. This arrived in time to replenish the gun dumps by nightfall, by which time the last desperate counterattack of the enemy had been thrown back.

Our line had been bulged in somewhat but never broken. At nightfall, the 3rd Division had practically all the high ground it had captured in the morning up to 1,000 yards west of Raillencourt, and commanded observation of all the eastern and northeastern exits from Cambrai. Elements of the 4th Division held the practice trenches southeast of Cuvillers, and from there the line bent back immediately west of Belcourt Village and Abancourt Station, thence following the line of the railway northwest to a point 500 yards south of Aubencheul-au-Bac. It had been a day of Homeric combat, especially on the front of the 3rd Canadian Division, which held up the attack of more than three times their number. From 5:00 PM onward throughout the night the enemy was quiet. As a precaution we put on a moderate counter-preparation at dusk and a heavy counter-preparation just before dawn, and, from the excessive number of signal rockets the enemy put up in response, he anticipated an attack from us, but his retaliation was feeble.

Our infantry was so exhausted after seven days of continuous fighting that it was decided to relieve the 1st and 4th Divisions and put the 2nd Division in the line. The next day passed off quietly except for a stiff counterattack in the evening by the enemy to endeavour to retake the high ground we had secured on the right, which commanded the exits from Cambrai. Warning of this attack was given by a deserter, therefore the Gunners were ready for it, lanyard in hand, and the assaulting troops were practically wiped out before they reached our line.

During these operations, from September 27 to October 2, the Corps had captured over two hundred guns, half of them heavy howitzers, and seven thousand prisoners, besides killing more of the enemy on the first day than on any other day in the War.

From October 3 to 8 the Canadian Corps marked time, waiting for the XVII Corps on the right to come up abreast. The 3rd Canadian Division still held the western and northern outskirts of Cambrai and the 2nd Division prolonged the line to the north of Abancourt. The 11th Imperial Division, with a refused flank, was north of that—towards the Sensée River. The latter division, under Brigadier-General Winter,[7] the C.R.A. who was acting in command, did very good work throughout these operations.

On October 7 and 8 the XVII Corps was fighting its way forward but was sheering off towards the southeast of Cambrai. By the latter date it held Niergnies, two miles south of Cambrai, but Faubourg de Paris still remained uncaptured. The XVII Corps had passed well to the south of it, and had as its next objective Awoingt, two miles southeast of Cambrai.

On October 8 the Canadian Corps Commander decided that the time was ripe to take Cambrai. At 1:30 AM, on October 9, the 2nd Canadian Division attacked directly south so as to cut the railway and roads leading east from the city, and by daylight had crossed the canal and reached their first objective, thereby giving them control of the remaining exits from the city. The 3rd Division pressed forward into the west and northwestern suburbs, and by 8:00 AM entered the city and took possession. The Germans had looted the whole city and burned a considerable portion of the centre, besides blowing up all the bridges over the canal except one on the north side, which was saved by a Canadian Engineer Officer[8] who rushed across and killed five of the enemy with his revolver as they were trying to blow the mine. The Canadian Engineers immediately began to build a temporary bridge where the Arras Road entered the city, and had it nearly finished by 3:00 in the afternoon.

Then occurred an unfortunate incident, which later led to considerable hard feeling. As soon as it was announced that the Canadians had captured the city, the XVII Corps was ordered to take over the place. With more alacrity than the occasion

---

7   Brigadier-General Sir Ormonde de l'Épée Winter, KBE, CB, CMG, DSO, who was appointed to command the 11th Divisional Artillery on October 13, 1918.

8   Captain (later Lieutenant-Colonel) Coulson Norman Mitchell, 4th Battalion, Canadian Engineers. Mitchell was awarded the Victoria Cross for this action.

called for, the xvii Corps rushed in to relieve the Canadians. On arriving at the temporary bridge already mentioned, an officious officer indignantly enquired of the engineer in charge how he came to be working in the xvii Corps area. Pickets were established throughout the city, and certain non-coms went so far as to order Canadian soldiers out, even interfering with men who had been told to search buildings for booby traps, and others who were engaged in endeavouring to put out the fires that were still burning. On orders from the Army, the Canadian troops were withdrawn, but individual Canadian soldiers hotly resented the arbitrary action of the military police, very naturally asking: "Who in the hell took this city anyway?"

There might have been further heard of this incident had it not been that greater events were rushing upon us. On October 6, Bulgaria having meantime unconditionally surrendered to the Allies, Germany sent a message requesting the president of the United States to arrange an armistice to discuss peace terms. The fall of Cambrai came at the psychological moment when the president was dictating his reply, and from thence on followed the series of negotiations that ultimately brought about peace. The interest in the War became subservient to the continual succession of momentous events that included the submission of Austria and Turkey, the destruction of the Turkish armies in Mesopotamia, the withdrawal of the U-boats, and eventually the arrival of German plenipotentiaries, on November 7, to discuss peace terms.

Coincident with the fall of Cambrai the whole German front commenced to fall back, from Diksmuide to Verdun, and the combination of the rapidly ensuing military successes, coupled with the daily arrival of wireless news foreshadowing the collapse of the War, kept the troops in a constant state of jubilation and excitement. Huge maps were posted in mess rooms and even on boardings in the village streets with the successive daily advances on all the Allied Army's fronts marked upon them for the information of officers and men. Bets were made as to the time when Peace would be concluded, and speculation was rife as to when the troops would return home. At the same time, it was interesting to note the impersonal and almost phlegmatic manner in which news was received by the troops. In the earlier stages of the War it would have been received with wild acclamation. But coming so suddenly, the veteran troops were slow to realize what it really meant. They had become so accustomed to their mode of life, and to the feeling that the War might go on for years, that it was with difficulty and with a certain amount of scepticism that all ranks oriented themselves to the new situation. For some time they did not put much stock in the prospect of an early end to the War, but were keenly alive to the military successes that ensued with bewildering rapidity. Those successes were something tangible that they could understand, and it was not until the absolute debacle of the Austrian Empire that the men in the ranks, whose eyes had been dazzled by the sudden dawn of Peace, began to realize that the War was actually about to stop.

The realization was not entirely free from a feeling of dim apprehension on the part of the soldier that the fabric of his existence was suddenly to be overturned, and that he had to face a great change for which he had in no way prepared.

Chapter 33

THE GRAND ADVANCE AND
THE CAPTURE OF VALENCIENNES

After the fall of Cambrai, the 2nd Canadian Division and the 11th Imperial Division continued the advance in a north-easterly direction towards the junction of the Sensée River and the L'Escaut Canal. The XXII Corps took over the line on the right and the 3rd Canadian Division went into reserve.

The 2nd Canadian Division, with the 11th Imperial Division on its left, cleared up the triangle formed by the Sensée River and the L'Escaut, even crossing the latter and capturing Iuwy. There they turned north, with their flank on the railway to Denain, and captured Hordain. The 11th Imperial Division on their left was pinched out, and the 2nd Division extended from the Sensée River to Fressies. The 56th Imperial Division extended the line farther to the west. Meantime, the VIII Corps, which through all these weeks had clung to Vimy Ridge obsessed by the idea that the enemy was going to attempt a counterattack in that direction, had at last commenced to advance, so that the 1st Canadian Division swung to the northeast and worked its way forward, until on October 16 its front was on the Canal de la Sensée, and its left in the vicinity of Douai.

On the morning of October 17, the retirement of the enemy commenced. The 1st Brigade of the 1st Division sent patrols into Douai, though it was not on their front, and found the place evacuated. The VIII Corps was notified and marched in. The 4th

Canadian Division was just coming into the line to relieve the 56th, and, without losing any time, the 2nd, the 1st and 4th Canadian Divisions advanced north and east respectively, on the right and left. Within the next forty-eight hours the 1st and 4th Divisions advanced, fighting for fifteen miles. The 2nd Division was pinched out on the right, and on the night of October 19–20 the 4th Division passed across its front and captured Denain.

On October the 20th, the 1st and 4th Canadian Divisions held the line from just east of Denain (on the right) to Hasnon on the Scarpe River (on the left), a distance of 13,000 yards. Most of the villages on the western portion of this advance were deserted, but the city of Denain contained 28,000 inhabitants who welcomed the Canadians with wild enthusiasm and gratitude on being liberated after four years in the hands of the Bosche. The troops were crowned with flowers and refreshments forced upon them by citizens already feeling the pangs of hunger. Women lifted their children to the necks of the Artillery horses, and shouted and cried, and marched beside the advancing troops, singing the great national anthem of their nation, and waving the guns on after their retreating foe. In a remarkably short space of time, French flags appeared in front of every house and the liberated inhabitants went nearly mad with joy.

Three days later the city of Denain tendered a reception to the Commander of the Canadian Corps and the 4th Division that had liberated them. The Prince of Wales, who had been attached to the staff of the Canadian Corps since October 8, accompanied the Corps Commander. The 10th Brigade lined the streets leading to the cathedral where the senior officers were received by the mayor and council and church dignitaries. General Watson[1] was presented with the city's flag; girls arrayed in the costume of the country presented armfuls of flowers to each senior officer; and an immense crowd of cheering civilians lined the streets. A service of thanksgiving was held in the cathedral at which as many as could get inside were present. High mass was celebrated, and after that the chief ecclesiastical dignitary delivered an address in which Providence was thanked for Britain's help, and the Canadian Corps was hailed as the Lord's special instrument for their liberation.

In all the other villages the scenes at Denain were repeated, and for the first time the Canadian soldiers commenced to realize what the struggle of the past four years meant to the inhabitants of France. They were accommodated in the most

---

1   Major-General Sir David Watson, KCB, CMG. GOC 4th Canadian Division.

comfortable billets, practically every man had a bed under a roof, and every soldier was waited on and treated like the hero he was.

It was at this time that the King of the Belgians, with his army, forced the Germans back from Oostende and Bruges, and the Army relieved Lille and captured Roubaix and the adjacent cities. To the south a general onslaught was made by other British, French and American armies, and Le Cateau, Laon, and other notable points were captured. There was a general feeling that instead of relaxing military operations in view of the enemy's appeal for an armistice, the utmost energy should be displayed in pushing him back to his own frontier.

Following the capture of Denain, the 1st Division was relieved by the 3rd, and they pressed forward to capture Valenciennes. In two or three days the Canadian Corps was up to the canal on the western outskirts of the city, having pushed through the Forêt de Raismes. The front extended from Condé, south along the canal, past Valenciennes and, including the suburb Anzin, to a point where the right flank was in touch with the xxii Corps, two miles southeast of Denain. The canal was unfordable and the bridges had been blown up. In addition to this, the Germans flooded a large area both north and southwest of the city. On this account it was quite impossible for the 3rd Division on the left to get on, and the 4th Division on the right was held up by the xxii Corps, which was three miles to the right rear. The situation was a repetition of Cambrai, with the difference that our left front faced floods that made either attack or counterattack on the part of the enemy impossible in that area.

A wait of nearly a week ensued, while the xxii Corps was trying to make a flank. Finally they got sufficiently forward to make an attack on the south of the city between the canal and the Rhonelle River.

The approach to the city of Valenciennes from the south was dominated by a height known as Mount Huoy, which was really the key to Valenciennes as it could only be attacked from the south or east. The xxii Corps attacked Mount Huoy and got it, but in the afternoon was driven off.[2] Finally it was decided that a portion of the 4th Canadian Division and six brigades of artillery should cross the canal east of Denain and make the attack on Valenciennes from the south, supported by the whole Corps Artillery. This was a very difficult operation, as the routes of approach were all under enemy observation from Mount Huoy. The large body of the Artillery required had to be brought up in the face of the enemy, together with sufficient ammunition

---

2   October 28, 1918.

to carry a barrage over a front 25,000 yards wide and 3,500 yards deep, the objective being the railway running east and west through the southern suburbs of the city. It was arranged that when this objective was reached the 3rd Canadian Division should force the passage of the canal on the western front of the city. Arrangements were made to have the heaviest possible artillery concentration to barrage the force to its objective.

With this end in view the 4th and 5th Artillery Divisions, reinforced by the 39th Division Artillery, were to barrage the German Infantry northward from Famars, while the 5th DA, from a position near La Sentinelle, put on an enfilade barrage just in front of the creeping barrage. The Heavy Artillery, consisting of five brigades, superimposed a barrage of 120 yards, a portion of which formed a semicircle in front of the attack to prevent any of the enemy getting away. The XXII Corps was to make a flank for this attack on the east side of the River Rhondelle, attacking towards Presneau and Saultain. The attack was launched at 5:15 AM on November 1. The Germans put up a good fight and employed a great deal of artillery, but our gunfire was so overwhelming that all their counter-battery work was beaten down, and our infantry reached their objective in the southern outskirts of the city with very slight casualties.

A very large number of the enemy was killed. The 10th Brigade counted eight hundred dead in the area they passed over, which, of course, included the destruction wrought by artillery fire. At the same time the 3rd Division succeeded in crossing the canal and got three companies into the southwestern part of the city with their flank in communication with the 10th Brigade. Heavy fighting took place for the village of Marly and the adjacent steel works, and this delayed matters so that when night fell the enemy was still holding the city with machine guns in the streets.

The situation was rendered precarious from the fact that the XXII Corps had not succeeded in protecting our flank. They had gotten forward fairly well early in the day, but in the afternoon were pushed back 1,000 yards so that the enemy was able to bring long-range machine gun fire to bear on our battery positions, which had been advanced beyond Mount Huoy. With the untaken city in front, the impassable canal and flooded area extending four miles along our left flank in rear, and the enemy almost within striking distance of our line of communication on the right, there existed every opportunity for them to cut off the whole Canadian Forces that had been sent across the canal. Our batteries were ordered to place their machine guns in readiness and take all precautions to prevent an enemy coup, which would certainly have taken place had the enemy not been so demoralized by our attack. The realization of the situation, however, did not affect the confidence of our troops in the slightest. During the night of November 1–2, they pressed on, captured Marly, and drove the enemy out of the streets of the city. At 8:00 AM on November 2 it was officially reported that the Canadian Corps held Valenciennes and a line about 1,000 yards beyond the eastern suburbs. During November 2 the enemy heavily shelled the whole of the city, though there were over five thousand civilians still remaining in it, and the whole place had remained untouched by our fire. One of the difficulties we were now confronted with was that, owing to practically all the towns and villages being filled with inhabitants, we could not shell them, whereas the Bosche used them as a sanctuary for his artillery and machine guns.

The bridges were immediately put in repair, and all the Corps Artillery and the 3rd Division passed through the city. The advance continued from day to day until by November our front was half way to Mons. On the night of November 6–7, the 4th Division on the right was relieved by the 2nd Division, which had three brigades of artillery in immediate support. The 3rd Division had four, while the 1st, 4th, and 5th DAs were held in rest immediately east of Valenciennes. All the Heavy Artillery, consisting of five brigades, passed through the city and were deployed to the east of it in depth.

It was on this day that news arrived that Germany had sent four plenipotentiaries from Berlin to meet General Foch and discuss terms of Peace. General Headquarters issued an order at 10:00 AM that if a flag of truce appeared on our front, it was to be detained and the fact reported to G.H.Q.

Chapter 34

HOW PEACE CAME

A few days after the capture of Valenciennes our guns were two-thirds of the way to Mons, which is twenty miles east of Valenciennes. As the Corps on our left was being held up and our flank was exposed, it was decided on November 10 to put on a corps barrage to the north of Valenciennes and get in rear of the enemy. I went forward to look over the ground, but learned that the enemy was falling back all along the line, and that the operation was unnecessary.

The road from Valenciennes to Mons runs through a number of villages, which in some places are so close together as to constitute one long street. It was necessary to know at once whether the retirement was a general retreat or if the enemy proposed to make a stand this side of Mons. So I continued on in my car until I crossed the border into Belgium, just beyond a village the Tommies called "Quivering Jane."[1] Here I found the whole civilian population standing in expectant groups in the street, and nearly every house in the village fairly blazing with Belgian flags—red, black, and yellow. They watched my motor approach in apprehensive silence, but when it got close enough for them to recognize the British uniforms, there were a few timid cheers (timid because the retiring Bosche had left the unpleasant news that the Canadians were addicted to atrocities far more terrible than the Belgians had suffered from

---

1   The village of Quiévrechain.

the Germans). I stopped my car and learned that the Bosche had only left the place two hours before. They assured me that he had gone "away back."

There were none of our troops about, but it was worth taking a chance to confirm the information, so we pushed on slowly, looking all ways for trouble. The road was wide and straight, and we could see Belgian flags in the next village. So we went on and were received with a sort of twittering cheer by the civilians along the sidewalks, who were all dressed in their Sunday best and obviously prepared for whatever might happen. When we stopped the car it was surrounded by a mob of men, women, and children, screaming and shouting and all waiting to shake hands with me. Women who could not get near the car held up babies to look at us, and the whole throng was tremulous with excitement. Learning that the Bosche was still farther away, we tried to get on, but by this time the crowd was so dense that we could barely move. At this moment another motor came racing up containing Major Crerar,[2] my Counter-Battery Staff Officer, who had been scouting for forward positions and had heard the news. He spoke French fluently and this relieved the situation. While he questioned the civilians, two men pressed their way through the crowd and announced that they were prisoners belonging to the King's Liverpool Regiment who had been captured last March and were escaping. They confirmed the reports regarding the enemy, and believed he had gone back to Mons. I asked for a flag to put on my car and half a dozen people rushed to the burgomaster's office. Leaving Major Crerar to follow with the flag I pushed off for the next village. He subsequently caught up to us with an immense banner on a spear-pointed pole, nearly twenty feet long. This flag had been made by a Belgian lady before the liberation of the village and is rather a curiosity in its way. The materials are black cloth, red shiny baize, and a sort of thick yellow muslin.

Meantime, we had not seen any of the patrols or scouts, and the only assurance we had of not running into the enemy was the display of Belgian flags in each successive village as we approached. A large cathedral loomed up in the next town, which we found was Jemappes, only two miles from Mons, and I was not at all sorry on arriving at the outskirts to come across two of our infantry scouts. They reported

---

2   Later General Harry Duncan Graham Crerar, CH, CB, DSO, CD, PC. Commander First Canadian Army 1944–1945. Crerar joined Morrison's staff on June 29, 1918. He was acting CBSO as of October 21, 1918, as McNaughton had moved up to be Acting Commander Canadian Corps Heavy Artillery. Both men were promoted (Crerar to Lieutenant-Colonel and McNaughton to Brigadier-General) and confirmed in their new positions on November 10, 1918.

that there were no Germans in the town, but as one of them immediately proceeded to climb a telegraph pole in order to get a better view of the street, the information could not be deemed official. However, as the people in the streets were cheering and waving flags, and waving to us to come on, we got our only rifle out from under the seat, put the orderly on a war footing, and unbuckled our holsters. The people were hysterical with excitement and tried to mob the car, but we put on, full speed ahead, only to be stopped a short distance farther by a huge crater where the enemy had blown the street. Somebody said that by going around a block we could avoid the crater and get into the Grande Place. Within sight of the *hôtel de ville*, an enemy plane appeared overhead and turned loose its machine gun, but as we were in a narrow one-way street with high buildings on each side and the plane was flying at right angles, is disappeared in a few moments. Our two cars swung into the Grande Place and pulled up in the lee of the hotel, out of sight of the plane, where we were immediately hemmed in by a tremendous crowd of civilians who paid no attention to the aeroplane but carried on like crazy people in their joy and excitement. It was not a pleasant situation because at any moment the enemy plane might swoop over and gun the crowd in an effort to get at us. It was impossible to explain the danger to the crowd on account of the noise, and, besides, they were carrying on as if they did not care whether they were machine-gunned or not.

Fortunately at this moment a burly old gentleman bore his way through the people and announced that he was the burgomaster, and invited us to come with him into the city hall. As we walked across the Place, the scene reached a climax when the people saw the badges on our shoulder straps and commenced to shout: "Vive Canada!" The words passed along like wildfire all over the square. The male portion of the population threw their hats in the air, and the women waved their handkerchiefs, and about a hundred men all tried to shake hands with me at once. Finally we were "borne by the joyous crowd" up the steps and into the *hôtel de ville*. The stout old burgomaster played up well, and as soon as we got inside, led me swiftly into his private office, where my staff officers eventually arrived more or less in a state of limpness.

Burgomasters and aldermen are the same all the world over. This old gentleman opened a rapid-fire conversation in Belgian-French, quite regardless of the fact that I did not understand a word he was saying, and then, suddenly looking over my shoulder, burst into a stentorian oration, though I was only standing a yard away. For a moment I did not know what had happened, but, looking over my shoulder, I found that the crowd had filled the corridor outside and were surging into the office. There was nothing for it, so I stood to attention and tried to look as much like a conquering hero and liberator of cities as I knew how. For nearly five minutes he fairly deluged me with unintelligible eloquence, only stopping for breath in the intervals when his voice was drowned out by the plaudits of his constituency.

The worst was not yet over. A pale young man with a droopy moustache, who introduced himself by saying "he knew Toronto" (he said it as though Toronto were a mutual acquaintance), ranged up alongside and proceeded to interpret the speech, concluding with the information that the burgomaster invited me to dinner. As it was obviously up to me to contribute something to the historical occasion, I went through the motions of delivering a speech in reply, calm in the assurance that nobody but my staff officers and the young man who knew Toronto understood a word I said. I must say for the civilians of Jemappes that they applauded liberally. One tangible advantage from this international episode was the information furnished from the young man who knew Toronto that the enemy was entrenched on the railway embankment three kilometres from the town, and evidently intended to make a fight for Mons. This was what I had come to find out, so, putting off the burgomaster's invitation till a more convenient season, we got back to our cars, which we found filled with flowers, and barged off amid a repetition of the flattering ovation that had greeted our arrival. As a matter of fact, thirty men of the Princess Pats had already passed through Jemappes, and although the fine regiment was relieved the next day, one company remained to enter Mons with the 42nd Highland Battalion less that forty-eight hours later.[3]

As it was obvious that the enemy intended to fight at least a rearguard action in front of Mons, the Infantry of the 3rd Division was pushed on, followed by the Field and Heavy Batteries, while the 2nd Division cooperated on the right with an encircling movement. By nightfall our troops were engaging the enemy in the suburbs of the historic town, while at the same time rumours were flying about of an impending armistice. There was a tacit understanding that Mons—where the War had started so far as the British Army was concerned—should be taken by the Canadians before Peace intervened.

Sunday, November 10, was a lovely autumn day. Again I went forward with the hope this time of actually getting into Mons. Colonel Gow, Canadian Deputy Minister of Militia in England, was visiting the Corps and he came with me.

---

3   No. 4 Company, PPCLI.

Though at that time in the Civil Branch, Colonel Gow had served in the field earlier in the War,[4] and his tastes ran to front line work. When we reached Jemappes the enemy was shelling the town, which indicated that he had not yet left Mons. Leaving the car under cover, we went forward about a mile, and there before us lay the historic town of Mons. It is a place with about 25,000 inhabitants, situated in low ground and commanded from the south and west by ridges and slag heaps that afford excellent observation posts for artillery. The Hun was holding the outskirts with machine guns, and his artillery fire from beyond the town was quite heavy. A large building in the middle of the place was blazing merrily. We afterwards discovered that with his customary mania for destruction, the enemy was burning the food supplies that had been requisitioned and stored in the building for the use of the city's inhabitants.

Proceeding out on the railway embankment, running about 2,000 yards north and south from the town from which the enemy had been driven the previous day, we sat down and studied the situation. Shells of all calibres were drifting over in an aimless sort of way and the only sign of method in the enemy's shooting was a languid bombardment of the apex of a pyramidal slag heap that looked right into the town. His shooting was so bad that only about one shell in ten hit the peak of the slag heap, while the others plumped into the poor little town of Jemappes, which, as already described, was crowded with civilians. It did not take long to size up the situation: the burning stores indicated that the enemy intended to evacuate, while the industrious rattle of machine guns, and the lack of method in the way he threw his shells about, indicated that he would not do so until he was good and ready, which would not be that day. We were much handicapped because we could not shell a town that was full of inhabitants, and had to content ourselves with bombarding the exits. On the other hand, the Infantry could have rushed the place—but it was not desirable to incur any avoidable losses with Peace so near. Obviously we would not get into Mons that day, and equally obviously the Infantry would hustle the enemy out of the city that night. One company of the Princess Pats was close into the suburbs and declined to be relieved because they were bound to get into the town before Peace was proclaimed.

---

4   Honorary Colonel Walter Gow, Deputy Minister of Overseas Military Forces of Canada, February 8, 1917–December 28, 1918. He was a first cousin of John McCrae. Gow had served with the 19th and 31st Battalions.

Shelling was never so dangerous as when the Hun was simply slashing his stuff about without any method, because you never could tell where he would put down his next crash. We therefore adjourned in search of lunch. There was a very handsome chateau not far away, and we decided to test Belgian hospitality, which was done by the simple method of entering the grounds, ringing the bell, and announcing that: "Mon général is hungry." This resulted in one of the surprise incidents that make happy memories. We were immediately surrounded by the family, consisting of an old gentleman and his wife, two grown-up sons, one of them a priest, and four daughters. You would think they had been waiting for us since the beginning of the War, and now the whole family proceeded to wait on us. In a suspiciously short time a delicious lunch was laid out, including such delicacies as roast duck, a huge pâté de fois gras, cake, fruit, and last but not least, the old gentleman disappeared down to the cellar and returned with a rimey bottle of old Burgundy. The gentlemen served us themselves, and the ladies sat around the table and said nice things about Canada and the Canadians. We had got through the soup and barely reached the roast duck when a German shell landed in the garden, followed by several more, so that by special request the ladies were induced to betake themselves to the cellar. The shelling stopped and they soon came back. As an accompaniment to the dessert, the Bosche put on another crash and another shell landed in the garden on the other side of the house. So once more we were robbed of the society of the ladies. When the shelling stopped they returned. After the coffee we toasted the host and hostess, the Allies, the King of the Belgians, and generally cemented the Entente Cordiale, the ladies daintily sipping a little wine with each toast and everybody clinking glasses. It was a charming Sunday afternoon. We told them the Kaiser had abdicated and that the Canadians would have Mons by morning, Peace or no Peace, and these hospitable people made us promise to be their guests again the next day. After four years of mud and slaughter, this was something like war deluxe.

The whole family came out on the lawn to see us off as the Hun was busy shelling in another direction, and we started off towards Mons. A few hundred yards down the road occasional shells were smashing through the buildings, but the streets were thronged with men, women, and children watching the shells coming over with more curiosity than fear. This was their first experience of battle and none in that particular section had been hit. A Canadian on a stretcher was being carried along. He had an ugly wound in the leg and the blood was dripping through the stretcher, but the boy was in great spirits, actually flirting with the girls in the doorways and jollying them in bad French, while they waved their handkerchiefs to him and "*vived*" Canada. That morning these same women had mobbed six Bosche prisoners and nearly battered their heads in with wooden shoes before the guards could rescue them.

We penetrated to within 500 or 600 yards of the enemy's line on the south side of Mons and got a view of the ground, crossing their fire in a dangerous manner. We decided that it was too close to the end of the War to take any chances. Besides, it was evident that there would be no surrender this afternoon.

Early next morning I was awakened by the sound of voices in the next room of our palatial billet in Valenciennes just in time to hear an officer say: "Peace has come." And I heard his batman reply: "Thank God, sir!" Almost immediately my own batman came in and informed me that Mons had been captured at 4:30 AM by the 42nd Battalion and one company of Princess Pats, and that the "Cease Fire" would sound at 11:00 AM.[5] There was practically no jubilation in the mess at breakfast. Everybody shook hands in a perfunctory way as the occasion seemed to demand some recognition, but it was quite evident that the realization of what had taken place came slowly. Perhaps the first thought was that the associations in close companionship of four years were about to be broken up. One blurted out, not flippantly: "Well, that was a perfectly good old War!"

Colonel Gow and I went down to Mons to see Peace ushered in on the front line. Already thousands of fugitives were repatriating themselves, and the highway was crowded for miles with strange and pathetic caravans of returning exiles. Every sort of vehicle, from a baby carriage to a motor lorry, was utilized. In some cases you would see a woman, a boy, and a dog hitched to a small cart piled up with the family belongings, with a little baby asleep on the top of it; then a top-heavy wagonette with an old man and a cow between the shafts and the wife and children following behind carrying bundles or pushing; here and there a handcart or barrow loaded with clothing and bundles had upset in the mud. Every road for miles was thronged with these people, crawling along like an army of ants to re-people the towns and villages. Many had marched all night and when we returned in the evening the throng was almost as great. Many pitiful scenes were to be witnessed from the side of the road. A frantic mother would search among her friends for a lost child, then would be ordered on; but before she took up her bundle she would scrawl with chalk on the

---

5   Mons was liberated by the Royal Canadian Regiment, the 42nd Infantry Battalion, and No. 4 Company, PPCLI.

wall, *Jean, little son of Mdme. Delemarle, is lost. His mother goes to Hasnon.* When these men and women fled, or were driven back, before the tide of war, they had scrawled messages of welcome to their oncoming deliverers, and, returning again to their homes, they used the doors and shutters of the houses for all sorts of news. *Dear Mary, your Father is dead, come to live with Annette and Paul* was one message with a heartbreak in it.

As a contrast to this ghastly procession, the villagers all along the road were *en fête.* Passing the chateau where we lunched the day before, we were showered with flowers. Near Mons, battalions were marching in column with bands playing and batteries of artillery were moving at a clanking trot along the cobblestone highways, either in pursuit of the enemy or to join the military celebration, which was to be held in Mons at the hour of the Armistice. Though the hour had not yet arrived, our advance troops were already following up the enemy several miles east of that city.

Entering Mons by the road we had attempted to follow the day before, we came upon dead Bosches lying in the gutters and on the sidewalks. Most of them were the victims of shellfire. The capture of the city had been so recent that the place was only partly cleaned up. Crowds of men, women and children placidly paraded along to get good places at the military ceremony, either taking no notice of this grim garnishment or grouping about the bodies as if they were an appropriate part of the function. In some instances the sight of them aroused such memories that men, whose faces were convulsed with hatred, deliberately spat upon them.

Mons has an imposing *hôtel de ville* with an immense cobblestone place in front of it, well-suited in every respect to the wonderful scene that was to follow. The buildings and roofs all around the square were black with the people of the city, which had only been wrested from the Huns six hours before. On the central balcony stood the burgomaster in ceremonial uniform, surrounded by the notables of the city. From every side street poured cavalry, infantry, and artillery, just as they had come out of the fight, and with the precision of long practice, they formed up in an imposing parade. In the centre was a squadron of the 5th Lancers, who had fought at Mons in 1914. All the rest of the troops were Canadians.

Slowly, the hand of the clock climbed towards the hour that was to mark the close of the greatest war in history, and there were the troops, grimed and unshaven and mud-stained, who had won back the city wrested from the Old Contemptibles in August 1914. The fight of the night before had been no bloodless victory. The enemy's dead were thick in the suburbs, and especially around the train station, where they had made their last stand. The Canadian Infantry had made it a point of honour, notwithstanding the cautions against casualties, to drive the enemy from Mons before the Cease-fire sounded. Their triumph would not have been half so sweet had they not celebrated it in the Grande Place of Mons.

There was little cheering though much suppressed excitement among the civilian multitude, until a few minutes before 11:00 AM, when the beautiful chimes of Mons Cathedral, high above the multitude in the square, commenced to chime and then pealed forth "La Marseillaise." In the crowded square below the cheering commenced, first rising like a growl and then pulsating to a mighty roar which lasted several minutes. Then there was a strained silence. All eyes seemed to be turned on the clock tower. Three minutes—two minutes—a word of command that echoed through the square—the crash of rifle butts on cobblestones—the flash of fixing bayonets—"Present Arms!"—the massed bands burst forth with "God Save the King"—everybody came to the salute—and the War was over!

Then came the shouting. The burgomaster made a speech and was cheered, the officer commanding the Brigade[6] replied briefly and was cheered. The troops were called to attention, took off their helmets and cheered. The massed bands played all the Allied national anthems and each in turn was cheered. But the best part of the show was the march past. It was not a regular review, but the mass of troops wheeled into column and marched away with the grim, sober air of men whose work is done. Every corps in turn was cheered. They may have received greater ovations among their own people later on, but none more heartfelt than that of the people they had rescued from bondage that morning.

In the afternoon another and more imposing military triumph was staged by the Canadian Corps, and, though much more imposing in size and dignity of arrangement, I must say that I enjoyed the spontaneous performance of the morning. The square was lavishly decorated with the flags of the Allies. The parade was dazzling, though the day was murky; the civic reception was spectacular and effective; the entry of the Corps Commander with his staff, mounted[7] and preceded by an escort of cavalry and followed by his battle standard, was a magnificent climax to the day of rejoicing. Sir Arthur Currie rode into the captured city along streets garnished

---

6   Brigadier-General John Arthur Clark, CMG, DSO and two bars, QC. GOC 7th Infantry Brigade September 12, 1918 –April 30, 1919.

7   Including Morrison on his horse, King.

with the enemy dead, not to triumph over, but to receive the thanks of its delivered citizens, and to congratulate and receive the congratulations of the men he had led to victory. It was a scene to stir the pulses of the most unemotional, and to illumine the imagination of the most prosaic.

After receiving the general salute, the Corps Commander and his staff dismounted and were met by the burgomaster and councillors of the city. After listening to a eulogistic address of gratitude and welcome, General Currie appropriately replied and then presented the city with his battle flag. The troops representing the 3rd Division, which had captured the city, marched past and presented a splendid appearance. General Currie and the senior officers present were escorted into the ancient council chamber where, by the light of tallow candles, they inscribed their names in a sort of golden book of the city, which they were proudly informed had never been opened throughout the four years of Hun occupation. It was quite an historic scene, the officers in their war-stained uniforms, and the city officers in black clothes and robes of office, standing around the great carved council table, their faces thrown into strong relief by a few sputtering candles in a quaint old candelabra, which was the only means of lighting, and which served only to make the darkness visible in the great wainscoted room.

So the War, as a war, ended for the Canadian Corps fighting to the last and successful to the last, while its enemies went down before it amid the crash of empires and the wreck of dynasties.

Chapter 35

THE OCCUPATION OF GERMANY

After the capture of Mons on November 11, the Canadian Corps, after a short rest, commenced the advance towards the Rhine where, in conjunction with the 11 British Corps, it was to take possession of the Cologne Bridgehead. The original intention was that all four divisions should proceed to the Rhine, but later this programme was changed so that only the 1st and 2nd Divisions actually proceeded into Germany, the 3rd and 4th remaining in the vicinity of Mons and Brussels. On November 24 the Corps Headquarters moved to Gosselies, a Belgian town of ten thousand inhabitants, where the Corps Staff was billeted in the handsome chateau of the Baroness Moile.

It was here that it first became evident that the portion of Belgium that had remained in the hands of the Germans for four years had suffered very little as the result of the occupation and the War. On the contrary, the inhabitants had prospered. Unlike northern France, occupied Belgium had been regarded as an integral portion of the German Empire and its people treated accordingly. Not only had the people plenty of food, but they sold their surplus to the Germans at very high prices. In like manner, the manufacturers had large contracts of munitions and their workmen were highly paid. Even unskilled labour, which, we were told, received only three or four francs a day before the War, was paid three or four times as much by the Germans.

In the small town of Gosselies there were twenty-two millionaires, chiefly profiteers. The inhabitants had no complaints to make of their treatment by the Germans, and on the contrary, seemed rather disappointed on the whole that the War was over and that they had been "liberated." The farms were rich in beef cattle, poultry, sheep and horses. Anything the Germans had appropriated had been well paid for. All this was in the nature of a revelation to the Canadians, in view of the propaganda of a "starving Germany," which was being lavishly circulated in order to work upon the sympathy of President Wilson, pacifists, and neutrals throughout the world, in order to secure better terms.

On November 28 the Corps Headquarters moved to Huy in order to keep pace with the march of the 1st and 2nd Divisions and 11 Corps troops, the latter of which included three brigades of Heavy Artillery. On December 1, Headquarters moved again to Vielsalm. The weather luckily remained mild, with a good deal of rain and fog. The country was very hilly and we had then entered the Ardennes. The roads were not very good, besides being winding and with continuous steep gradients and descents. Had there been snow or ice on the roads, the advance would almost have been rendered impossible for wheeled transport. The Ardennes is a wild, hilly region covered in many places with pine forests, and is sparsely populated. Very few billets were available and the troops had to bivouac in the open. Added to this, there had been great delay in the repairing of railways, so that there was a continuous shortage of food and forage. Altogether it was a very hard march, and at times the troops were without food for twenty-four hours at a stretch.

On December 7 the Corps Headquarters moved from Vielsalm to Schleiden, crossing the frontier into Germany between these places.

The actual crossing of the frontier was an historical event, and, personally, I looked forward to it with a good deal of interest. It was a raw December day, and as our motors proceeded along the muddy forest road, the trees were dripping with moisture from the melted snow, which had fallen lightly on the previous day. So far as we were concerned there was little of the spectacular in our entry into Germany. There was the boundary post near the dreary road, and a few stolid German children, looking over a farm gate, stared vacantly at the motors as we rolled by.

Our first billet in Germany was at Schleiden, at the chateau of Count von Spee, a cousin of Admiral von Spee who lost his life at the Battle of the Falkland Islands. We reached there about noon, after a three-hour run through farming country with occasional small villages. Count von Spee's residence was a large building of modern construction, looking more like a large hotel than a private house. The count himself stood in the main hall and proceeded to welcome us more in the guise of a friendly host than the proprietor of an enemy billet. He spoke English quite well, and I must say that his assumption of friendly equality decidedly annoyed me. I was prepared for sulky ill humour or even open resentment in our enemy billet, but not for the smooth and brazen pretence of hospitality with which we were received. In the anteroom allotted to us was conspicuously displayed a large portrait of his naval kinsman, and on the central table was an enormous volume, beautifully illustrated, recording the glories of Germany throughout the ages, up to and including the coronation of William I at Versailles in 1871. As there were no other books in the room, it would appear that this volume had been laid out for our special benefit.

The inhabitants did not appear at all unfriendly and food seemed plentiful. The people were well-dressed and well-fed. There were cattle in the fields and plenty of poultry in the farmyards, besides a large butter factory in operation at Schleiden. As yet there was no evidence of "starving Germany." Along the roads, guns and broken-down motor lorries and wagons had been abandoned, and in most cases the retiring army had endeavoured to destroy them, contrary to the terms of the Armistice. In some instances motor lorries had been deliberately sawed into pieces. Among the inhabitants were many ex-soldiers, still wearing their uniforms but disguised in bowler hats with their shoulder straps removed.

We remained at Schleiden nearly a week while the troops were moving forward. On December 11 the Corps Headquarters were established in the Schaumburg Palace at Bonn, which is an attractive university city of ninety thousand inhabitants. The German Crown Prince had been educated there, and the Kaiser's sister[1] still occupied the palace that became Corps Headquarters.

On December 12 the Cavalry, led by the Canadian Corps Commander and his staff mounted,[2] made the official crossing of the Rhine at Bonn. We moved on to the bridge at 9:30 AM, the Corps Commander, preceded by a squadron of Cavalry and followed by his staff, presenting a very brave appearance. Behind Sir Arthur Currie rode an orderly carrying the battle flag on a lance. It was a thrilling moment as we moved onto the great bridge, the Infantry band stationed at the farther side playing a popular marching tune. The sidewalks along the route were crowded with Germans

---

1   Princess Margaret of Prussia.
2   Again including Morrison riding King.

observing the pageant with much interest and without any show of resentment except that the men did not removed their hats as the battle flag went by. On arriving at the far side of the bridge, the Corps Commander with his staff wheeled to the right and took the salute of the Cavalry Brigade as it marched past and proceeded farther into Germany to form a screen around the nineteen-mile perimeter of bridgehead.

When this ceremony was over the cavalcade rode back, and as the citizens somewhat obviously refused to raise their hats, as is the established custom in Germany with reference to their own officers, troopers were detailed to ride along the curb to demand that courtesy, and—if necessary—to knock hats off with the flat of their swords. This was the enemy's first mild taste of subjugation, and our troopers took much pleasure in demonstrating this lesson in courtesy. It had a rather amusing sequel. After the parade, the burgomaster was sent for and instructed that all citizens must accord to Canadian officers the same courtesy which they had been accustomed to render to German officers, on penalty of punishment.

The next day, December 13, was a Friday, and the rain poured down dismally. This day was allotted to the crossing of the Rhine at Bonn and Cologne by the 1st and 2nd Divisions of Infantry and the 3rd Artillery of the Corps. During the preceding night fifty guns of our heavy artillery arrived after a march of forty-seven miles on the previous day. Throughout the darkness the heavy guns rumbled over the cobble-stoned streets of the two cities, and at daylight they occupied the bridge crossings. Beside each gun were twenty rounds of heavy shell. The guns were trained on the farther side of the Rhine, and tremendously impressed the inhabitants who stood literally in the tens of thousands watching them throughout the day, as if they expected any moment that a bombardment would open.

At 9:30 AM General Currie and his staff took up a position at the Bonn bridge, and General Sir Herbert Plumer occupied a similar position at the Cologne bridge. Promptly at 9:30 AM, the heads of the columns debouched on to their respective bridges and came tramping across in magnificent array, with colours flying and bands playing. The troops were specially prepared for the occasion: every bit of brass and steel shone like gold and silver, and their uniforms, although war-worn, were cleaned to the last button; guns and harnesses were spotless and, notwithstanding the steady downpour of rain, the columns, which poured over the Rhine until 3:00 PM, presented an appearance that wrung expressions of admiration even from the German civilians. No attempt was made to break the step of the marching columns, so that before the 1st Brigade had crossed, the big suspension bridge was swinging under their rhythmic tread until it was feared that the copper trolley wires overhead might snap. To prevent any results from such an accident, it was ordered that the electric currents be turned off. So for six hours the columns poured across the Rhine. But for the noise of the bands and the words of command as the troops passed the saluting point, the column marched in proud and grim silence, even the horses stepping as if they realized the importance and splendour of the triumph.

Beyond the bridgeheads definite zones were established, on perimeters of about twenty miles, and for the next seven weeks we remained on duty as part of the Army of Occupation.

The regulations prevented fraternization on the streets, but it was impossible to prevent it in the billets, where the German population, generally speaking, was excessively friendly and anxious to be kind to the men. On Christmas, men who were in billets were showered with presents and entertained at lavish Christmas dinners. Large numbers of others who were in barracks were invited out by the inhabitants, with whom they had become acquainted in one way or another, and were treated with the greatest kindness and hospitality. Even in the royal palace, the princess sent into the mess on Christmas Eve a large Christmas tree ornamented with candles, and made presents to Prince Arthur of Connaught,[3] to the ADCs, and to the prince's equerry. The orderlies, chauffeurs, and grooms, in the residence next door where they were billeted, each received half a dozen presents from the mistress of the house.

Under these circumstances, and as time wore on, the situation on the Rhine became peculiar if not disquieting. The civilian population generally observed the rule against fraternizing with the soldiers on the streets, but they invited them to their homes and treated them with such unaffected kindness as proved quite disarming. A considerable proportion spoke English, or at least enough to make themselves understood, and they lost no opportunity of ingratiating themselves with the troops. All this was done in such a manner that neither officers nor men could resent their attentions without appearing boorish. Added to this the men had been a long time from home and its comforts, and, if the truth be told, they had experienced no such treatment in France or Belgium. On the contrary, the French and Belgian civilians had never put themselves out to be agreeable to our men, nor even attempted to learn their language during the four years they had been among them, always forcing

---

3   Major, Prince Arthur of Connaught, KG, KT, GCMG, GCVO, GCStJ, CB, PC. Aide-de-Camp to Sir Douglas Haig, attached to the Canadian Corps HQ. Prince Arthur was a first cousin of His Majesty King George V.

them to speak French. The Germans were quite the opposite. The prices were kept down—even food was more plentiful and less dear than in France—and no efforts were spared to enhance the comforts of the men and make them feel that they were welcome guests rather than hostile invaders. It is scarcely an exaggeration to say that the treatment of the troops in France and Belgium was as might have been expected in Germany, whereas the treatment in Germany was what might reasonably have been expected in France or Belgium.

Our stay in Germany was not without its relaxations. Excellent performances of grand opera were put on nightly at the Royal Opera House in Cologne; even the small opera house in Bonn essayed a production of *The Geisha* in German. The officers at Bonn commandeered the Kaiser's fine game preserve five miles southwest of that place, and got a lot of good hunting. Twice a week the chief gamekeeper was ordered out with about thirty beaters and conducted drives through the forest that resulted in the killing of wild boar, deer, foxes, pheasants and miscellaneous game. The head forester was arrayed in a uniform after the manner of the Kaiser himself when he went hunting, the crowning glory being a velour hat with a large tuft of feathers in the band. He carried a hunting horn and a knife for administering the *coup de grâce*. The beaters were a villainous-looking lot of demobilized soldiers. Their demobilization consisted in tearing off their shoulder straps and putting on bowler hats. As the line of these beaters approached the hunters, making raucous noises and pounding on the trees with their clubs, many an officer's finger unconsciously closed on the trigger as he saw their grey field uniforms appearing through the brushwood. But they were exceedingly docile, and the old forester did everything possible to give us good sport.

For some months the Canadian Corps had been honoured by having HRH the Prince of Wales[4] and HRH Prince Arthur of Connaught attached to Headquarters Staff as ADCS.

The Prince of Wales joined the Headquarters mess during October, when the Corps was occupying a wooden hut in the deep trenches of the Drocourt–Quéant Line. The first night, at dinner, the prince behaved with such modesty and charm that he won all hearts immediately. He was seated at the right of the Corps Commander, but expressed a preference to be allowed to occupy a place among the "Subs"[5]

---

4   Later His Majesty King Edward VIII.

5   Subalterns (i.e., second lieutenants and lieutenants).

at the foot of the table, and at the close of the dinner he smartly sprang to his feet and proceeded to hold the door open, and most respectfully to bow the Corps Commander out. This most tactful and courteous act made an excellent impression, which was continued and deepened throughout his stay with us. In the series of battles that ensued he evinced such elation under fire that at the capture of Valenciennes those who were responsible for his safety had practically to order him back to Headquarters, where the language he used, striding up and down the mess room, endeared him still further to the junior subs.

Prince Arthur had held a commission in the Scots Greys, but came to the Canadian Corps early in 1917 and continued on duty there, with the exception of a brief absence in Japan, until the end of the War. One unpleasant incident that occurred during our stay in Germany had the sting taken out of it by Prince Arthur. The Military Governor of Cologne had issued, for reasons known only to himself, a military telegram making Cologne out of bounds to Canadians. The offensive order was later withdrawn, but meantime, the Military Governor had sent to Prince Arthur an invitation to dine with him in Cologne. The prince answered the invitation with a polite note in which he reminded the governor that the Canadian troops were confined to the Canadian area except when on duty, and as accepting an invitation to dinner could not be regarded as proceeding to Cologne on duty, he must, as an officer of the Canadian Corps, beg leave to decline.

Chapter 36

DEMOBILIZATION

Early in January it was decided to demobilize the Canadian Corps, and the 3rd Division commenced its march to Étaples, which was to be the point where the personnel was to be reorganized for transportation to Canada. On the tenth day of the new year the 1st Division was relieved at Cologne. By January 26 the 2nd Division and the Corps' troops had been relieved, and the Corps Staff left Germany and proceeded via Cologne to Aix-la-Chapelle, then to Andenne on the River Meuse, midway between Liège and Namur.

A pleasing incident occurred as we were nearing the frontier between Germany and Belgium. It was difficult to be sure exactly when we had crossed the frontier. We had stopped several civilians to make inquiries but found we were still in Germany, until at last we overtook a tattered and miserable looking individual on the road. My staff officer[1] called to him to come over to the car, but he was not very ready to obey the summons. The Major shouted at him angrily, and he finally came. "Take off your cap," thundered the Major, but instead of obeying, the man drew himself up and replied with quiet dignity, "I don't have to take my cap off, I am a Belgian." Then we knew we were out of Germany, and were not sorry for it.

At Andenne the corps mess was in a large but not particularly attractive château where we experienced the most grudging civility. A few days after our arrival

---

1   Major D.A. White, DSO. Staff Officer to the G.O.C.R.A. Canadian Corps May 8, 1918–April 15, 1919.

I happened to notice a number of bullet holes in the window of one of the rooms, and, on inquiry, was informed that on August 21 and 22, 1914, this small village of two or three thousand inhabitants had been the scene of an unprovoked massacre by Bosche soldiers. A woman living next to the office told me that on August 21, the Bosche soldiers gathered all the women and children together in the market place and put a cordon of sentries around them, where they remained in the broiling heat until the evening. In the meantime they heard a lot of shooting in the village, and when this woman returned to her home she found her husband and son shot to death in the little yard behind the house. These were only two of several hundred unoffending civilians who had been murdered. After rounding up the women and children the soldiers had gone about the streets shooting every man or boy on sight. When the unfortunates took refuge in cellars, the soldiers threw gas or smoke bombs down, and when the men were driven out they were deliberately killed with a bullet or bayonet. In the window of a shop in the village there was a large frame draped with crepe containing the names of the people who had been murdered, to the number of 227, plus 40 who had never been found and were supposed to have been burned to death in the houses near the river bank, which had been set on fire.

In coming out of Germany we crossed the Belgian border at its northwestern corner. Before we had proceeded 200 yards within the Belgian frontier we came on traces of wrecked houses and graves, indicating that the atrocities had commenced almost immediately after the German Army entered Belgium. As we understood there had been practically no resistance, on account of the surprise of the invasion, until the German troops reached the vicinity of Liège, yet many houses along this road had been destroyed, obvious evidence that the atrocities were deliberately commenced to terrorize the Belgians before there was any military resistance offered. As there had been no fighting in that area since August 1914, and the ruins were overgrown with grass, it was certain that it was during the advance of the German Army and their retiring. The damage was done. Having come from the Rhine and through Aix-la-Chapelle, where everything was as untouched as if there had never been a war, the evidence of these wanton outrages immediately as the Belgian border was crossed made a very painful impression.

On February 1, Corps Headquarters moved from Andenne to Jodoigne. At that time the 1st Division was quartered in the vicinity of Huy, the 2nd near Namur, the 4th Division at La Hulpe south of Brussels, and the 3rd Division was proceeding with demobilization near Tournai. The process of demobilization seemed very slow to the eager troops who had been so long from home. The weather, too, was unusually severe, with continuous rain and snow. But the troops put in a busy winter. Balls, *fêtes sportives*, boxing tournaments, and special performances at the Royal Opera House in Brussels, helped to keep all ranks from thinking too much of home. Discipline was well-maintained and the troops were kept in good spirits by every legitimate means. Excursions by motor lorry were organized to allow visits to Antwerp, Waterloo, Brussels, Liège and other points of interest. Generous leave to local points were granted; concert parties put on nightly performances; schools were organized; and libraries were put in circulation. There was among all ranks an eagerness to prepare themselves for their return.

By the end of March the major part of the 3rd Division had reached Canada, the 1st Division was in England, and the 2nd Division had begun to move down to Le Havre preceded by three brigades of Heavy Artillery. On March 31, Field Marshal Sir Douglas Haig paid his last visit to the Corps, and the general officers gathered to say "Farewell" to the chief who had commanded them with such distinction. The Headquarters Staff was demobilized shortly afterwards.

It was almost four years since the old 1st Division took over its first bit of firing line in front of Fleurbaix. Those were glorious years—glorious for every man who had the least share in winning the victory, and glorious for Canada. The troops were returning covered with honour. All that was depressing was left behind, for their faces were set towards home, and the land they sailed for was "God's Country."

By the end of August[2] practically all fit men were home, and within a very few weeks Canada's veterans had been silently absorbed into civilian life. In the secret places of their hearts they carried memories of which they could not speak, of comrades whose fortune it had been to "... go down with unreluctant tread. / Rose-crowned into the darkness!"*

Canada's sons had kept faith with the 56,000 of their dead who sleep "In Flanders Fields."[3]

From the poem "The Hill" by Rupert Brooke[4]

---

2   1919.

3   This number only refers to the dead of the Canadian Corps, not all Canadians who died in the Great War.

4   Morrison's note.

ACKNOWLEDGEMENTS

First and foremost I wish to thank John and Shaun Fripp and their family for their support of this project, and for their generosity with Edward Morrison's Great War treasures: his typewritten manuscript, letters, officer's book, and photographs. The manuscript, an invaluable resource, is a record of an Artillery Commander's service and experiences throughout the Great War in its entirety. There is nothing else like it.

Next, the words *thank you* are simply not adequate for the Herculean amount of work done by First World War artillery expert Major (Retired) Marc George, of Brandon, Manitoba, without whose painstaking efforts this book would not be the rich resource that it now is. People, events, dates, terminology, weaponry, and actions are now identified with detail throughout that would have probably taken me many extra weeks, if not months.

Many thanks to Steve Clifford of Victoria, British Columbia,[1] whose generosity in sharing wonderful, recently discovered photographs of officers at Valcartier in 1914, and of the 16th Battalion Canadian Scottish in 1914 and 1915, have greatly enriched the book. I'm also grateful to John Frederick at the University of Victoria Libraries Special Collections for supplying me with photographs from the W.O.H. Dodds

---

1   Read his blog, *Doing Our Bit*, at www.militaryandfamilyhistory.blog.

Collection. My thanks to Kathleen Wall at McCrae House and Guelph Museums for providing photographs for yet another book. I am grateful to Steve Harris for steering me to the right source for battle maps, and to Jason Nisenson in the library at The Military Museums in Calgary, Alberta, for scanning the battle maps needed to illuminate the actions described.

Finally a big thanks to Clive Prothero-Brooks at the Royal Canadian Artillery Museum in Shilo, Manitoba, for providing me with the photograph of "the Knight," Sir Edward Morrison.

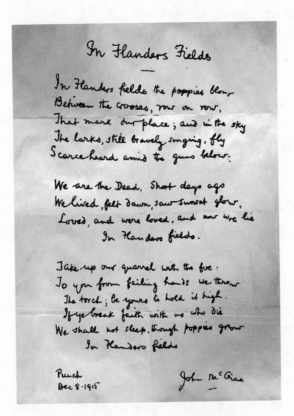

Handwritten copy of John McCrae's "In Flanders Fields."
SUPPLIED BY SUSAN RABY-DUNNE, INFLANDERSFIELDS.CA

INDEX

command structure, 161, 164,
171, 175–76, 181, 191, 216
Connaught, Duke of, 27n5, 28
Connaught, Prince Arthur of,
241, 242
conscription, 147, 169–71
Constantine, Charles Francis,
94n17
Contalmaison, 96
convoys, 29, 31–33
Cosgrave, Lawrence Vincent
Moore, 46, 81, 82, 85, 100,
119, 157–59
Cotton, Charles Penner, 89, 91
Coulotte, 130, 133
Courcellete, 99, 101, 105,
106, 172n1
Craig, Charles Stewart, 72n4,
74, 76
Crerar, Harry, 13
Crerar, Harry Duncan
Graham, 228
Crest Farm, 153, 156, 161
Crimea, 189
Crow's Nest, the, 204
Currie, Sir Arthur, 13–14, 22,
79, 95, 132, 134, 150, 153, 156,
169, 179, 192, 197, 212, 223,
235–36, 239–40

Damery, 200
Decline Farm, 156
demobilization, 244–46
Denain, 222, 223–24
Desire Support Trench, 112–13
Desire Trench, 106n3, 112–13
Devizes, 37
Diksmuide, 44, 131, 132, 220
dirigibles, 78–79
Domart, 192–93
Douai, 222–23
Douai Plain, 125, 128, 134, 146
Double Crassier, the, 135, 136
Doullens, 178
Drake, B.F., 78
Dranoutre, 79
Drocourt–Quéant Line, battle
of the, 203–9

"Duck's Bill," 72–74
Duisons, 191
"dum-dum" bullets, 167
Dundonald, Lord, 36, 53
Durkee, Adelbert Augustus, 57–58
Dury, 206

Edward VIII, 79n10
Egypt, 132, 187
Electric Generating Works, 130
Éleu-dit-Leauwette, 133
Épincy, 214
Escourt-St-Quentin, 211
Estaires, 181, 182, 185–86
Etaing, 207
Eterpigny, 204

Fabeck Graben, 101
Fanshawe, Sir Hew Dalrymple,
87n7
Farbus, 121
Farquhar, Francis Douglas, 27
Festubert, battle of, 68–71
Flers-Courcelette, battle of. See
Somme, battle of the
Fleurbaix front, 47–53
Flexicourt, 192
Foch, Ferdinand Jean Marie, 55,
61, 181, 183, 189, 226
Folkestone air raids, 131
Fontaine, 215
fortresses, 96–97
Fortuin, 150
Fosse 4, 143–44
Foster, William Wasbrough,
103, 200
Fotheringham, John Taylor, 96
France, 42–43, 48–49, 78, 170,
176, 187–88, 223–24, 241–42
Franks, George, 93, 94n19
Fransart, 200
fraternization, 47
French, Sir John, 68
French Army
1st Army, 197
11th "Iron" Division, 55, 56, 61
45th (Algerian) Division, 57,
62, 64

in battle of Amiens,
196–97, 198
represented on Versailles
Council, 176
Territorials, 43
Fresnoy, 126, 127, 128, 130
Frezenburg, 152
Fricourt, 96
Fripp, Emma Thacker Kaye,
11, 22
Fripp, Herbert, 11, 22
Fripp, Herbert Downing,
94, 100n7
Fripp, John, 22
Fripp, Shaun, 22
Fromelles, 49n20
fuzes, 118, 124, 158

garrison artillery, 121n9
gas attacks
at Bourlon Wood, 215
at second Ypres, 56–57,
60–66
at the Somme, 114
at Vimy Ridge, 120
Gentelles, 192
George V, 93–94
German-Americans, 47
German Army: cavalry, 44
German Army: corps
13th Württemberg, 89–90, 91
Prussian Guard, 27, 40, 47,
60, 140–42
German Army: divisions
1st German Guards, 141–42
Prussian Guard, 27, 40, 47,
140, 141–42
Germany
collapse of resistance, 220
occupation of, 237–43
view of 1917 Canadian federal
election, 170
Gheluvelt, 161
Givenchy actions, 50, 68, 70–76,
181–82
Goldberg, 164
Gosselies, 237, 238
Goudberg, 153

AUTHOR BIOGRAPHY

Born in London, Ontario, **Sir Edward Whipple Bancroft Morrison**, KCMG, CB, DSO (1867–1925), was a military officer and a journalist. He served overseas in the Boer War and World War I, being promoted to major-general in 1918, and was made a Knight Commander of the Order of St. Michael and St. George in 1919. Morrison worked for the *Hamilton Spectator* and the *Ottawa Citizen,* leaving the *Citizen* in 1913 to take up full-time military duty. (He would return to the paper after the War.) His memoir of the Boer War, *With the Guns in South Africa,* was published in 1901. His memoir of the Great War was written between 1918 and 1925, but Morrison died before it could be published. Excerpts appeared in the *Ottawa Citizen* in 1928, three years after his death, but the memoir was never published in its entirety, until now. Morrison married Emma Thacker Kaye Fripp in 1911. His eldest stepson, Herbert Fripp, served as his Aide-de-Camp and worked on his staff for much of the Great War. Herbert's sons, John and Shaun Fripp, came to inherit much of Morrison's war memorabilia, including his unpublished memoir. It is with their permission that this book is in existence today.

Susan Raby-Dunne is a military historian, composer, veterans' advocate, and WWI and WWII Battlefield Guide. She is the author of *John McCrae: Beyond Flanders Fields,* which was nominated for the Golden Oak Award, and the author of *Hell Burned Through: The Art and Story of a Lancaster Rear Gunner.* Her military musical version of the poem "In Flanders Fields" debuted on CBC radio and internationally in 2006. She is the Canadian representative of the American charity Soldier's Heart. After years of ranching and breeding horses, she now devotes herself to writing. She lives in Longview, Alberta.